Praise for
Every Young Man's Battle

"*Every Young Man's Battle* does the best job I have ever seen on the subject of sexual temptation. Once upon a time we lived in a world that didn't talk about secrets, and that world has brought us to the mess we are in today. Young men must have an honest, blunt, and unashamedly Christian look at their sexuality. This book will save thousands of future marriages."

—JIM BURNS, president, YouthBuilders

"I have never read a book as direct and open as *Every Young Man's Battle*. The profound principles communicate the authors' personal experiences and provide the hope that anyone can overcome a day-to-day battle with impure thoughts. *Every Young Man's Battle* helps you see the importance of taking control over your eyes, your mind, and your heart so that you can completely honor God in every facet of your life."

—SCOTT BULLARD, of musical recording group Soul Focus

"It's encouraging to see some real men stand up and sound the alarm to young men. Stephen, Fred, and Mike's courage to tell their stories exposes what has unfortunately become a dirty little secret among men in the church. The battle cry of the day is for men of all ages to live a pure and holy life, and this book will crush Satan's strategy by giving the troops the guts to talk about what has been taboo in the church for so long. The authors' poignant stories paint a picture of battle in which all men can relate and offer hope and camaraderie to win the war."

—TROY VANLIERE, artist/manager (representing NewSong, Carolyn Arends, Soul Focus, Jadyn Strand, and Glad)

"There has been a gaping void in the search for holiness, and *Every Young Man's Battle* addresses those issues where others have been comfortably silent. If there is even a spark of desire for purity in your life, this book will kindle that fire… It *is* possible to walk in victory, as you will surely find out after reading the Every Man series."

—MATT BUTLER, of musical recording group NewSong

Every Young Man's Battle

STEPHEN ARTERBURN

FRED STOEKER WITH MIKE YORKEY

WORKBOOK INCLUDED

Every Young Man's Battle

Strategies for Victory
in the Real World of Sexual Temptation

WATERBROOK
PRESS

EVERY YOUNG MAN'S BATTLE
PUBLISHED BY WATERBROOK PRESS
12265 Oracle Boulevard, Suite 200
Colorado Springs, CO 80921

ISBN 978-0-307-45799-8

Published in association with the literary agency of Alive Communications Inc., 7680 Goddard Street,
Suite 200, Colorado Springs, CO 80920, ww.alivecommunications.com.

Published in the United States by WaterBrook Multnomah, an imprint of the Crown Publishing Group,
a division of Random House Inc., New York.

Library of Congress Cataloging-in-Publication Data
Arterburn, Stephen, 1953–
      Every young man's battle : strategies for victory in the real world of sexual temptation / Stephen
Arterburn, Fred Stoeker with Mike Yorkey. — 1st ed.
            p. cm.
      1. Young men—Religious life. 2. Chastity. 3. Sex—Religious aspects—Christianity. I. Stoeker,
Fred. II. Yorkey, Mike. III. Title.
      BV4541.3 .A78 2001
      241'.66—dc21

                                                                              2001055759

Printed in the United States of America
2012

10 9 8 7 6 5

SPECIAL SALES
Most WaterBrook Multnomah books are available at special quantity discounts when purchased in bulk
by corporations, organizations, and special-interest groups. Custom imprinting or excerpting can also be
done to fit special needs. For information, please e-mail SpecialMarkets@WaterBrookMultnomah.com
or call 1-800-603-7051.

contents

foreword

by Stephen Arterburn

Being part of the Every Man series has been one of the great joys of my life. If I'd written and published only this one series, I would've been completely fulfilled. I owe all this to Fred, who lived out this message long before he was called by God to write about it.

Now, it may sound strange to some, but I believe Fred had one of those rare experiences where God interrupts what we're doing and gives us a new mission. I'm quite confident God spoke to him directly. Fred's coming to me with his manuscript was also part of God's plan, and I'm so glad for it! As a result, my life has been filled with words I could never replace, in the form of e-mails, letters, hugs, crying eyes, and expressions of gratitude. Here are a few comments from the men:

- "Thank you—you've saved my marriage."
- "I am now the man I always wanted to be, living the life I always wanted to live."
- "Oh! This feeling of freedom. I feel so clean!"
- "I don't know where I would be today if it were not for this book."
And from the wives:
- "Thank you for giving the man I married back to me."
- "We would not still be married if not for this book."
- "I wish you could see the man my husband has become today."
- "My man was totally transformed reading your book."
I've received these kinds of messages every day:

I never go into Christian bookstores, but I was jogging one day and stopped in one. Staring back at me was your book. I was compelled by it. I ran home, got my money, and came back and bought it. It changed everything!

Somebody gave me this book about five years ago, and right before I was about to go back online, there it was looking up at me from the floor. I picked it up and read it through my tears. Our marriage has been healed.

Years ago at New Life, we started an Every Man's Battle Workshop weekend. More than six thousand men have attended since that time. For a few men, it was just a way to get someone off their backs. But for almost all, it's been the start of a whole new life. One of my favorite stories is of a husband who came because his wife demanded it. After the conference he confessed his affair. He was truly repentant and said he would do anything to make it up to her. She asked him to sign over all the property and assets to her—because the name on them wouldn't matter if he was truly finished with his lust and adultery. She asked him to shave his chest, and she asked him to get braces on his teeth. He did all three because he realized his actions had humiliated her and he was willing to do anything to humble himself and win back her heart. I speak with them both regularly, and they are doing well.

I'm so glad *you* have come upon this book. For some reason God has put it in front of you. I'm not just hoping you'll read it; I'm hoping you'll live it. And while I know personally that every marriage can't be saved, I know that every man can reclaim his sexual integrity and every spouse can fully heal. Every man can walk with his head held high—free, honorable, and a man after God's own heart.

It doesn't really matter what you've done; it's no worse than what others have done. And it doesn't matter where you've been; others have been down that path before. What matters is what you are willing to do now and what you will choose to do. You may have thought you were entitled to do the things you did, but now your entitlement is to live clean, renewed, and without even a hint of impurity. I challenge you to join the millions across this country who have reclaimed their integrity, their faith, and their respect. If Fred and I can do it—those who know us would confirm this—you can certainly do it too.

acknowledgments

I'd like to thank Andy Turcotte, Steve Beeman, Richard Pickrell, Ron Strack, and Mark Oberbeck for your great insights into the hearts of young men and women. You are wonderful pastors and I'm amazed at your friendship.

I thank my prayer team as well. Pastor Palmer and Deacon Mike Swaim have lifted me in the darker moments. I thank Vicky Cluney, Diana Koontz, and Ray and Joyce Henderson, who never stop praying or believing. And the head of the prayer pack is my wife, Brenda. What a warrior. What a woman!

I thank my friends who have understood my absence at important events because of the deadlines. I thank you younger friends of mine who have opened your hearts to tell some of your deepest stories, all for the sake of Christ. I've changed a few details to protect your privacy, but God knows who you are, and He is forever grateful.

Gary Meyer, you've always been there to make me laugh, even if it meant eating a cricket or waking me with horns and drums at two in the morning. Thanks for accepting me as your "intense friend."

Mike Yorkey, you are a master. I'm lost without you. And thanks to Dan Rich, Thomas Womack, Michele Tennesen, and all of WaterBrook Press. Stephen Arterburn, what can I say? Your support and encouragement are ceaseless. It is amazing to me.

My mother-in-law, Gwen, has carried the ball many times when we needed a first down. She's a real gamer. Jasen, Laura, Rebecca, and Michael, you are the finest children on the planet. You've sacrificed much. God will make it up to you, now and forever.

—*Fred Stoeker*

breaking the silence code

(by Stephen Arterburn)

There's a time-honored code that almost every male I've known has followed. I'm positive that my father and my brothers followed what I call the
"Sexual Code of Silence." The code states that it's okay to joke about sex
or even lie about it, but other than that, it's your solemn duty—as a male—
to keep silent whenever a *serious* discussion about sex takes place.

Since everyone is determined not to talk about this, or maybe is embarrassed to do so, you probably don't have a clear picture of what healthy sex
is all about. In fact, you're probably thinking that some very wonderful
things are not normal and that some very normal things are pretty weird.
That's one of the reasons we wanted to write this book for you. We wanted
you to have accurate information about a wonderful subject that's prone to
misinformation and ignorance. You're a sexual being and deserve to know
what's right and true about your sexuality so you can have the greatest
chance possible for a fantastic sexual relationship with the person you marry.

It's sad that in the Christian community, where we have access to God's
truth, we operate with so many lies and myths about sex. Some teens and
young men with a low sex drive think they're not real men, when in reality
they may have a chemical or hormonal variance that lowers the drive. Some
teens and young men with a strong sex drive may view themselves as
slightly crazy and in need of major help to squelch their urges.

You may be vacillating between those two extremes, especially if you're in the middle of your adolescent years. Because your body is in a constant state of growth, you feel driven one minute and almost asexual the next. Don't let this concern you. You're right on schedule, and everything you're experiencing is normal.

One of the most difficult assignments you'll ever have is to integrate your sexuality with the emotional, spiritual, social, and relational person you want to be. Many have the tendency to see their sexuality as something shamefully separate and distinct from themselves, but that shouldn't be the case at all.

Let me illustrate by using a good old hypocrite as an example. You probably know some people who are very religious when they go to church on Sunday, but you'd never know they were Christians by the way they act during the rest of the week. Sure, they say all the right words and go through the right motions on Sunday, but that part of their lives is reserved for Sunday. Come Monday morning, they sound more like they went to hell on Sunday rather than church. Those people haven't fully integrated their spiritual life with the rest of their lives.

The same could happen to you in the area of sexuality. This is an area you want to fully integrate with your Christian walk. When you do, you'll have a much healthier outlook regarding relationships with the opposite sex, premarital sex, and even what your marital relationship will be like in bed.

I have a friend whose son turned twelve a couple of years ago. He's a great dad, and he has a great kid. When the boy turned twelve, it's as if the spigot labeled Hormones was turned wide open. Stuff was happening inside his body, but he didn't understand why he was experiencing certain feelings. All he knew was that he had some urges that were difficult to control. The young boy then did a very courageous thing. He approached his father and said, "Dad, I just feel like taking off my clothes and standing in front of a girl naked."

That was an honest expression of feelings and an accurate description of what it felt like to be a twelve-year-old boy. The fact that he could comfortably talk with his father about his feelings indicated that he wanted some answers to what was happening to him. All of us would benefit from a similar attitude.

In fact, *attitude* is everything when it comes to winning the battle for sexual integrity. If there's a single Bible verse that captures God's standard for sexual purity, this is it: "But among you there must not be even a hint of sexual immorality, or of any kind of impurity" (Ephesians 5:3).

For teens and young adults, this is a scary verse that prompts more questions. What does a "hint" mean? How far can I go with a girl when we're alone? How far can I go with myself when I'm alone? Is masturbation okay?

These are great questions, and we'll answer them straight up. That's why you're going to find *Every Young Man's Battle* to be the most honest and forthright resource on teen and young adult sexuality out there.

Ready to get started? So are we. We're going to begin by letting Fred tell you his story and, as we say in Texas, it's a humdinger.

where are we?

when football was king

FROM FRED: THE START OF MY STORY

Growing up amid the Iowan cornfields, I made football my god. The sport dominated everything about me, and I happily played and practiced year-round. I even liked two-a-days in hot, muggy August. Football was such a big part of my life that I let the noble sport dictate what I did off the field. After the games, I never joined my teammates at Lake McBride for the keg-ger parties. Drinking beer, I believed, would weaken my focus and soften my drive. As for girlfriends, I viewed them as high-maintenance commitments that would distract me from my goal—becoming an all-state quarterback.

Like any red-blooded football player, however, I had more than a pass-ing interest in sex. I'd been hooked on *Playboy* centerfolds ever since I found a stack of the magazines beneath my dad's bed when I was in first grade. I also discovered copies of *From Sex to Sexty,* a publication filled with naughty jokes and sexy comic strips.

When Dad divorced Mom, he moved to his bachelor pad, where he hung a giant velvet nude in his living room. I couldn't help but glance at this mural-like painting whenever we played cards during my Sunday after-noon visits. On other occasions, Dad gave me a list of chores whenever I dropped by to see him. Once, while emptying the trash can in his bedroom, I came across a nude photo of his mistress. All this caused sexual feelings to churn deep inside me.

Hollywood movies filled me with lustful curiosity and burning passion. In one film, Diana Ross poured a bucket of ice on her boss's belly just as he orgasmed, which seemed to intensify the experience. My mouth dropped open. *What's up with this?* I pondered such scenes in my mind for days upon days. On those rare occasions that I went out on a date during the off-season, these deep churnings often stirred and bubbled over. Too often, I'd push a girl's boundaries while I tried to get a hand under her bra.

Still, my passion for football kept my sexual yearnings in check. I performed well on the gridiron and was named "Athlete of the Year" at Thomas Jefferson High School—a 4-A powerhouse in Cedar Rapids. I received full-ride scholarship offers from the Air Force Academy and Yale University.

I had bigger dreams, however—PAC-10 football, even if it meant trying out for the team as a walk-on. I wouldn't settle for anything less. Soon I stood before my locker at Stanford University, staring in awe at the familiar white helmet with the red *S* and the name Stoeker taped across the front. Strapping on my helmet and chin strap, I proudly raced onto the field in my attempt to win a spot on the team. Before long everyone in the country would know my name when I tossed long rainbow passes into the end zone. I was living my dream.

In one afternoon, that dream shattered into a thousand pieces. I was one of eight quarterbacks warming up that day. From the corner of my eye, I saw Turk Shonert, a blue-chip recruit from Southern California, throwing thirty-five-yard bullets! Three other quarterbacks zipped the ball through the air as if it were on a string. These QBs were so good that all four would later start at Stanford *and* play in the NFL.

I, along with Corky Bradford, an all-state quarterback from Wyoming, and my dormmate at Wilbur Hall, stared in disbelief. There was no way either of us had the skill level to compete with these blue-chippers. When my football dreams died that afternoon, I turned my attention to…women. Pictures of naked women.

As I settled into normal college life without sports or dreams, my churning sexuality broke through every dike, and I was soon awash in pornography. I actually memorized the date when my favorite soft-core magazine, *Gallery,* arrived at the local drugstore. I'd be standing at the front door at opening time, even if I had to skip class to do it. I loved the "Girls Next Door" section in *Gallery,* which featured pictures of nude girls taken by their boyfriends and submitted to the magazine for publication.

While I waded into porn waters up to my neckline, I somehow kept sexual intercourse on some higher moral dry ground. From where I stood, making love was something *special* for when you were married. I still felt that way after I returned to Iowa following my freshman year. I got a summer job on a roofing crew to make some quick, big cash, and I began dating an old friend named Melissa, entering a relationship that quickly mushroomed into a heavy love affair. When I wasn't pounding nails on someone's roof, Melissa and I spent endless hours together. Just before I got set to return to Stanford for my sophomore year, we decided to spend a secluded weekend together at Dad's property on Shield's Lake in southern Minnesota.

Beneath a bright, full moon on a crystal-clear night, we lay down to sleep with a cool breeze blowing gently over us. The setting was romantic, and I was getting more excited by the minute. I quietly reached for Melissa, and she knew exactly where I was headed. Melissa looked up at me with a deep sadness in her big brown eyes, the moonlight framing her innocent face. "You know that I'm saving myself for marriage—hopefully ours," she said. "If you push forward with this, I want you to know that I won't stop you. But I will never be able to respect you as much as I do right now, and that would make me very sad for a very long time."

Laying her virginity on the line, she had delivered the ultimate pop quiz. How would I answer? Who did I love most—her or me? My head spun. My desire and passion pounded away as I gazed into that sweet face glowing softly at me. We became silent for a long time. Finally, I smiled. Snuggling in next to her, I dozed off to sleep, passing her test with flying colors. Little did I know that it was the last test I'd pass for many years.

When I left Melissa behind on my drive back to Stanford University, a deep loneliness settled in. Far from home and with few Christian underpinnings, I wandered aimlessly through my days, feeling sorry for myself. Then one day during an intramural football game, my eyes caught sight of a female referee. She looked like a grown-up version of my childhood sweetheart, Melody Knight, who had moved to Canada when we were in the third grade.

I was in love! Since there was nothing holding us back, it wasn't too long before we were in bed making love. I justified it because I was having sex with the girl I *knew* I would marry. It seemed like such a small step away from my values. Sadly, the flame of our relationship burned out as quickly as it began, but sadder still: This small step led to many more steps down the hill.

The next time I made love, it was with a girl I *thought* I would marry. The time after that, it was with a good friend that I thought I could love and *maybe* marry. Then came the pleasant coed I barely knew who simply wanted to experience sex before she left college.

Within twelve short months, I'd gone from being able to say no in a secluded camper on a moonlit night to being able to say yes in any bed on any night. Just one year out of college in California, I found myself with four "steady" girlfriends simultaneously. I was sleeping with three of them and was essentially engaged to marry two of them. None knew of the others.

Why do I share all this?

First, so you'll know that I understand the fiery draw of premarital sex. I know where you're living. Second, if you're already sleeping around but know that you shouldn't, I bring you hope. As you'll soon see, God changed my whole mind-set about having sex before marriage.

distance from God

Even as I bounced from bed to bed during my single days, I didn't notice anything wrong with my life. Oh, sure, I attended church sporadically, and from time to time the pastor's words penetrated my heart. But who was he? Besides, I loved my girlfriends. No one was getting hurt, I reasoned.

But my stepmother noticed something was wrong. My dad had eventually remarried, and when I visited back home in Iowa, she occasionally dragged me across the river to the Moline Gospel Temple in Moline, Illinois. The gospel was preached in that church, but to me the whole scene was ludicrous. I often laughed cynically, just thinking of the people there.

After graduating from Stanford University with an honors degree in sociology, I took a job in the San Francisco area as an investment adviser. One day in May, I stayed late at the office. Everyone else had gone home, leaving me alone with some troubling thoughts. I swiveled my chair around and propped up my feet on the credenza to gaze into a typically grand California sunset. As the sun dipped beneath the horizon, God somehow interrupted the scene with the horrible revelation of what I had become.

TAKE A LOOK AT...YOU!

This was a different experience for me. Oh, I knew who God was and had even prayed on occasion that I wanted Him closer in my life, but nevertheless I'd be right back in bed the following evening with the French graduate student—or one of the others. I never really meant those prayers. Then again, my word never meant much back then, and I knew it.

My friends understood this as well. Corky, one of my buddies, had coined a slang term for this character flaw of mine. To "Fred-out" was to promise to be somewhere and then not show up, and this colorful phrase became part of the vocabulary in my circle of friends. After those earlier prayers, I'd simply "Fred-out" on God.

But not this time.

I don't know how He did it on that evening in my San Francisco office, but God showed me how hopelessly ugly I'd become through my sin. Tears of sorrow and despair streamed down my face. Where once I was blind, now I could see. Instantly, I saw my deep, deep need for a Savior. Because of the Moline Gospel Temple, I knew who to call upon. My prayer that day flowed from the simplicity of a certain heart: "Lord, I'm ready to work with You if You're ready to work with me."

I stood up and walked out of the office, not yet fully realizing what I'd just done. But God knew. In the first two weeks, it seemed as if the heavens moved everything in my life, and in no time I had a new job back in Iowa and a new life ahead of me. And I left the girlfriends behind!

But it wasn't the new life *ahead* of me that would transform me…it was a new life *in* me. Though I still didn't know it for sure, an event on my trip home to Iowa revealed that God had moved in. I stopped in Steamboat Springs, Colorado, to visit a couple of Stanford buddies. The father of one owned a ranch just outside Steamboat, so I was looking forward to grabbing a few days of relaxation and Rocky Mountain high as I passed through.

When I arrived, I needed to make a pit stop, so I headed straight for the bathroom. When I opened the door, I found the walls papered with *Playboy* centerfolds, and I was instantly repulsed.

I stood there shocked.

Shocked by the centerfolds? No, I was shocked by my revulsion. *Where in the world did this reaction come from?* I wondered. After all, we're talking Fred Stoeker, the guy who'd memorized the dates when porn magazines hit the local drugstore. The one who skipped class to lust over the pages. The one who *lived* for centerfolds, saving them for last like some sweet dessert. I'd never been repulsed by a centerfold in my life.

As I mused over this development for several days, I didn't put two and two together and connect this "new me" to the prayer in my office, but I should have. Looking back, I can see that it clearly was a sign that my heart was changing. When you're saved, God gives you a new heart for Him. He lives in you and gives you the strength you need to do everything and anything He calls you to do, including His call to sexual purity. This new life flowed with no effort from me, and the new inclinations to do God's will came without any attention on my part.

As I recall, during the two weeks between my sunset prayer in San Francisco and that moment when I stepped into the *Playboy*-decorated bathroom, I hadn't prayed again, attended church, or read my Bible. The Holy Spirit simply took me at my prayerful word and began working with me right where I was.

THE DESIRE TO DO RIGHT

It took a second event a number of weeks later to finally confirm to me that God had indeed transformed me by giving me a new heart that beat with a desire to do right and to live holy. After I settled into an apartment in Ankeny, Iowa, my nights were monotonous and long. A man accustomed to entertaining four girlfriends isn't used to having his nights free!

In no time, thoughts of Janet began to swirl in my imagination. She was an old friend from high school, and I'd been enamored with her for years. Back then, I'd been too busy with football to start a relationship with her, but I'd often dreamed of sleeping with her.

I soon tracked her down and—what luck! She was still single and living in Omaha. I called her and, after some cheerful banter, she invited me to meet her at her favorite dance bar. Need I say more? After closing time, we found ourselves alone in her apartment. One thing led to another, and we slipped out of our clothes and slipped into her bed. We began kissing, but a strange thing happened: I couldn't get an erection! *That* had never happened before. Deeply humiliated, my head spinning, I slunk out to the parking lot and slumped into my car.

Then I clearly heard the Spirit whisper into my heart, "By the way, I did that to you. I know it hurt you, but this practice can't be tolerated anymore in your life. You are Christ's now, and He loves you." He didn't have to say it twice—on the spot I recommitted myself to staying pure! (I was glad I did, because a few months later I met Brenda, and we committed to saving intercourse until our wedding night.)

Wide-awake now to my salvation, I wasted little time finding a church home. A proper fear and respect for this new life in me had taken root, and I immediately fell in love with the Spirit's whisper in my life. I wanted to grow in Christ and experience the abundant life of joy that He had waiting for me.

Before I continue with my story (in chapter 5), let's take a time-out and explore some important principles of sexuality that I think you'll find interesting and immediately applicable to your life. We'll begin with a discussion of God's view of our sexuality.

oneness with God

As a young man, you probably have many questions about this mysterious thing called sex, even though you've been exposed to a lot about sex in today's media and films.

In the old days, we would say that most of us learned about sex "in the gutter." The phrase isn't around today, but many of your fathers received their first sex lessons on some street corner or in a locker room shower. That's where we listened to older and "wiser" guys unlock the mysteries of what happens between a man and a woman—or what you can do to yourself. Of course, that still happens today, and this story from Tyler is fairly typical:

> I was walking home with Billy one afternoon after school, and he suggested picking up something to drink. I didn't really like Billy, but I felt sorry for him because he didn't have many friends. I could tell he was trying so hard to be nice. After we bought our drinks, he told me about something called masturbation. I'd never heard that word, so he explained what it was. He said all the guys in our class had been experimenting. I couldn't get what he told me out of my mind, so that night I tried it. Having an orgasm was like nothing I'd ever felt before, and I really liked it. But the thought of God looking on while I did it made me feel kind of rotten.

Maybe you haven't gone more than a week without masturbating since you were a freshman in high school. With questions about sex looming on every side, maybe you've begun experimenting with your girlfriend, unsure of where God's boundaries lie but determined not to look for them too hard.

A few years ago, Brad told us, "I know making love is wrong before marriage, but I guess anything short of that is fine. I love to get up under a bra." Brad's "under the bra" experiments eventually ended in regular intercourse with his fiancée, and those sexual experiments took on a frustrating life of their own and resulted in significant problems. "We've been having sex for over a year, and I'm confused," Brad said. "I think we should break it off, but now I feel obligated to marry her since we've been having sex for so long. I wish we hadn't gone so far. Now I'm worried she might not be the one for me."

We live in a culture where the sexual boundaries have been obliterated, disappearing like the chalk lines marking the batter's box after six innings of play. John, an all-around sports star and leader at school and church, recently sat in on an abstinence course taught by his youth pastor—but he wasn't buying. Afterward, he got into a heated argument with his youth pastor. John finally said, "Okay, I'll commit to this abstinence thing, but there's no way I'm giving up blow jobs. I've had dozens of them, and I really like them."

But maybe you're not like John at all. You're a good kid. You play drums loudly in the youth worship band, and you're such a handsome, winsome guy that other parents say they'd love to have you marry their daughter some day. On the outside, you look great. Yet privately, in terms of your sexuality, your conscience has dimmed to the point where you're not quite sure what's right or wrong anymore.

LAYING DOWN THE TRUTHS

Perhaps intercourse once seemed wrong, but you recently got it on with that girl in English class, and you didn't feel guilty at all. Purity once seemed right, but now whenever the youth speaker talks about keeping yourself pure until marriage, the idea sounds quaint and archaic—so "twentieth century."

If any of this sounds like you, then you're sinking in a sexual quicksand. You still bang the drums in the worship band, but you really don't *feel* the worship anymore. Instead, you feel distant from God.

But we're getting ahead of ourselves. Regardless of where you stand right now, let me use my (Fred's) story as a starting point to lay a foundation for the rest of this book. It's an underpinning of six basic truths upon which we all need to agree:

1. *Attraction to Girls Is Natural*

Attraction to the female body is a natural, God-given desire. Just as it was natural for me to want to hang around girls in college, so it's natural for you to find a girl's beauty tugging at your eyes for attention.

The temptation, however, is to fulfill these desires and attractions in a wrong way and to go beyond a natural and normal outlook. That means viewing a girl more as an extremely interesting collection of body parts rather than as a precious child of God. We refuse to believe you don't know the difference. You know when you're thinking about her mostly as a pair of breasts walking by, and little else.

We'll be tempted in many wrong ways to play with these natural desires and attractions to girls. Obviously, stripping off her clothes in the basement at the after-game party is a wrong way, but it's just as wrong to stare lustfully at her and fantasize in your mind. Neither practice is any more pure than the other.

2. *Sex Is Exhilarating*

This one's not too hard to accept, is it? There's nothing in the world like an orgasm. No feeling hits you harder or draws you back faster, whether through masturbation or sex with a partner. When I was fourteen, my sister's boyfriend, Brock, said to me with a wicked little grin, "Once you taste the candy, you'll never say no again. So you better not taste it!"

Brock was right. Once you travel down the freeway of premarital sex, you can't back up. If you want your purity back, then you'll have to exit that freeway entirely.

3. Sex Is a Slippery Slope

If you don't ram a stake into the ground and declare, "This is as far as I go, and I won't go any further," then you'll lose your footing on the slippery slope of sex. Remember how I let myself go in college? Because of the pleasure, sexual escalation was natural. Besides, why should I *not* have sex? I wasn't committed to Christ, and I saw no reason (until God later intervened) to stop having sex. Looking back, it was amazing how I made such sweeping rationalizations for my behavior:

- "It's okay because I really love her. I *know* I'm going to marry her anyway."
- "Why wait until marriage? We're already married in our hearts."
- "Sex isn't wrong for everyone. God is really concerned only about adultery."

Maybe you've said the same things to yourself…the same things that non-Christians say to themselves! That alone should make you feel a bit uncomfortable. It's amazing how we can justify our actions to ourselves and to God. These rationalizations allow our consciences to gradually become accustomed to the sexual freeway we're traveling.

4. God Has Standards of Sexual Behavior for His Children

God takes sexual standards seriously, and He wants to be heard on the matter. When I tried to continue in my sexual ways after committing my life to Christ, God humbled me in Janet's bedroom. God sure got my attention that night. We're talking Joe Stud not being able to perform when it counted the most! If He's this interested in our purity, then we need to get just as interested.

Clearly, premarital intercourse is outside His standards. But what about oral sex? Mutual masturbation? Petting? French-kissing? Where are the boundaries? We'll get to the details later, but first we want to tell you that God has already rammed His *own* stake into the ground:

> Among you there must not be *even a hint* of sexual immorality, or
> of any kind of impurity, or of greed, because these are improper
> for God's holy people. Nor should there be obscenity, foolish talk
> or coarse joking, which are out of place. (Ephesians 5:3-4)

That, my friend, is quite a stake. Not even a *hint?* Hmm. Do your Christian friends act in this manner? Probably not. Today's teens and young men are often indistinguishable from their non-Christian peers, sharing their tastes in popular music, dirty jokes, and attitudes about premarital sex. Kristin, a teenager, told us,

> Our youth group is filled with kids faking their Christian walk.
> They're actually taking drugs, drinking, partying, and having sex.
> If you want to walk purely, it's easier to hang around with the non-
> Christians at school than to hang around with the Christians at
> church. I say that because school friends know where I stand, and
> they say, "That's cool—I can accept that." The Christian kids mock
> me. They laugh and ask, "Why be so straight? Get a life!" They pres-
> sure my values at every turn.

We're not pointing a special finger at teenagers. Young adults in their late twenties are no different from Christian teens. Linda, a single career woman, says her adult singles group at church has "players"—men and women who send signals that they're ready to play in the bedroom.

Married couples have also fallen short. There isn't a day in which I (Steve) don't take a call on my daily radio talk show from a husband or wife asking how he or she can recover from an adulterous affair or a partner's sexual addiction.

5. God's Love Is Not Based upon Your Ability to Meet His Standards

God's love for you is unconditional; it never changes. Before you were formed in the womb, He loved you. You're the apple of His eye. His love for you has no limits, and His love for you never wanes. If you masturbate, that fact doesn't lessen your value to Him. If you get up under a girl's bra, God doesn't regret having sent His Son to die for you.

This is true for all of us. When I (Fred) couldn't put my porn magazines down, He still loved me. When I lay in the arms of another Saturday-night date, He still loved me. When I continued to ignore Him, He chased me desperately, aching to reach me before it was too late and my heart was too hardened.

6. Rules Are Part of a Vibrant Relationship with Christ

I recall how the Holy Spirit whispered to me, "This practice can't be tolerated anymore in your life. You are Christ's now, and He loves you." The implication was that continued sexual activity would hurt my intimacy with Christ.

When you break His standards, the Lord doesn't reject you, but you can't be as close to Him. Soon after I prayed that prayer in my office, God told me *No more* in regard to my sexual exploits. Did I feel as though I'd taken an elbow to the chops? Yes. But by the grace of God, I didn't say, *Hey, what's the deal? You're taking my freedom away! You're killing me!* Instead, I said, *You got it, Father.* This new life in me was moving me His way. I had a desire to be closer to Him. And in order to get closer to Him, I had to be not so close to those women in my life.

When I got close to God, what He said about interpersonal relationships started to make a whole lot of sense. I quickly found that God's rules weren't just sets of arbitrary, kill-joy regulations. Instead, His rules set me free to live fully and to avoid dangerous traps.

For instance, after I moved back to Iowa, I continued to maintain a phone relationship with one of my girlfriends back in California, the one I was most serious about. My friends and family fully expected us to marry someday since we'd been an item for three years. Then at church I heard the pastor say that Christians shouldn't be unequally yoked with nonbelievers. Since I was a Christian, and she wasn't, this news presented a problem.

My reaction? *You got it, Father.* I called her and explained the verse in the Bible about being unequally yoked. "I really need you to explore this and to seek God," I said, "or I don't know how we can keep our relationship going."

"Okay, I'll read my Bible for thirty days, and we'll see," she promised. A month later, I heard from her, right on cue. "I've done what I promised," she said. "But I just can't buy this stuff at all."

"I'm sorry to hear that," I responded. Then I quietly said that we should go separate ways. God's rule freed me to break off the relationship and allowed Him to find someone better suited to be my wife. Less than a year later, God introduced me to Brenda, and my life has never been the same.

CHOOSING SEXUAL PURITY—AND INTIMACY

At a single moment, salvation gave us a new life and a new desire to be sexually pure for the first time. But this new desire alone will not bring full intimacy with Christ. We must say yes to this new desire and refuse to ignore it. We must choose oneness and intimacy with Christ. We must choose sexual purity.

It is God's will that you should be sanctified: that you should avoid sexual immorality. (1 Thessalonians 4:3)

It's not enough to *seem* or to *feel* Christian. We must *be* Christians in action. We can't expect to practice with the youth band by day and then slide nude under the sheets with the cute keyboardist by night. We can't expect to circle and hold hands in emotional prayer at church by day then wallow in cybersex by night.

When we turn on the computer and masturbate over naked, nameless lovers lying across our screen, we aren't like Christ. We aren't moving toward Him. While His love for us never changes, our intimacy with Him wanes. Distance grows. But when we choose sexual purity and walk in the light, we're one with God's essence. Intimacy grows. True relationship flourishes.

When we call ourselves Christians but don't act like it, He forcefully objects. Luke 6:46 says, "Why do you call me, 'Lord, Lord,' and do not do what I say?"

God is aching for you to be one with Him. The whole plan of salvation was designed that He might have a close relationship with you. Have you met the terms? Do you love His standards? When God asks you to change your behavior, do you say, *You got it, Father*? If so, that's a mark of growing intimacy.

Let's go to the source and check out what the Bible has to say on the subject of sexual impurity. Did you know that in nearly every book of the New Testament we're commanded to avoid sexual impurity? Here's a selection of passages that teach God's concern for our sexual purity. Highlighted in italics are key words indicating what we're to avoid in the sexual realm:

But I [Jesus] tell you that anyone who *looks at a woman lustfully* has already committed adultery with her in his heart. (Matthew 5:28)

For from within, out of men's hearts, come evil thoughts, *sexual immorality,* theft, murder, *adultery,* greed, malice, deceit, *lewdness,* envy, slander, arrogance and folly. All these evils come from inside and make a man "unclean." (Mark 7:21-23)

You are to abstain from...*sexual immorality.* (Acts 15:29)

So let us put aside the deeds of darkness and put on the armor of light. Let us behave decently, as in the daytime, not in orgies and drunkenness, not in *sexual immorality* and *debauchery,* not in dissension and jealousy. (Romans 13:12-13)

I am writing you that you must not associate with anyone who calls himself a brother but is *sexually immoral* or greedy, an idolater or a slanderer, a drunkard or a swindler. With such a man do not even eat. (1 Corinthians 5:11)

The body is not meant for *sexual immorality,* but for the Lord. (1 Corinthians 6:13)

Flee from *sexual immorality.* (1 Corinthians 6:18)

I am afraid that when I come again...I will be grieved over many who have sinned earlier and have not repented of the *impurity, sexual sin* and *debauchery* in which they have indulged. (2 Corinthians 12:21)

So I say, live by the Spirit, and you will not gratify the desires of the sinful nature.... The acts of the sinful nature are obvious: *sexual immorality, impurity* and *debauchery.* (Galatians 5:16,19)

But among you there must not be even a hint of *sexual immorality,* or of any kind of *impurity,* or of greed, because these are improper for

God's holy people. Nor should there be obscenity, foolish talk or coarse joking, which are out of place. (Ephesians 5:3-4)

Put to death, therefore, whatever belongs to your earthly nature: *sexual immorality, impurity, lust, evil desires* and greed, which is idolatry. Because of these, the wrath of God is coming. (Colossians 3:5-6)

It is God's will that you should be sanctified: that you should avoid *sexual immorality;* that each of you should learn to control his own body in a way that is holy and honorable, not in *passionate lust* like the heathen, who do not know God.... For God did not call us to be *impure,* but to live a holy life. (1 Thessalonians 4:3-5, 7)

See that no one is *sexually immoral.* (Hebrews 12:16)

Marriage should be honored by all, and the marriage bed kept pure, for God will judge the adulterer and all the *sexually immoral.* (Hebrews 13:4)

For you have spent enough time in the past doing what pagans choose to do—living in *debauchery, lust,* drunkenness, *orgies,* carousing and detestable idolatry. (1 Peter 4:3)

In a similar way, Sodom and Gomorrah and the surrounding towns gave themselves up to *sexual immorality* and perversion. They serve as an example of those who suffer the punishment of eternal fire. (Jude 7)

Nevertheless, I [Jesus] have a few things against you: You have people there who hold to the teaching of Balaam, who taught Balak

to entice the Israelites to sin…by committing *sexual immorality.*
(Revelation 2:14)

Nevertheless, I [Jesus] have this against you: You tolerate that woman
Jezebel, who calls herself a prophetess. By her teaching she misleads
my servants into *sexual immorality.* (Revelation 2:20)

But the cowardly, the unbelieving, the vile, the murderers, the
sexually immoral, those who practice magic arts, the idolaters and
all liars—their place will be in the fiery lake of burning sulfur.
This is the second death. (Revelation 21:8)

Isn't that something? Drawing from these passages, let's summarize
God's standard for sexual purity:

• Sexual immorality begins with the lustful attitudes of our sinful
nature. It's rooted in the darkness within us. Therefore, sexual
immorality, like other sins that enslave unbelievers, will incur
God's wrath.

• Our bodies weren't meant for sexual immorality, but for the Lord,
who has both created us and called us to live in sexual purity. His will
is that every Christian be sexually pure—in thoughts and words as
well as in actions.

• Therefore it's holy and honorable to completely avoid sexual
immorality—to repent of it and flee from it, as we live by the Spirit.

• We shouldn't be in close association with other Christians who per-
sist in sexual immorality.

• If we entice others to sexual immorality (maybe in the car's backseat
or in her bedroom when her parents aren't home), Jesus Himself has
something against you!

Clearly, God expects us to live according to His standard.

nobody escapes
from adventure island

Not too many decades ago, guys were married off at about the same age
you were when you took your driver's test.

Taking a wife at age sixteen had to help the ol' hormones! But that was
a different time and a different era, and getting married at sixteen today is
no more realistic than beating Shaquille O'Neal in a game of one-on-one.
It's just not going to happen.

So you've been dealt some lousy cards. Not only do teens go through
puberty sooner, but they're caught in a system of education that keeps them
in school through high school and often four years of college. Even when
you finally graduate after sixteen years of schooling, you're expected to post-
pone marriage even further while you take a few years "getting settled" into
your career. And during all that time, you're expected to remain as celibate
as a castaway until the day you say "I do."

"It's definitely weird," says Danny. "I feel like God made me a sexual
being, but He's asking me to live as though I'm not." We feel for you,
Danny, and for the countless young men who share your frustration. Some
even claim that in these changed times God no longer expects them to live
by His old standards of purity, because He never intended this postponement of marriage in the first place.

We hate to pile on here, but the postponement of marriage isn't the
main cause, or even the worst result, of this change. The most dangerous

assault on our sexual purity from this cultural change is our new view of ourselves and our teen years. A couple of hundred years ago, teenagers who married continued to work on the family farms or in the family trade. People in those days saw no distinction between the teen years and the adult years. Young people grew up quickly in those days because they had to! You weren't given a year to go backpacking through Europe, and you knew that the decisions you made today would affect your tomorrows.

Likewise, the Bible doesn't refer to the teen or adolescent years as we think of them. Once you reached thirteen years or so, God considered you a man. You were treated in that manner by parents and by your elders.

We've lost this mind-set, and it's killing our purity. These days, teens are often treated like kids. Even if you're in graduate school, you can still hear others saying that you're "not ready" to get married. They're usually thinking financially or maybe emotionally, and maybe they're right. But you're certainly ready to have sex!

The truth is, as young men we often treat ourselves as kids. If we viewed ourselves as men like God does, we'd always view our sexual decisions today as having an impact on our tomorrows. But we usually don't do that. There remains this huge gap between the *physical* ability to do sexual things (which happens during puberty) and the *legal* ability to do sexual things (at least in God's eyes), which is ours only at marriage. Facing this enormous chasm, it's easy to view the physical and the legal as two thoroughly separate realms. In other words, you think that what you do during the teens is completely different from—or has no effect on—what happens during your adult years.

Nothing could be further from the truth.

STILL HOOKED ON THE BIFURCATION MYTH?

Bifurcation. Do you know what that word means? Well, neither did I (Steve) until I learned it from a dentist. Here's what happened. One day

I sat down across the table from my friend Shane at a cafeteria on the Baylor University campus. As we talked, I bit down hard on a chicken-fried steak, one of my favorite meals. Shane instantly heard what I felt, and he groaned. I did as well. One of my molars apparently chomped into a piece of metal lodged in that steak. Pain and embarrassment flushed over me as I spit out a sharp, shiny chunk of steel.

"That must have hurt," said my friend.

"Oh, you got that right!" I moaned. "I really did a number on my tooth."

"Do you think you need to see a dentist?"

"I hate dentists, but I'm hurting so bad..."

A short while later my dentist pried open my mouth and noticed I was missing a portion of one of my molars. He went to work, and within an hour I had a temporary crown capping my chicken-fried steak saga...or so I thought.

Over the years that tooth continued to bother me. When I finally said something to Dr. Farthing, he peered at the tooth for a long time. Then I heard him utter the word "bifurcation" to his assistant. Then he explained it to me. "Bifurcation means that something has completely split into two separate parts. A cracked tooth is one thing. A bifurcated tooth is another. Cracks can be fixed, but bifurcated teeth must be pulled because they're either dead or dying."

I nearly needed a diaper when I heard him say the word "pulled." Not only did he yank the offending tooth; he also had to perform a bone graft and set an implant. In the midst of all this oral construction work—and the accompanying agony of our new "painless" dentistry—I had plenty of time to meditate on bifurcation. I began to realize that this word described the way I once thought about life in general. I'd always assumed that the school years and the adult years were completely bifurcated—split apart and completely separate.

The bifurcation myth says that you can do what you want as a teenager because after you move into adulthood, it won't matter. That myth caused me many problems, and it will create havoc for you as well, if you believe it.

You see, there's no line that you step over from the teen years to the adult years. God knows that; it's why He sees you as a man right now. You must begin to see yourself this way too, because the person you become as a young man is the person you'll drag into adulthood. Your likes and dislikes—from food to music to movies—will follow you. More important, your character will be formed, just as a concrete foundation outlines a house.

Since life-bifurcation is a myth, the decisions you make today *will* impact everything in your future. The sexual desires you feed as a teenager will be the same desires you'll want to feed when you're forty. Decision-making is a two-edged sword: The right decisions you make today will help you make the right decisions when you're older. Wrong decisions today get you traveling down a path that leads to more horrible mistakes tomorrow. These decisions will carry right over into marriage, and you'll live one life in front of your wife and one life behind her back, trapped by the sexual habits you form now. You likely haven't even met your future wife yet, but know this: If you believe that today's sexual decisions are harmless to your future, bifurcation is rotting the roots of your future marriage right now.

Because of this bifurcation myth, you may not be one bit horrified by the story of my (Fred's) college years—the porn magazines, the multiple sex partners, the all-around good times. You may even be a bit jealous. "Wow, Fred had it all! He had sex anytime and anywhere, then he fell into God's arms and walked off scot-free. That's for me!"

We've heard upperclassmen return from college totally frustrated because they "missed out" on all the excitement. "My friends lived it up while I missed out on all the fun and wild times," exclaimed one college graduate. In his mind, he had a free get-out-of-jail pass but, like an idiot, he didn't use it. He believes that missing out on a backseat rendezvous with Betty Jo "B. J." Blowers actually screwed up his life.

It's as though he was raised by watching the Disney animated classic *Lion King*. Remember the young lion Simba in that film? (Okay, we know you prefer more manly fare like *Gladiator* or *Pearl Harbor*, but humor us.) If you recall, Simba took off and turned his back on the Pridelands and everything he knew, hooking up instead with some buddies for some R&R in "paradise." *Hakuna matata*...no worries. He and his buddies did whatever they pleased, whenever they pleased. The young lion had everything but responsibility.

Suddenly, Simba's evil uncle, Scar, took over the Pridelands, which caused total disarray and ruin. With everything on the line, Simba did the right thing. He turned his back on the playboy lifestyle, gathered up the troops, led them to victory, married Nala, stood regally at his coronation, and took his rightful place of greatness among the animals. In only a day, Simba moved without a hitch from the questionable character of his young days to his mature adult days. And most of us figure that's the way it'll also work for us.

So we often take off for our own sexual paradise beyond the Pridelands of our Father's kingdom. *Hakuna matata*. When the guys start swapping tales in the locker room, we want to share our own stories. Why not? The laws of "you reap what you sow" appear to have been suspended.

STILL PLAYING FREELY?

So we play, with little concern. Randy, a Christian and now seventeen, ran off to "paradise" at age thirteen. Not long ago, he broke up with his girlfriend, saying he was giving up on the dating scene for a while. A few weeks later, some friends saw him walking arm in arm with his old girlfriend again. Later, one friend asked him, "Randy, what's up with that? I thought you broke up with her."

"Oh, she's not my girlfriend," he casually replied. "We're just humping buddies." Randy may think things are cool, but those actions will catch up with him. It's impossible to form the proper respect for women in the shadow of such sin, let alone a proper respect for God. And what will happen long-term if Randy's wife doesn't match up sexually to his former girlfriend?

Jason has a father who travels for four or five days at a shot and a mother who works until 5:30 every day. That means he has two hours after school each day "with no mom around and a junior high girl down the street who comes over to my house every afternoon and lets me do anything I want to her. What's the big deal? It's fun, and she wants it."

Lisa, who grew up in the church, recently approached her youth pastor with a question. "I've been giving oral sex to different boys at our parties for quite awhile now. I don't know why, but I just thought I should ask you about it. Is that wrong for me to do?"

Stumbling a bit, the youth leader asked, "Were these your boyfriends?"

Lisa responded, "No, I wasn't dating any of them. It's just casual with us. All the guys know me for it, and that's why they come to the parties. I feel quite a bit of pressure to keep giving them what they want, now that they expect it. I've become quite popular because of it. Still, I thought maybe I should ask you about it, just to make sure it was okay."

Maybe you haven't traveled this deeply into paradise. Maybe you just hang on the fringes with *Playboy* or regularly visit that hot adult Internet site. Maybe you're experimenting with fantasy, lusting over that girl at school and repeatedly thrilling to intense wet dreams with her. In any event, you've left the Pridelands.

Hakuna matata? No worries? Guess again. If you're not concerned, then you should know that life isn't like *The Lion King*. It's more like *Pinocchio*, another Disney classic. Pinocchio knew it was the right thing for all boys to go to school. On his way to class, however, he met some scoundrels who painted a wonderful picture of spending the day at Adventure Island, a sort of amusement park just offshore. They gave Pinocchio and his buddy Lampwick free passes for the ferry ride to Adventure Island, but neither knew that at day's end all the boys would be turned into donkeys and be sold to pull carts in the coal mines for the rest of their lives. Like Pinocchio, maybe you think Adventure Island will bring you great amusement at no charge, although you know you're not supposed to go there. But there *will* be a price to pay at the end of the day, and it will be a heavy one.

First, what you view today will stay in your mind a long, long time—maybe forever. There's an old saying: "It takes twenty seconds to look at a *Playboy* and twenty years to forget what you saw." I can still remember the nude spread of Suzanne Sommers in the surging mountain stream as if it were yesterday. I still remember the short, full-bodied Asian girl standing nude in the wheat field in *Gallery* after she won the "Girl Next Door Contest." I can still see the nude *Playboy* model cloaked in a clear plastic raincoat as the shower cascaded over her. Every detail, from the color and cut of her hairstyle right down to the curvature of her spreading thighs are imprinted in my brain. I guess the old saying is wrong. I saw those images twenty-*three* years ago, and I still haven't forgotten.

Second, we pay the price whether we know it's coming or not. I've watched a ton of gory movies in my day, but few screams in those films have matched Lampwick's shriek of raw terror when his hands were turned into hooves. He didn't see it coming. If you think the law of reaping and sowing has been suspended during your teen years, then Satan gleefully uses this to his advantage. He does everything in his power to hook you sexually before marriage.

Maybe you aren't concerned. Maybe you think God will forgive you and that everything will be over once you marry. He'll forgive you, all right, but it's not over. Sin comes with inescapable consequences that follow you. You'll have to pay the price at the same toll bridge as the rest of us. Jim told us this:

I've been a Christian since the age of nine, and I've been sexually active since I was twelve. Now I'm in my late twenties, and I'm on the Internet constantly viewing the worst kinds of pornography. The lustful thoughts and acts will one day destroy me if I can't find a way to control it. Though I'm a Christian, it's always two steps backward and one step forward due to my sexual sin. I regret the things I do but then go right back to them. I never can focus my extra energy on Him, no matter how desperately I desire it.

Here's what Tom, a college student, said:

I've been struggling with sexuality for over a year now. I had a long-time girlfriend in high school that I made love to for a couple of years. Since we broke up, I've longed for another girlfriend, but I haven't found anyone, which has been frustrating. So frustrating that my feelings for girls have turned primarily to lust. I'm really ashamed of the things I do and think about, and I'm often ashamed to face God. I don't know how I'll ever get free.

Tanner says he's addicted to pornography:

It began when I was in high school, and it chases me through the years. I've tried to pray and read my Bible, but because of my sin, I have no desire to do these spiritual disciplines. I'm desperate and need help. I'm studying to become a pastor, and I'm close to ordination, but I feel convicted and guilty. My deepest desire is to serve God and be a man of God, but I don't know what to do. I cannot get free.

And Derrick feels as though he's living like a public saint and a private sinner:

The hypocrisy is ripping me apart, and the absence of God is like a living hell for me. I need help. I'm dying on the inside. I just don't know what to do or where to go. I don't live for God, I don't witness, and I don't pray. People say that the definition of hell is "eternal separation" from God. I feel that I have that right now, so I guess I'm in hell!

The end of the day at Adventure Island has arrived for these men, and they struggle against binding cords like donkeys pulling coal cars through dark mines, day after draining day. Some of you already feel the cords wrapping you tighter and tighter.

As the cords tighten, you struggle and struggle, and you may be ready to give up. You hope that you'll someday be free from sexual sin, expecting to grow out of it as naturally as you grew into it. Kind of like outgrowing acne. With each birthday, you wait for your sexual impurity to clear up, but nothing changes. So you wait some more, hoping that your future wife will arrive in time to help you fight your way back to purity.

But if you've got the idea that marriage will save you, you're foolishly mistaken.

STILL LOOKING FOR A SEXUAL NIRVANA?

If you're looking for sexual nirvana…marriage isn't it. When Mark signed up to attend the premarriage class that I (Fred) teach, he told me that his life was a mess. "I've been hooked on sex for years, and I'm counting on marriage to free me," he said. "I'll be able to have sex whenever I want it. Satan won't be able to tempt me at all!"

When we got together a few years later, I wasn't surprised to hear that marriage hadn't fixed the problem. "You know, Fred, my wife doesn't desire sex as often as I do," he said.

"Oh, really?"

"I don't want to seem like a sex addict or anything, but I probably have as many unmet desires now as I did before marriage. On top of all that, some areas of sexual exploration seem embarrassing or immodest to her. Sometimes she even calls them 'kinky.' I think she's rather prudish, but what do I say?"

In our experience, you can't say much!

To hear that marriage doesn't eliminate sexual impurity comes as a surprise to teens and young singles. Ron, a youth pastor in Minnesota, said that when he challenges young men to be sexually pure, their response is, "That's easy for you to say, Pastor. You're married! You can have sex any time you want!"

If only it were so.

First of all, sex has different meanings to men and women. Men primarily receive intimacy just before and during intercourse. Women gain intimacy through touching, sharing, hugging, and communicating deeply. Is it any wonder that the frequency of sex is less important to women than to men, as Mark woefully discovered? Because of the differences between men and women, forming a satisfying sex life in marriage is hardly a slam dunk. It's more like making a half-court shot.

Second, your wife may suddenly become much different from the woman you courted. Larry, a strapping, handsome young pastor in Washington, D.C., has a great Christian heritage. His father is a wonderful pastor, and Larry was thrilled when God also called him into the ministry. When Larry met Linda, a striking blonde bombshell, they appeared meant for each other, a regular Ken and Barbie set. After their wedding day, however, Larry found Linda to be far more interested in her career than in fulfilling him sexually. Not only was she disinterested in sex, she often used it as a manipulative weapon to get her own way. Consequently, Larry doesn't have sex very often. Twice a month is a bonanza, and once every two months is the norm. No sexual nirvana there.

Third, your wife may not care to help you in your battle. After a recent speaking engagement regarding *Every Man's Battle,* I noticed a man remaining behind in his seat. When everyone else had milled out, he came up to me and said, "My wife approached me this week and said, 'Jim, I have something to tell you, but I don't really know how to bring it up. I'll just say it straight out. I just don't like sex, and I really wish I didn't have to do it anymore.'

"I was stunned. I didn't quite know what to say, so I replied, 'Honey, is it something I'm doing wrong, or is there something I can do better?'

"She said, 'No, it's not what you're doing. All my friends feel this way. Every one of them.'"

You're probably saying to yourself, *Yeah, right, but that'll never happen to me.* Really? Marveling at Jim's story, I passed it on to one of my pastors as we chatted in his office. "See that chair over there?" he asked. "That's my counseling chair. Do you know what complaint I hear most often from married men?"

"No, what is it?"

"'I'm just not getting any sex anymore.' It's overwhelming!"

Marriage won't free you from the coal mine. If you've been impure before your wedding day, you can expect it to crop up after the honeymoon. If you're single and watching sensual R-rated movies, wedded bliss won't change this habit. If your eyes lock on passing babes, they'll still roam after you say "I do." If you're masturbating like gangbusters now, you'll find that putting that ring on your finger won't keep your hands off yourself.

You see, *before* your marriage, Satan does everything he can to *get* you to have sex with your girlfriend; *after* marriage, he does everything he can to *keep* you from having sex with your wife.

Do we need to repeat this point? If so, please read the above paragraph again.

And so, in spite of marriage, don't be surprised when your sexual sins keep spilling over everywhere just like they did when you were single. Joe told us he loves women's beach volleyball:

At night, I've had shockingly vivid dreams with these women. Some have been so exhilarating and so real that I wake up the next morning certain that I've been in bed with them. Heavy with guilt, I wonder where my wife is, sure she has left me over this affair and wondering how I could have done such a thing. Finally, as the cobwebs clear, it slowly dawns on me that it was just a dream. But even then I feel uneasy. You want to know why? Because while I know it was just a dream, I'm not at all certain it wasn't some form of adultery.

John wakes up early to watch those morning exercise shows, though he doesn't care much about fitness:

The truth is, I feel absolutely compelled to watch, to catch the close-ups of the buttocks, breasts, especially the inner thighs. And I drool. I sometimes wonder if the producers doing those closeups are just trying to hook men into watching their shows. Every day I tell myself that this will be the last time. But by next morning, I'm right there at the TV again.

Gary is a church music director. He's married and has a three-year-old girl, and he and his wife are expecting another child. He teaches marriage classes and leads the youth choir. "I have a great job," he says, "and a great life at my church. My wife says everyone puts me on a pedestal because of my dedication to the choirs and my hard work." All is well, right? He's escaped, right? Listen to what Gary had to say:

All this, and you would think I'd be at least spiritually happy, but I'm not. I feel so unworthy, undeserving, and ashamed. I know in my heart that something is not right. I, too, look at those bra and lingerie ads in the newspaper as if they were placed there solely for my plea-sure. I surf channels on the TV and stop and linger on the sexy shows. I pray and pray that God could take this from me, but yet I struggle to say no. *Baywatch,* swimsuit issues, secretaries wearing tight sweaters…it doesn't matter.

I know what you're thinking. *These guys are perverts and weirdos!* But these men are not weirdos; they're your next-door neighbors, your friend's father—maybe even your father. They're Sunday school teachers, ushers, and deacons. Even pastors.

They are today what you will become tomorrow. Today, you're making the same decisions they once made as teens. They're saying, "Don't do what we did!"

Your sexual decisions now *will* carry over into adulthood. The biggest blunder you can make as a young man is to believe that you're different from other guys and somehow stronger. You may think, *I'll never do what these guys are doing.* All we know is that there are countless married men with lovely wives sleeping in sexy negligees in their bedrooms while they masturbate at the computer.

What makes you so certain you won't do the same?

Growing older won't free you from sexual impurity, and marriage won't free you either. Sooner or later, you'll have to commit to purity if you want a true relationship with Christ and with the women in your life. Why not now?

Before we get into an action plan, we need to talk further about the roots of sexual bondage, which we'll do in the next two chapters as we take up Fred's story once again.

how we got here

stopping short

Let's return to the rest of Fred's story.

A couple of years into my wonderful new life in Christ, I began experiencing something every Sunday morning during our church worship service. I'd look around and see other men with their eyes closed, freely and intensely worshiping the God of the universe. Myself? I sensed only a wall of separation between the Lord and me.

I just wasn't right with God. As a newer Christian, I couldn't imagine what was happening. Everything had been going well, and I had changed so much. *Maybe it's a temporary slump,* I reasoned. *After all, relationships ebb and flow.* But time passed, and nothing changed.

The true reason for that distance slowly dawned on me: In spite of all that had changed, there was still a hint of sexual immorality in my life that surfaced each Sunday morning when I settled into my comfy La-Z-Boy and opened the Sunday morning newspaper. I would quickly find the department store inserts and begin paging through the colored newsprint filled with models posing in bras and panties.

The models were always smiling. Always available.

I loved lingering over each ad insert. *It's wrong,* I admitted to myself, *but it's such a small thing, a far cry from porn.* So I continued peering through the pages, fantasizing. Occasionally, a model reminded me of a girl I once knew, and my mind rekindled the memories of our times together. I rather enjoyed my Sunday mornings with the newspaper.

As I examined myself more closely, I found I had more than a hint of sexual immorality hiding out in my life. Even my sense of humor reflected it. Sometimes a person's innocent phrase—even from our pastor—struck me with a double sexual meaning. I would chuckle, but I felt uneasy. *Why do these double meanings come to my mind so easily?*

I remembered that the Bible said such things shouldn't even be mentioned among the saints. I was worse...I would even laugh at them! And my eyes? They were ravenous heat-seekers searching the horizon, locking on any target with sensual heat.

Young mothers in shorts, leaning over to pull children out of car seats...

Foxy babes wearing tank tops that revealed skimpy bras...

Joggers in spandex, jiggling merrily down the sidewalks...

Smiling secretaries with big busts and low-cut blouses...

WHAT HAD HAPPENED TO ME?

I was left wondering, because I knew I'd started out so well. You see, I'd found a church home and began attending a wonderful marriage class taught by Joel Budd. Except for that embarrassing no-performance night with Janet that I mentioned in chapter 3, I didn't date during that year under Joel's teaching. I might have been the only man in history to attend a married couples' class for a whole year without even having so much as a single date! But just before the twelve-month mark, I prayed this simple prayer: *Lord, I've been in this class for a year and have learned a lot about women, but I don't know any Christian girls. Please show me a woman who embodies these godly characteristics.*

I wasn't asking for a date, girlfriend, or spouse. I just wanted to meet someone with these godly characteristics so I might understand them better.

God did far more than that. One week later, He introduced me to my future wife, Brenda, and we fell in love. Shortly after we began dating seriously, Brenda and I decided to stay pure before marriage, out of our commitment to Christ. She was a virgin—and I wished I were. As God continued to work in my life, Brenda and I married, honeymooned in Colorado, then settled into a new apartment building on the edge of a cornfield in a Des Moines suburb. Was this a little slice of heaven or what? I surely thought so.

Time passed and, at first, I was feeling good. While I was once engaged to two women simultaneously, I was now happily married to one woman. While I once drowned in pornography, since my wedding day I hadn't purchased a pornographic magazine. Given my track record, this was remarkable.

I threw myself into my leadership roles at church, and my Christian image shined brighter and brighter. By worldly standards, I was doing great. With just one little problem. By God's standard of sexual purity, I wasn't even close to living His vision for marriage. Clearly I'd taken steps toward purity, but I was learning that God's standards were higher than I'd ever imagined and that my Father had higher hopes for me than I had dreamed.

It soon became clear that I'd stopped far short of holiness. There were the ad inserts, the double meanings, and the heat-seeking eyes. My mind continued to daydream and fantasize over old girlfriends. These were more than a hint of sexual immorality.

When I confided in a close friend, he replied, "Oh, come on! Nobody can control his eyes and mind, for heaven's sakes! God loves you! It must be something else." But I knew differently.

I finally made the connection between my sexual immorality and my distance from God. Having eliminated the visible adulteries and pornography, and having avoided physical adultery, I looked pure on the outside to everyone else. But to God, I had stopped short, and I'd ignored His voice repeatedly as He prodded me in these areas. I'd merely found a comfortable middle ground somewhere between paganism and obedience to God's standard.

DESPERATION SETS IN

God desired more for me. He'd freed me from the pit, but I'd stopped moving toward Him. I had stopped short. Having seen my distance from God, I decided it was time to begin moving closer again.

I expected the journey to be easy. After all, I had decided once before to eliminate pornography and affairs, and those things were gone. I figured I could stop the rest of this sexual junk just as easily.

But like the other men we spoke of earlier, I couldn't do it. Every week I said I wouldn't look at those ad inserts, but every Sunday morning the striking photos compelled me once again. Every week I'd vow to avoid watching R-rated "sexy" movies when I traveled, but every week I'd fail, sweating out tough battles and always losing. Every time I gazed at some glistening jogger, I'd promise never to do it again. But I always did.

What I'd done was simply trade the naked photos of *Playboy* and *Gallery* for the sensuous ad inserts and other magazine ads. The sin remained because I'd never really changed, never fully rejected sexual sin, never escaped sexual slavery.

A couple of months slipped by, then a couple of years. The distance from God grew wider, and my impurity still ruled me. My faith waned further with each failure. Each desperate loss caused more desperation. While I could always *say* no, I could never *mean* no.

Something was gripping me, something relentless, something I couldn't shake. And my friendship with Christ? Our relationship had changed. He hadn't changed, but I had. I had stopped short of His standard, and I had stopped moving closer into intimacy. I'd said no in my spirit too often, and that stopped the flow of His inner power. I was in bondage.

God's standard is that we avoid every hint of sexual immorality in our lives. If we followed this standard, we would never experience sexual bondage. So we should be amazed that so many Christian guys are under that bondage.

Our heavenly Father is amazed. Here's our paraphrase of some questions God asked (in Hosea 8:5-6), revealing His amazement:

What is going on here? Why are my children choosing to be impure? They are Christians, for heaven's sakes! When are they going to start acting like it?

God knows we can choose to be pure. So why don't we? We aren't victims of some vast conspiracy to ensnare us sexually; we've simply chosen to mix in our own standards of sexual conduct with God's standard. Since we found God's standard too difficult, we created a mixture—something new, something comfortable, something mediocre.

What do we mean by "mixture"? Perhaps a good example is the muddled definition of "sexual relations" that surfaced in the famous sex scandal involving former President Bill Clinton. After the president stated under oath that he did not have sexual relations with Monica Lewinsky, he later explained that he didn't view oral sex as being in that category. So by his definition, he hadn't committed adultery.

That represents quite a contrast to the standard Christ taught: "But I tell you that anyone who looks at a woman lustfully has already committed adultery with her in his heart" (Matthew 5:28). Why do we find it so easy to mix our standards of sexual sin and so difficult to commit to true purity?

Because we're used to it. We easily tolerate mixed standards of sexual purity because we accept mixed standards in most other areas of life.

AUTHENTICITY OR JUST ACCEPTANCE?

Question: What's your aim in life—authenticity or acceptance?

What's the difference between those two? To aim for acceptance is to live your life by the question, "How far can I go and still call myself a Christian?" You want to *seem* to be a Christian, but you also still want to be accepted by your friends at school and in the youth group, without seeming weird or fanatical. Authenticity requires a different question, which can be stated like this: "How holy can I be?"

I was the perfect example of someone who wasn't shooting for Christian authenticity. I was teaching classes at church, chairing activity groups, and attending discipleship classes. My church attendance was exemplary, and I spoke the Christian language fluently. I looked authentic enough when I compared myself with my peers.

But by using our peers as examples and seeking acceptance, we merely cover our sinful tracks. Pete and Mary attended my premarriage class, and Pete impressed me from day one. He lapped up anything I said, nodding in assent at even the most difficult teachings regarding the husband's responsibilities, such as servanthood.

At the end of the seventh week, Pete and Mary stopped me after class. "Your discussion on sexual purity really hit home last week," Pete began, "especially when you said that viewing pornography and X-rated movies won't strengthen a couple's sex life. My first wife used to rent X-rated movies for me, and we'd watch them together before going to bed. Eventually, that hurt us." I nodded while I waited for him to continue. "Mary and I won't do this in our marriage."

So far, so good.

But I could see that Mary, stepping in, wanted to express her viewpoint. "We've been having an ongoing struggle over what we watch together," she said. "We'll often rent a movie to watch at my apartment, but you know how it is. Most of the popular movies have some pretty racy scenes, and I'm feeling more and more uncomfortable with this. When it gets steamy, I tell Pete we need to turn it off, but he gets angry, arguing that we've invested good money in the rental and it's a waste to shut it off. So I head off to the kitchen to do some work while he finishes watching."

Tears welled up in her eyes as she looked down. "I don't feel these movies are good for us," she said. "I've asked Pete to stop for my sake, but he won't. We make it a practice to pray together before he goes home, but after these movies, I feel dirty and cheap. These movies are coming between us."

Of course, Pete was embarrassed. At least in this area, *he had stopped short of authenticity.* By the standards of his peers, he knew he could watch popular movies with racy sexual situations and still "seem" Christian, while being accepted as well. That's all he needed.

To his credit, Pete asked me what he should do. I told him to follow Mary's lead and not watch the sexy videos, and he agreed to do so. That's authenticity.

So…are you being authentic? I once asked Thomas, a youth pastor, to describe the level of authenticity he saw within his young flock.

"Not much," was his terse reply.

I asked him to expound. "They seem to have great intentions," he noted. "They desire to be used by God. Trouble is, they won't step out. When I ask them, 'Why aren't you hungrier for God?' I know the answer already. They don't want to stand out. They don't want to put out the effort. They just want to be accepted. They want more *of* God, but they don't want to be more *like* God. To them, sexual purity seems too high a wall to climb, so they give up. In general, the desire to be like Christ is not really there."

"Why is that?"

"If they were authentic," said Thomas, "they would say, 'Christ saved me, so I want to be pure.' But most are lazy and apathetic about this, not willing to do what it takes. It's all emotion to them. They leave Wednesday night service pumped up and wanting to be different, but by second period Thursday morning they've given up. An authentic teen would say, 'I want to be free from sin.' But most of my kids would say, 'It would be nice to be free from sin,' but they won't pay the price. An authentic teen would say, 'I want to be a man of God.' Most of *my* guys would say, 'It would be nice to be a man of God if He would do it for me.'"

Which are *you* going to choose?

Many choose acceptance over authenticity because they feel that the latter has a large price tag. They're right about the size of the price tag. You empty your wallet to become authentic. What's worse, in spite of the price, authenticity doesn't necessarily remove the struggle against sexual sin. I recently spoke with Tara, who had returned for the summer from a Christian college. I'd heard that she had committed herself even more deeply to the Lord. Intrigued, I cornered her to ask what was up in her life. She happily gushed on about God's plan for her life.

In time, she added, "You know, I saw a group of guys down at my campus using your book *Every Man's Battle* as a teaching tool. I was so excited to tell them I knew you."

"Great to hear that," I said.

Then, after a pause, she leaned in with a stage whisper and said, "I'm really in love with Jesus, but I have to admit that sexual temptation is still a struggle for me with my boyfriend."

"Of course it is," I commented. "I understand completely. But if you keep being authentic with God about how difficult it is, He'll meet you more than halfway."

A smile came to Tara's face, and I wished her all the best.

TOGETHER ON THE MIDDLE GROUND

Tara is ready to fight. Are you?

So often there's no challenging voice calling us to obedience and authenticity. Instead, we move nearer our peers, often sitting together on the middle ground, a good distance from God. When challenged by His higher standards, we're comforted that we don't look too different from other Christians around us. Trouble is, as we've seen, we don't look much different from non-Christians either.

When we look like non-Christians, we haven't been taking God's standards seriously. It's proof we've mixed in our own standards. Mixture can destroy a people. When the Israelites left Egypt for the Promised Land, God told them to cross the Jordan River and destroy every evil thing in their new homeland. That meant killing all the heathen people and crushing their gods to powder. God warned them that if they failed to do this, their culture would "mix" with the pagans and they would adopt depraved practices.

But the Israelites weren't careful to destroy everything. They found it easier to ease up and stop short. In time, the idols and unrighteous people who were left undestroyed became a snare. The Israelites became adulterous in their relationship to God and repeatedly turned their backs on Him.

As promised, He removed them from their land. But just before the destruction of Jerusalem and the final deportation of her inhabitants, God prophesied this about His people in their coming captivity:

> Then in the nations where they have been carried captive, those
> who escape will remember me—how I have been grieved by their
> adulterous hearts, which have turned away from me, and by their
> eyes, which have lusted after their idols. They will loathe themselves
> for the evil they have done. (Ezekiel 6:9)

When we entered the Promised Land of our own salvation, we were told to eliminate every hint of sexual immorality in our lives. Since entering that land, have you failed to crush sexual sin? Every hint of it? If not, you'll someday loathe yourself for that failure, like I did. I didn't crush my sexual sin, and I became ensnared.

PURSUING THE RIGHT RESPONSE

Israel's King Josiah was only twenty-six years of age when he faced a similar situation of neglect for God's standards. In 2 Chronicles 34 we read how a copy of God's Law—long forgotten—had been found during a large-scale renovation of the temple. Then King Josiah listened as this Law was read aloud to him, bringing inescapably to his attention God's standards and the people's failure to live up to them.

Josiah didn't say, "Oh come on, we've lived this way for years. Let's not get legalistic about all this!" No, he was horrified. He tore his robes as a sign of grief and despair. "Great is the Lord's anger," he said as he immediately acknowledged his people's negligence and sought God's further guidance. God quickly answered with these words about Josiah's reaction:

> Because your heart was responsive and you humbled yourself before
> God when you heard what he spoke against this place and its people,
> and because you humbled yourself before me and tore your robes
> and wept in my presence, I have heard you, declares the LORD.
> (2 Chronicles 34:27)

At this point, notice how Josiah immediately led the entire nation in a thorough return to obedience to God's standards:

> Then the king…went up to the temple of the LORD with the men
> of Judah, the people of Jerusalem, the priests and the Levites—all
> the people from the least to the greatest. He read in their hearing
> all the words of the Book of the Covenant, which had been found in
> the temple of the LORD. The king stood by his pillar and renewed the
> covenant in the presence of the LORD—to follow the LORD and keep
> his commands, regulations and decrees with all his heart and all his
> soul, and to obey the words of the covenant written in this book.
>
> Then he had everyone in Jerusalem and Benjamin pledge them-
> selves to it; the people of Jerusalem did this in accordance with the
> covenant of God, the God of their fathers.
>
> Josiah removed all the detestable idols from all the territory

belonging to the Israelites, and he had all who were present in Israel serve the LORD their God. As long as he lived, they did not fail to follow the LORD, the God of their fathers. (2 Chronicles 34:29-33)

No mixture there. Knowing that God's standard is the standard of true life, Josiah rose up and tore down everything that opposed God.

But it certainly wasn't easy.

READY TO COUNT THE COST?

And what about you? It won't be easy for you, either. But now that you've heard about God's standard of sexual purity, are you willing, in the spirit of Josiah, to make a covenant to hold to that standard with all your heart and soul? Will you tear down every sexual thing that stands in opposition to God? Will you aim for authenticity and obedience, where you're truly called to go?

If you've been living a life of mixed standards, you probably have mixture in your *sexual* standards as well. It's likely you have at least a hint of sexual impurity in your life. In that case, you're not ready to pay the price of true obedience—like avoiding the sensuality found in many Hollywood films. Like avoiding sexy thoughts about the "goddesses" at your school. Like training your eyes to look away from string bikinis, full-busted sweaters, and the hot-looking babes who wear them.

A spiritual battle for purity is going on in every heart and soul. The costs are real. Obedience is hard, requiring humility and meekness, very rare elements indeed.

We were told about James, a respected teen in his youth group, who refused to promise to stay sexually pure when pressed to do so. "There are too many unforeseen situations out there for me to make such a promise," he said. Translation: "I want to keep my options open."

James has stopped short. Have you?

The point is this: Sexual impurity has become rampant in the church because we've ignored the costly work of obedience to God's standards as individuals, asking too often, "How far can I go and still be called a Christian?" We've crafted an image that may seem sexually pure, while permitting our eyes to play freely when no one's around and avoiding the hard work of purity.

From my (Fred's) college days, one man's example of this still serves as a warning to me. During my freshman year at Stanford, I became homesick. A dorm buddy who grew up in the shadow of the university felt sorry for me and asked me to his parents' home for dinner. They were extremely wealthy, and their home was stunning. What a great night! Not only was I served my first artichokes (which fascinate me to this day), but the mother was a strikingly pleasant host. That evening I learned that the father, a prominent local businessman, held a high position in their church and believed in the importance of family time.

A few weeks later, I was sitting in a barber's chair when my friend's dad walked into the shop. Being somewhat shy, I didn't say anything. Because of my wet hair and the barber's drape around my neck, he apparently didn't recognize someone he'd met only one time. Sitting down to wait his turn, he picked up a *Playboy* magazine. I was stunned! I watched to see whether he was "just reading the articles," but he immediately turned the magazine sideways to catch Miss March in her full glory.

Is this you? Is there a secret, dark side to your Christian image? If you're a teen, are you going on missions trips during the summer but still fondling some girl's breasts in the backseat of a car? If you're in college, are you leading a Bible study on campus but fantasizing day and night about the naked women you see on the Internet?

Who are you, really?

A search for the comfortable middle ground is an inadequate approach to God. We must count the cost of purity—and pay it. If we don't kill every hint of immorality, we'll be captured by our tendency as males to draw sexual gratification and chemical highs through our eyes—something we'll discuss in the next chapter. But we can't deal with our maleness until we first reject our right to mix standards.

just by being male

Before Brenda gave birth to our fourth child, I (Fred) became convinced through prayer that the child would be a boy, our second son. I was so certain of this that I told her and a few close friends that I was *sure* it would be a boy.

As delivery day neared, the pressure rose. "Why did I tell everyone?" I whined. "What if it's a girl? What if I'm wrong?"

With the start of Brenda's labor pains, the pressure seemed to double every minute. Finally, standing under the bright lights of the delivery room and watching Brenda bear down in the last moments before birth, I knew the moment of truth was near.

The baby came out face up. *Good,* I thought. *I'll have a perfect view.* Anxious, I gently urged Brenda, "Come on, sweetheart. Push a little more."

The shoulders emerged. Just a few more inches, I thought. And then? *Arrrggh! What are you doing, Doctor?* He turned the baby toward himself at the last moment, just as the hips and legs popped out. Now I could only see the baby's back. *C'mon, c'mon,* I cried out inside.

The doctor and nurse said nothing. It was maddening! Methodically and efficiently, they dried the baby, suctioned the throat, and slapped a silly little cap on the newborn. When the doctor finally presented our new child to me, the legs were flopping apart. Immediately I looked down; I just had to know.

"It's a boy!" I exclaimed. Most definitely.

And being a boy means having certain qualities that come "hard-wired" with the package.

WE DO HAVE THESE TENDENCIES, GUYS...

Why the prevalence of sexual sin among men? We got there naturally— simply by being male.

My son Michael is now fifteen years old, and his older brother, Jasen, is twenty-three, and I can assure you that both are definitely males. As I've raised them, I've been aware of the natural tendencies inherent to maleness that will touch every aspect of sexual purity for them, just as they do for me. In other words, our very maleness—and three male tendencies in particular—represents the second main reason (in addition to "stopping short") for the pervasiveness of sexual impurity among men.

Male Tendency #1: We're Rebellious by Nature

When Paul explained to Timothy that "Adam was not the one deceived; it was the woman who was deceived and became a sinner" (1 Timothy 2:14), he was noting that Adam wasn't tricked into eating the forbidden fruit in the Garden of Eden. Adam knew it was wrong, but he ate it anyway. In the millennia since then, all of Adam's sons have tended to be just as rebellious.

Author George Gilder in his 1973 book *Sexual Suicide* reported that men commit more than 90 percent of major crimes of violence, 100 percent of the rapes, and 95 percent of the burglaries. Men comprise 94 percent of our drunken drivers, 70 percent of suicides, and 91 percent of offenders against family and children. Most often, the chief perpetrators are single men.

Our maleness brings a natural, uniquely male form of rebelliousness. This natural tendency gives us the arrogance needed to stop short of God's standards. As men, we'll often choose sin simply because we like our own way. We think we're different. We think we can handle it. But as we saw in the last few chapters, mixing standards and choosing our own way will ensnare even the finest Christians with the deepest hearts.

Male Tendency #2: We Have a Strong, Regular Sex Drive

The human male, because of sperm production and other factors, naturally desires a sexual release about every seventy-two hours or so. How does this cycle impact sexual purity of the eyes and mind? It means your body isn't reliable to help much in the battle for sexual purity and obedience. We easily identify with Paul:

> When I want to do good, evil is right there with me. For in my inner being I delight in God's law; but I see another law at work in the members of my body, waging war against the law of my mind and making me a prisoner of the law of sin at work within my members. What a wretched man I am! (Romans 7:21-24)

Our bodies often break ranks, engaging in battle against us. This traitorous tendency pushes our sexual drive to ignore God's standards. When the engine of our sexual drive combines with our natural male arrogance to go our own way, we're primed and fueled for sexual captivity. The means of ignition, meanwhile, comes from the third male tendency, which is the most deadly.

Male Tendency #3: We Receive Sexual Gratification Through Our Eyes

Our eyes give us men the means to sin broadly and at will. We don't need a date. We don't ever need to wait. We have our eyes, which we can use to imbibe sexual gratification at any time. We're turned on by female nudity in any way, shape, or form.

We aren't picky. It can come in a photograph of a nude stranger just as easily as in a romantic interlude with a naked girlfriend. We have a visual ignition switch when it comes to viewing the female anatomy.

Women seldom understand this because they aren't sexually stimulated in the same way. Their ignitions are tied to touch and relationship. They view this visual aspect of our sexuality as shallow and dirty, even detestable. "When I first heard about how men are, it seemed so wild and unlike anything I could imagine," said my wife, Brenda. "I had a hard time believing it and occasionally even wondered if men were making it up. I don't want to sound mean, but because women don't generally experience this problem, it seems to us that most guys don't think about anything but sex."

Because women can't relate, they have little mercy on us and rarely choose to dress modestly. Walking the halls of any public high school in America can leave a guy gasping for breath! But visual sexual gratification is no laughing matter in your fight for sexual purity. Given what the sight of nudity does to the pleasure centers of our brain, and given the fact that it's pretty easy to see many naked or near-naked women these days, it's no wonder our eyes and mind resist control.

We're Talking Visual Foreplay

Let's restate this third natural male tendency in different words so you don't miss the point: *For males, impurity of the eyes is sexual foreplay.*

That's right. Just like stroking an inner thigh or rubbing a breast. Remember: Foreplay is any sexual action that naturally takes us down the road to intercourse. Foreplay ignites passions, rocketing us forward by stages until we go all the way.

God views foreplay outside marriage as wrong. We get a glimpse of this in Ezekiel 23:3, where God, portraying the waywardness of His chosen people, uses the picture of virgins in passionate sin: "In that land their breasts were fondled and their virgin bosoms caressed." If you've ever argued that God doesn't address "petting" in the Bible, let this verse serve as a corrective to your thinking. Just as instructive is the overall thrust of New

Testament teaching on sexual purity (which we listed at the end of chapter 3) and the application of those standards, mentally as well as physically. From God's viewpoint, sex is far more than being inside a woman.

What acts constitute foreplay? Clearly, caressing the breasts is foreplay. Why? Intercourse is sure to follow. If not with her tonight, then at least with masturbation later back home. If not with her tonight, then maybe tomorrow night when her will has weakened.

Masturbation while fantasizing about specific girls or over certain pictures is the same as doing it. Remember the standard Jesus set?

> You have heard that it was said, "Do not commit adultery." But I tell
> you that anyone who looks at a woman lustfully has already commit-
> ted adultery with her in his heart. (Matthew 5:27-28)

For married men, lustfully thinking of another woman is the same as having physical adultery. If that's true, then for single men, lustfully thinking of women must surely be the same as doing it as well. How much more so if you're masturbating while you do it!

What else is foreplay? Mutual stroking of the genitals is foreplay. Even stroking the top of the thigh can be foreplay. (Young men may not see it that way, but fathers do! If I saw a boy stroking my daughter's thigh, I wouldn't just wink and turn away.) When a girl lays her head in the lap of a teenage boy, that's foreplay. You may think that's a mild form, but that'll get your motor running at levels too high for young motors. Even slow dancing can be foreplay if certain parts of the body are in close contact.

This isn't to say that young couples can't relate physically in ways that aren't foreplay, such as holding hands, walking arm-in-arm, or even engaging in a short kiss. But heavy kissing around the neck and chest leads naturally to taking off some clothes, which leads to mutual masturbation, which leads to intercourse.

You may be asking, "What does all of this have to do with my eyes?" Impurity of the eyes provides definite sexual gratification. Isn't that fore-play? When you see a hot movie scene, is there a twitch below your belt? What are you thinking when you're on the beach and suddenly focus on a jaw-dropping beauty in a thong bikini walking past you? You gasp while Mission Control drones, "We have ignition!" You have her in bed on the spot, though only in your mind. Or you file away the image and fanta-size about her later.

You stare at a sexy model and lust. Your motor revs into the red zone, and you need some type of release or the engine's going to blow. You're preparing your body for intercourse, even if it's "false intercourse" with a jar of Vaseline.

No doubt about it: Visual sexual gratification is a form of sex for men. As males, we draw sexual gratification and chemical highs through our eyes. Alex remembers the time he was watching TV with his sister-in-law. The rest of the family was at the mall.

> She was lying flat on her stomach on the floor in front of me, wear-ing tight shorts, and she'd fallen asleep watching TV. I was on the chair, and I happened to look down and see her upper thigh and a trace of her underwear. I tried to ignore it, but my heart started rac-ing a little, and my eyes kept looking at the back of her upper thigh. It got so exciting that I began to stare and get really excited. I had to release it somehow. I masturbated while she slept, right out in the open.

In Alex's case, impurity of the eyes was clearly foreplay, which led to further sin. It's critical to recognize visual sexual impurity as foreplay. If viewing sensual things merely provides a flutter of appreciation for a woman's beauty, it would be no different from viewing the awesome power of a thunderstorm racing over the Iowa cornfields. There would be no sin and no problem. But if it *is* foreplay, and you *are* getting sexual gratification, then it defiles your body and your relationships:

> Flee from sexual immorality. All other sins a man commits are outside his body, but he who sins sexually sins against his own body. Do you not know that your body is a temple of the Holy Spirit, who is in you, whom you have received from God? You are not your own; you were bought at a price. Therefore honor God with your body.
> (1 Corinthians 6:18-20)

And it's certain that you'll be paying a cost that you may not even be aware of:

> Do not be deceived: God cannot be mocked. A man reaps what he sows. The one who sows to please his sinful nature, from that nature will reap destruction. (Galatians 6:7-8)

THE EYES GRIP THE THROAT

Our eyes, then, explain why no one escapes, and the problem never goes away without a fight. Before we experience victory over sexual sin, we're hurting and confused. *Why can't I win at this?* we think. As the fight wears on, and the losses pile higher, we begin to doubt everything about ourselves, even our salvation. At best, we think that we're deeply flawed, or worse, evil persons. We feel very alone, since men speak little of these things.

But the answer lies more in our eyes than in our souls. Most likely, your "addictive" behaviors are not rooted in some deep, dark, shadowy mental maze or weakness. Rather, they're based on pleasure highs that enter through the eyes. Men receive a chemical high from sexually charged images when a hormone called epinephrine is secreted into the bloodstream. This locks into the memory whatever stimulus is present at the time of the emotional excitement.

Likewise, our "mind's eye" can cause the same chemical high through fantasy. We've counseled men who became emotionally and sexually stimulated just from entertaining thoughts of sexual activity. A guy dead set on purchasing *Hustler* at his local 7-Eleven is sexually stimulated long before he even steps into the convenience store. His stimulation began in his thought process, which triggered his nervous system, which secreted epinephrine into the bloodstream.

Why can't we say no easily? Why do our eyes bounce toward sensual women so quickly? Why do our minds run to fantasy? The answer is *because we're compelled by the chemical high and the sexual gratification it brings.*

We're simply saying that the ability of the male eyes and mind to draw true sexual gratification from the world around them begins to explain why sexual sin is so common. In fact, it explains many things.

First, it explains why young men experiment with masturbation early in life. With all this "foreplay" of the eyes going on, and with no guidance on what to do with the feelings, the result is understandable. There's no sense in feeling deep shame over it, as if you're some weird pervert or something. You aren't.

Second, this explains why Paul places sexual sin in its own unique category:

Flee from *sexual immorality.* All other sins a man commits are outside his body, but he who sins sexually sins against his own body.
(1 Corinthians 6:18)

The means to sin rests *in our bodies*—we can't walk away from our eyes and mind like we can walk away from drugs. This also explains why prayer alone is often not enough for total victory. We can go to the altar of prayer and be freed, but if we stop short and never fully close the gates of our eyes to sensual pollution, the sewage seeps right back in day in and day out. The chemical highs return, and we're captured again.

So while we're to pray about sexual sin on the *spiritual* front, we have our orders on the *physical* battlefront as well. We're commanded to actively avoid sexual sin by choice—"to flee." It isn't unspiritual or "fleshly" to take an active role in this battle and to build defenses. We're commanded to do so by God. What's more spiritual than obedience?

Third, it explains why even married guys remain hooked after their weddings. Married or not, you must train your eyes and mind to be pure, or they'll keep doing what comes naturally.

THESE GUYS KNOW ALL ABOUT IT

Recently, I had breakfast with some guys from Columbia, Missouri, who had read *Every Man's Battle* as part of a men's group at their church. The book includes the following test to help readers determine the level of their addictive sexual cravings:

1. Do you lock on when an attractive woman comes near you?
2. Do you masturbate to images of other women?
3. Have you found your wife to be less sexually satisfying?
4. Are you holding a grudge against your wife—a grudge that gives you a sense of entitlement?
5. Do you seek out sexually arousing articles or photo spreads in newspapers or magazines?
6. Do you have a private place or secret compartment that you keep hidden from your wife?
7. Do you look forward to going away on a business trip?
8. Do you practice behaviors that you can't share with your wife?
9. Do you frequent porn-related sites on the Internet?

10. Do you watch R-rated movies, sexy videos, or the steamy VH1 channel for gratification?

As we gobbled our eggs and sausage, we talked about how the guys did on this little cravings quiz. A few of the sixteen men admitted that they answered yes to eight or nine questions, and not one man scored any lower than four. It doesn't take much imagination, then, to see why the bifurcation myth is so dangerous. While a graduation ceremony or a wedding reception may mark your move across the line into a new, separate adult life in your own mind, the addictive cravings for these sexual chemical highs know no boundaries. Your eyes and brain go with you into whatever future you choose.

Let us share some other stories with you along these lines. Thad is recovering from drug dependency at a local Christian ministry. He says this:

> I've been trying hard to get my life in order. At the drug center, I've learned more about myself and my addiction to drugs, but I've discovered a second, unexpected thing: I have a problem with looking at women.
>
> I want to be free, but I'm becoming frustrated and angry with the church. The Bible says women should dress modestly, but they don't. The women soloists are always wearing the latest, tightest fashions. I look at them, but all I see are curves and legs. You know, that one who always wears the slit way up the thigh? That thigh flashes with every step she takes. Believe me, I notice!

Kerry, an eighteen-year-old high school student, told us he absolutely dreads going to his bedroom:

> I always study in the living room as late as I can. I stall before returning to my room because I know what's going to happen. Before too

long, I have the computer booted up. I tell myself that it'll only be for a minute while I check e-mail, but I know I'm lying. I know what I really want. I'm hoping to view a little sex scene or two as I flip around with the mouse. I tell myself that I'll only look for a minute or two, or that I'll stop before I get carried away. Then my motor gets going and I want more and more, sometimes even opening the really X-rated sites.

The RPMs are going so high that I have to do something, or it feels like my engine will blow. So I masturbate. On a few occasions I fight it, but if I do, later when I turn the lights out, I'm flooded with lustful thoughts and desires. I stare wide-eyed at the ceiling. I see nothing, but I literally feel the bombardment, the throbbing desire. I have no way to get to sleep, and it's killing me. So I say, *Okay, if I masturbate, I'll have peace, and I can finally get to sleep.* So I do, and guess what? The guilt is so strong I still can't get to sleep. I wake up totally exhausted in the morning.

What's wrong with me?

What about you? Maybe it's true that when you and a babe reach a door simultaneously, you wait to let her go first, but not out of honor. You want to follow her up the stairs and look her over—check out her butt. Maybe you've driven your car to the parking lot of a local gym after school, watching scantily clad classmates bouncing in and out, fantasizing—even masturbating—in the car. Although you wonder what's wrong with you, you just can't help yourself.

IT'S A QUESTION OF MALENESS VS. MANHOOD

If we get into sexual sin naturally—just by being male—then how do we get out? Well, we can't eliminate our maleness, and we're sure we don't want to.

For instance, we'll eventually want to look at our future wives and desire them sexually. They'll be beautiful to us, and we'll be sexually gratified when we gaze at them, often daydreaming about the night ahead and what bedtime will bring. In its proper place, maleness is wonderful. The full constellation of male traits is an awesome, special creation of God that prepares us to lead and protect our homes with courage and strength. We can't afford to eliminate that!

Yet our maleness is also a major root of sexual sin. So what do we do?

We must choose to be *more* than male.

We must choose manhood.

If you've ever heard a youth speaker urge you to "be a man about it," he was encouraging you to rise up to a standard of manhood. He wants you to fulfill your potential, to rise above your natural tendency to mix your standards and take the easy way out. That's why he said, "Be a man."

Our heavenly Father also exhorts us to be men, even during these early years of your lives. He wants us to be like Him. When He calls us to "be perfect as your Father in heaven is perfect," He's asking us to rise above our natural tendencies—the impure eyes, fanciful minds, and wandering hearts. His standard of purity doesn't come naturally to us, but He calls us to rise up, by the power of His indwelling presence, and get the job done.

Before the army he commanded entered an important battle, Joab said to the troops of Israel, "Be of good courage, and let us play the men for our people" (2 Samuel 10:12, KJV). In short, he was saying, "We know God's plan for us. Let's rise up as men and set our hearts and minds to get it done!"

Regarding sexual integrity, God wants you to rise up and get it done. At some point, you'll have to make this decision. There's no escaping this fight, as we've already clearly shown you. Isn't it time to make a stand?

If you say yes then you must follow the lead of your role models, something we'll discuss in the next chapter.

PART III

choosing
authentic manhood

you can choose
true manhood

Many of us don't have decent role models, even in our own fathers. At worst, our fathers don't care about God's sexual standards. For instance, after I proposed to Brenda, my dad pulled me aside and quietly said, "Son, I know what the Bible says about premarital sex, and you and I are both Christians and everything. But sex is too important for you to get married without having intercourse with Brenda first. You can't afford to marry a frigid girl."

Dad might have been a good role model in many ways, but in the arena of sexuality, he was a disaster.

I wasn't alone. Tyler, a junior in our youth group, has a strong mother fighting for his purity, but when Tyler's father loans him his pickup truck for dates and hands him the keys, he never fails to remind him, "Don't forget, Ty, I've put a supply of condoms in the glove box for you." Then when Tyler returns the keys, his father asks, "Did you get laid?"

Brandon told me about being with a bunch of guys playing Nintendo late one Saturday night. He was supposed to be home at 11 P.M., but he fell asleep and didn't wake until 3 in the morning. Horrified, he raced home in his car to find his mom on her knees praying desperately for his safe return, tears streaming everywhere. And where was dear old dad? He'd gone to bed hours earlier, smirking at his wife's prayers and saying brightly, "Quit worrying! He's probably found some cute girl and is getting laid for the first time. It's about time for him to grow up."

Even the best fathers fear discussing the topic and can't bring themselves to convey the truths they deeply long to share with their sons. Kenny told me, "I remember when I was in high school and my father and I were driving home from a fishing trip in southern Missouri. I noticed his hands tightening the grip on the steering wheel, and then he said it: 'Son, you're getting older. Do you have any questions about girls?'

"And in my great wisdom at age fifteen, I emphatically said, 'No!' And nothing else was said the whole trip. In fact, the subject was never brought up again. I didn't know anything then, and I'm still learning years later. What a loss," Kenny concluded.

So who will be your role model?

FOLLOW THESE HANDS AND EYES

We hope your own father will be an excellent role model for you. If that's not possible, or it's highly unlikely, the Bible provides role models who can fill your father's shoes if necessary. As we look to these people, what we can learn about the meaning of true manhood, especially regarding how we deal with our eyes and minds and bodies?

For example, let's focus on hands for a moment. In a newsletter, author and speaker Dr. Gary Rosberg told of seeing a pair of hands that reminded him of the hands of his father, who had gone on to heaven. Gary continued to reminisce about what his father's hands meant to him. Then he shifted his thoughts to the hands of Jesus, noting this simple truth: "They were hands that never touched a woman with dishonor."

As I (Fred) read this, sorrow tore at my soul. Oh, how I wished I could say that about my own hands! I have degraded women with my hands, and I regretted the sin. As I thought about it more, however, I realized that since my first year of salvation, I haven't touched a woman in dishonor. That made me feel good!

I pondered Gary's words a little longer. Jesus' hands never touched a woman with dishonor, but Jesus said lusting with the eyes is the same as touching. Given that Jesus is sinless, I suddenly realized that Jesus not only never touched a woman with dishonor, He never even looked at a woman in dishonor. Could I say that?

Actually, I couldn't. Though I had received salvation, I was still looking at women in dishonor.

"Oh, don't be so hard on yourself," you might say. "It's natural for guys to look. That's part of our nature." But what you're doing is stealing. The impure thought life is the life of a thief. You're stealing images that aren't yours. When you looked down the blouse of a woman who isn't your wife, you were stealing something that wasn't yours to take. When you had pre-marital sex, you touched someone who didn't belong to you. It's just like walking down Main Street behind someone who drops a hundred-dollar bill, and you pick it up. If you choose to keep the money instead of saying, "Hey, Mister!" then you've taken something you're not entitled to.

Similarly, if a well-built woman bends over and shows you her breasts while you continue to stare at her, you're a thief. You need to leave that valuable creation in the hands of God and her husband or her future husband. When we're thieves with our eyes, we're grabbing sexual gratification from areas that don't belong to us, from women who aren't connected to us. In this arena, Jesus, having never looked on a woman with dishonor, is clearly our role model.

"Well, sure!" you say. "He was God. It's unfair to expect me to live like Him!"

Maybe. But if, because of His deity, Jesus' personal standard seems unattainable to you, let's look at another manhood role model from Scripture in the area of sexual purity.

JUST A MAN, A GREAT MODEL

His name was Job, and though you wouldn't think it, this man is the essential role model of sexual purity in Scripture. Job's story unfolds in the Old Testament, where in the first chapter of the book that bears his name, we see God bragging about Job to Satan:

> Have you considered my servant Job? There is no one on earth like
> him; he is blameless and upright, a man who fears God and shuns
> evil. (Job 1:8)

Was God proud of Job? You bet! He applauded His servant's faithfulness in words of highest praise. If you walk in purity, blameless and upright, He'll speak just as proudly of you. But if you don't, this passage from Scripture may actually discourage you when you compare your life with Job's. Don't be discouraged. Instead, learn from Job.

First, we need to learn more about how Job did it. In Job 31:1, we see Job making this startling revelation: "I made a covenant with my eyes not to look lustfully at a girl."

A covenant with his eyes! You mean he made a promise with his eyes to not gaze upon a young woman? It's not possible! It can't be true!

Yet Job was successful; otherwise, he wouldn't have made this promise:

> If my heart has been enticed by a woman, or if I have lurked at my
> neighbor's door, then may my wife grind another man's grain, and
> may other men sleep with her. (Job 31:9-10)

Job had been totally successful, otherwise he couldn't have made this statement from his heart. He knew he had lived right, and he knew his eyes and mind were pure. He swore to it upon his wife and marriage, before God and man.

Let's go back to the beginning of the story and read the opening verse of the book of Job: "In the land of Uz there lived a man whose name was Job. This man was blameless and upright; he feared God and shunned evil."

Job was just a man! As you realize that, these precious words should gloriously flood your soul: *If Job could do it, so can I.* God wants you to know that even with your manhood and all its bothersome tendencies, you can rise above sexual impurity.

MAKING YOUR OCULAR COVENANT

When I (Fred) first gave serious consideration to Job's example, I meditated upon his words for days on end. Job and I were different in only one way— our actions. God called him "blameless." I wasn't blameless, but since I was a man, just like Job, there had to be hope.

After a few days, my mind turned to the word *covenant.* What was that? I learned that a covenant is an agreement between God and man. So how would I go about making one? And if I did make a promise to God, could I be counted on to keep my word?

And then there was the issue of my eyes. Could I really expect my eyes to keep their end of the bargain? Eyes can't think or talk! How do they keep a promise?

Day after day, my mind returned to this covenant concept, trying to intellectually grasp it, all the while remaining in my sin. Yet something was stirring deep in my soul.

Then it happened. I remember the moment—the exact spot on Merle Hay Road in Des Moines—when everything broke loose. Minutes before, I had failed God with my eyes for the thirty-millionth time. A female jogger, her glistening body capturing my eyes as I drove past her, made me all excited. Yet as soon as I passed her, my heart churned in guilt, pain, and sorrow. Driving down Merle Hay Road, I gripped the wheel and through clenched teeth, I yelled out: "That's it! I'm through with this! I'm making a covenant with my eyes. I don't care what it takes, and I don't care if I die trying. It stops here. It stops here!"

I made that covenant and built it brick by brick. Later, Steve and I will show you the blueprint for building that brick wall, but for now, study my breakthrough:

- I made a clear decision.
- I decided once and for all to make a change.

I can't describe how much that decision meant to me. Floods of frustration from years of failure poured from my heart. I'd just had it! I wasn't fully convinced I could trust myself even then, but I'd finally engaged myself for battle. After making a covenant with God regarding my eyes, all my mental and spiritual resources zeroed in on a single target—my impurity.

DON'T FOLLOW THIS SISSY

You may be thinking, *Who in their right mind would ever make a covenant with his eyes like this? It seems crazy.* What I did on Merle Hay Road may seem odd to you. But remember, acts of obedience often appear strange, even illogical.

To help you understand where I'm coming from, let's look in the Bible at the story of a man who just didn't get it. His name was Zedekiah, the greatest sissy in the Bible. He was reigning as the king in Jerusalem when the Babylonians were threatening to capture and destroy the city and bring an end to the nation of Judah.

Zedekiah's lack of manhood rose to the surface in the events described in Jeremiah 38. Jeremiah, as God's prophet, knew what the outcome of the Babylonian invasion would be, and he made it known by stating:

This is what the LORD says: "Whoever stays in this city will die by the sword, famine or plague, but whoever goes over to the Babylonians will live. He will escape with his life; he will live." And this is what the LORD says: "This city will certainly be handed over to the army of the king of Babylon, who will capture it." (Jeremiah 38:2-3)

When Zedekiah heard about this, he let his officials throw Jeremiah into a deep cistern to shut him up. He later ordered his servants to lift the prophet out, but he still kept Jeremiah under arrest. Then one day, with Jerusalem under siege, the king summoned Jeremiah to a secret meeting. The prophet told the king what to do.

This is what the LORD God Almighty, the God of Israel, says: "If you surrender to the officers of the king of Babylon, your life will be spared and this city will not be burned down; you and your family will live. But if you will not surrender to the officers of the king of Babylon, this city will be handed over to the Babylonians and they will burn it down; you yourself will not escape from their hands." (Jeremiah 38:17-18)

Surrender! God, through Jeremiah, was asking the king to do something very difficult, something that made no sense. Who in their right mind would ever leave the fortress and go over to the enemy? It seemed crazy. Still, God's Word was clear. The city would fall whether they stayed or left.

Zedekiah expressed his fear, but Jeremiah remained firm, saying, "Obey the LORD by doing what I tell you. Then it will go well with you, and your life will be spared" (Jeremiah 38:20). But Zedekiah, indecisive and fearful, failed to obey. The right thing to do was too illogical, too costly. The results for himself, his family, and his nation were tragic.

MAN'S MAN OR GOD'S MAN?

When it comes down to it, God's definition of real manhood is straightforward and simple: Hear His Word and follow it. It's not someone deciding that "it's my way or the highway" or "I'll do what I want when I want."

Have you ever known a guy whose beard is so heavy that he uses two blades to shave in the morning—one for each side of his face? By late afternoon, his four o'clock shadow is so thick that he has to shave again. Four blades in one day! For those of us who are "smooth men," we hold this tough guy in awe.

But God cares nothing about that. When God looks around, He's not looking for what everyone else calls a man's man; He's looking for "God's man." His definition of a man—someone who hears His Word and acts upon it—is tough, but at least it's clear.

Meanwhile, the results of failing to be a man according to God's definition could have a tragic end. The fact is, as Galatians 6:7-8 tells us, God is not mocked: You reap what you sow, both the good and the bad.

By now you understand God's command that you should eliminate every hint of sexual immorality from your life. If you do that, as Job did through his covenant with his eyes, then you're God's man. If you don't eliminate every hint, are you headed for trouble? Surely.

Earlier in the book of Jeremiah, we read these desperate words spoken by the prophet to the people: "How long will you be unclean?" (13:27). That's the question for you as well: How long will you choose to be sexually unclean? How long will you keep shutting down the new life within you?

We've seen what God expects through these role models. We've seen it can be done. Jesus and Job were authentic men, and they didn't mix standards even when their lives were on the line. Are you God's man, hearing the Word and doing it? If you want to turn things around, authenticity with God is the place to start.

what's it going to be?

Many single guys wonder how they can be expected to toe God's line. To some, it seems impossible to please God in their sexuality. There are just too many obstacles, in spite of our role models.

But all things are possible through Christ—if we have faith in Him, we can do it. The first half of Hebrews 11:6 says, "And without faith it is impossible to please God." *Oh that's just great! I don't have any faith!* We're not talking some superspiritual, emotional faith, where if you claim, "I'm going to be pure"—and claim it long, loud, and early—then your positive mental attitude will carry the day. No, we're talking about the kind of faith found in the rest of that verse:

> And without faith it is impossible to please God, because anyone
> who comes to him must believe that he exists *and that he rewards*
> *those who earnestly seek him.* (Hebrews 11:6)

Sure, you have faith that God really exists, but do you believe that God rewards those who earnestly seek Him? If you do, you'll also believe that your relationship with God is worth the sacrifice of giving up sex with your girlfriend. Is your relationship with God as gratifying as her breasts on Friday nights?

Since many of us go for the gusto today, we go for the breasts. Even if some of us *say* we believe in that stuff about God, we don't *live* like we do.

That's why, when given the choice between meeting God's standard and being accepted by Him, or ignoring those standards and being accepted by our peers, we choose our peers every time. We don't really have the faith that God exists or believe that He'll reward those who earnestly seek Him.

ACTING AUTHENTICALLY

Evidence of that mind-set flourishes everywhere we turn. A lot of us talk a good game while sitting on the bench, but when given the chance to play, we keep our eyes on the babes in the stands, not on the pitcher holding the ball.

Granted, there's a lot to look at in the stands. Even Christian girls push their wardrobes far beyond modesty, sporting short shorts, tight T-shirts, and bare midriffs. You can get an eyeful and even masturbate from the memory when you get home later that night.

Sex is everywhere—even in church settings. The custodial staff at my church has even found used condoms and torn condom wrappers in some classrooms on the mornings after youth group meetings. Can you believe that? While it sounds like I'm making this up, there's no reason to doubt that Christian youth are just as sexually active as their non-Christian peers. Surveys and research back it up.

One Wednesday evening at a youth group meeting, several boys were laughing hysterically as they waited for things to start. The youth pastor approached the group. "What's up, guys?" he asked.

"Sorry, but we all saw a great video over the weekend at Brent's house," said one of the high school juniors. "It was the most hilarious movie, wasn't it Brent?"

"It sure was," he said, grabbing his stomach as he giggled.

"What was the movie?" asked the youth pastor innocently.

"American Pie."

"What was so funny in the movie?" asked the youth pastor. "I haven't seen it."

All four guys started smirking. Said one, "There's a part where the guy masturbates into an apple pie. It was hilarious!"

"Masturbating into an apple pie? I'm not sure that type of humor is appropriate for Christians," said the youth pastor.

A dark scowl came over Brent's face. "Oh, you're just like our parents," he sneered. "Get real."

Those teens would rather watch the girls in the stands than get into God's game. What about you? Are you like those guys whose favorite video is *American Pie*?

KNOW YOUR TEAM

You may be playing in God's game, but when the final out is made, you forget whose team you're on. One summer Jeremy went on a missions trip to Costa Rica, and he was genuinely touched by the poverty and squalor he witnessed in that Third World country. He dug trenches to build new school classrooms for eight hours a day, and by night, he was gripped by the prayer times with the missionaries. He thought he was a changed person.

When Jeremy returned home, it wasn't more than two evenings before he was back into his old routine with the guys. Watching raunchy R-rated videos like *American Pie*. Fantasizing about Lindsay as he lay awake at night. Sure, he had a great experience in Costa Rica, but that was there and now he was here.

Three weeks later, he found himself in the backseat of his car, half drunk, with a girl unzipping his pants. In an alcohol-induced fog, he couldn't remember being touched by God's presence among those poor people in Costa Rica. That seemed so long ago. Nor could Jeremy remember what he'd read in his Bible that week:

The *acts of the sinful nature* are obvious: sexual immorality, impurity.... But the *fruit of the Spirit* is love, joy, peace, patience, kindness, goodness, faithfulness, gentleness and *self-control*. Against such things there is no law. Those who belong to Christ Jesus have crucified the sinful nature with its passions and desires. Since we live by the Spirit, let us keep in step with the Spirit. (Galatians 5:19,22-25)

Jeremy is expressing sexual immorality, not self-control. He's not concerned with being intimate with God. If interviewed at that moment, he would say things like these:

- "I can't commit to keeping my pants on. There are just too many unforeseen circumstances that might make me want to go to bed with a girl, so I won't make that promise."
- "God cannot possibly have meant 'not a hint.'"
- "It's impossible for me not to look at one of my classmates in a string bikini."
- "Just because she won't let me order doesn't mean I can't look at the menu."

If you think like this, you're not coming to God on His terms. God is aching for you to be one with Him, that He might use you. He wants to give you a voice in His kingdom. He wants to show you His power.

So when He defines His terms of sexual purity, don't say, "God can't possibly mean that!" because He does. Christ is looking to see whether you can be trustworthy—capable of handling more for His kingdom. Luke 16:11 says, "So if you have not been trustworthy in handling worldly wealth, who will trust you with true riches?"

If you aren't trustworthy in handling fleshly passions, how can you be trusted to handle things of greater value? Jesus said that if you were faithful in the little things, He would entrust you with bigger things. In this, God isn't primarily referring to what He's called you to *do* in His kingdom. He's primarily concerned with what He's called you to *be* in your character.

Maybe you've asked God to reveal His will for your life, but how are you doing with that "little" part of His will that He has already revealed to you?

It is *God's will* that you should be sanctified; *that you should avoid sexual immorality*; that each of you should learn to control his own body in a way that is holy and honorable, not in passionate lust like the heathen, who do not know God; and that in this matter no one should wrong his brother or take advantage of him.... For God did not call us to be impure, but to live a holy life. Therefore, he who rejects this instruction does not reject man but God, who gives you his Holy Spirit. (1 Thessalonians 4:3-8)

God has already laid down His life as an example to us:

Therefore, since Christ suffered in his body, arm yourselves also with the same attitude, because he who has suffered in his body is done with sin. As a result, he does not live the rest of his earthly life for evil human desires, but rather for *the will of God*. For you have spent enough time in the past doing what pagans choose to do—living in...lust. (1 Peter 4:1-3)

It's time to fulfill God's will for your life. Focus on the "little" things He has entrusted to you. He wants to reward you as you earnestly seek Him.

MOCKED FOR HER STANDARDS

Sure, authenticity and earnestness have a price. A few years back, Cyndi was known throughout her church as a girl who lived purely and radically for God, a high-school student with high standards. I'll never forget a conversation I (Fred) had with her. "Is it hard to hold such high standards like you do?" I asked.

"Oh, I don't mind being mocked," she replied. "Christ was mocked plenty. That's just part of it."

Wow, I said to myself. We sat silently for a while as I pondered her statement. Then I glanced up at her and found her staring wistfully into the distance. Suddenly, her face crumpled slightly, and a large tear rolled out of the corner of her eye.

"I so ache to find a friend, anyone, who's like me," she whispered.

How can this be? I thought. *How can we all be so mushy in our standards that those walking straight are lonely?*

I asked her youth pastor, Larry, "Why aren't the other youth drawn to Cyndi? I would be."

"Oh, they respect her to no end," said Larry. "Of course, some will always mock, but her peers rarely choose radically committed Christians as role models. That represents too much sacrifice and too much risk of not being accepted. They prefer to hang out with guys who play sports and have a lot of girlfriends. You know, one who's both Christian and worldly simultaneously."

Everyone with beliefs gets mocked, not just Christians. Don't be so afraid of it! That's just a part of life. When I was playing football, I was radical in my commitment to be the best quarterback in the state. In the winter before my senior year, I decided that I needed to improve my balance on the football field.

I devised a plan. I noticed that the snowplows at school piled up the snow into a huge twenty-foot-high berm that ran for the length of the parking lot. On the top of this mountain was a ten-foot-wide plateau that jutted with boulders and jags of snow and ice. Strapping my cleats on and tucking a ball under an arm, I'd take off running from one end to the other. At full speed I cut in and out between the jags and boulders, pretending they were linebackers and defensive backs.

Early on, I paid a heavy price. The ice cuts and bruises really hurt, and

I took more than a beating. Still, as the weeks went by, I clipped the jutting ice less often. My ability to cut and change directions became sharper and faster with each passing day.

My teammates sometimes dropped by to watch. They laughed and mocked me, all right. But I had faith that I would be rewarded for my efforts, and I *was* rewarded. The next fall, when it was third-and-two or fourth-and-one, who wanted me to run the option play and keep the ball? Answer: The very same teammates who watched me run for those tough yards on the snow berm. They knew I'd never go down easily.

I did all that for football, a "god" that existed only in my mind. Our own God is real, and He'll truly reward those who earnestly seek Him—or practice for Him! If you would step out for God with even a fraction of the commitment I had on that ice plateau, you would be an all-star in God's kingdom.

And remember one more thing: While authenticity has its price, inauthenticity for the sake of acceptance has a high price as well—as we've seen in the many stories told earlier in the book. The effects of your sin will follow you into adulthood. Since both have their price, why not pay the price for something great? Why not fight? God *will* reward you.

NO PLANS TO SURRENDER

We came across a newspaper story about a World War II vet named B. J. "Bernie" Baker who was told he was dying of bone cancer. Given only two years to live, he told the doctors to fight the disease with everything possible. "Give me the treatments," he said. "I'll keep living my life." Meanwhile he and his wife found time for a motor-home drive to Alaska, a fishing excursion to Costa Rica, and several trips to Florida.

Nine years after the diagnosis, he was struggling with shortness of breath and loss of strength, but he said, "I'm going to keep fighting. Might as well."

Those words weren't uttered in resignation. They were the words of a fighter, a real man, a soldier who faced bombs and machine-gun fire in the South Pacific before returning to America and eventually starting Baker Mechanical Company with two pipe wrenches and a $125 pickup truck. (It would become one of the largest companies of its kind in America.) The cancer hit him hard, but he had no plans for surrender.

Might as well keep fighting. What was Bernie's alternative?

To quit and die.

What about you and your battle with your impure eyes and mind? What's your alternative to fighting?

To become ensnared and die spiritually.

When you talk to courageous men from Bernie's generation, World War II veterans who embody the title of Tom Brokaw's book *The Greatest Generation,* they say they don't feel like heroes. They simply had a job to do. When the landing-craft ramps fell open, they swallowed hard and said, "It's time." Time to fight.

In your struggle with sexual impurity, isn't it time? Sure, fighting back will be hard. It was for us. When we began our fight, we fully expected to take a beating at first, and we did. Our sins had humbled us. But we wanted victory over those sins and the respect of our God.

Your life is under a withering barrage of machine-gun sexuality that rakes the landscape mercilessly. God has trained you for battle and given you the weapons, along with the promise that courageous young men of God can stop the fire.

But right now you're in a landing craft, bobbing and inching closer to shore and a showdown. You can enter the fray now, or you can dawdle until this withering barrage leaves your spiritual landscape devastated, which means you'll have to fight later among deeper ruins and more desperate conditions. But the showdown will come. You can't stay in the landing craft forever. Sooner or later, the ramp will drop, and then it will be your time to run bravely into the teeth of the enemy. God will run with you, but He won't run for you.

It's time to plunge ahead and go like a man.

GOING TO WAR, GOING TO WIN

Several years ago I counseled a high-school sophomore named Ben who said he wanted sexual integrity. But his words were just words. "I'm still buying the *Playboys*," he said recently. "I guess I just don't hate them enough."

Similarly, I'm reminded of seventeen-year-old Ronnie, who was masturbating several times a day. His pastor told me, "Ronnie says he wants to be free, but he doesn't feel any compunction to put in any effort on his own. He'll give up his sin, but only if God does it."

Later, Ronnie rushed into his pastor's office in terror, saying, "Pastor, you've got to help me! You know the fantasies I have while masturbating? Two weeks ago, they suddenly turned homosexual, and I can't make them stop!" That was the moment when Ronnie needed to stand up and fight.

We've known those who have failed in their battle for sexual purity, and we know some who have won. The difference? *Those who won hated their impurity.* They were going to war and going to win—or die trying. Every resource was leveled upon the foe.

There will be no victory in this area of your life until you choose manhood with all your might. In the arena of sexual purity, you're at your own point of decision.

Look in the mirror. Are you authentic? Are you proud of your sexual fantasizing? Or do you feel degraded after viewing cyber porn or sex scenes in films?

Is a low-grade sexual fever burning? Like any low-grade fever, it doesn't disable you, but you aren't healthy, either. Spiritually, you can sort of function normally, but you can't push hard. You just get by. And if this fever doesn't break, you'll never fully function as a Christian. Like the prodigal son, you need to come to your senses and make a decision. Here are some more questions to ask yourself:

- How long am I going to stay sexually impure?
- How long will I rob my friends in the youth group with my fake Christianity?
- How long will I stunt the growth of intimacy and oneness with God, an intimacy I promised Him years ago?

God's view is simple here. You need to face those questions and make a decision. Yet you're hesitating. We know you are, because we hesitated for years. You're thinking, *Wait a minute; I'm not ready.* Or, *It just isn't that easy!*

Fine. We'll agree that choosing to stop sinning isn't any slam-dunk, easy decision. Once you're ensnared, the obstacles loom huge. But listen to the following words spoken by preacher Steve Hill, who was addressing his escape from addiction to drugs and alcohol as well as from sexual sin:

> There's no temptation that is uncommon to man. God will send you a way of escape, but you've got to be willing to take that way of escape, my friend.
>
> I was an alcoholic to the max. I would drink whiskey, straight whiskey, every day. And I was a junkie. Cocaine up my nose, in my arm—I did it all, friend. But God never delivered me from the desire and the love of drugs. He never did. What happened is that I *decided* to never touch the stuff or drink booze again.
>
> Those of you who are into pornography may be asking God to take away your lustful desires. You are a man with hormones. You feel things. You have since puberty, and you will until the day you die! You are attracted to the opposite sex.
>
> I'm not saying that God cannot take the desire from you. He can! He's just never done it in my life or in the tens of thousands of

people I've worked with over the years. That includes pornographers. Ninety-nine percent of them had to *make a decision*. They had to make a decision to not walk by magazine racks of adult magazines, and they had to make a decision to stay faithful to their wives and their families.

We agree. It's time to make a decision.

THIS IS YOUR MOMENT

Consider the example of Eleazar, one of David's "three mighty men," whom we learn about in this brief record of a tough battle against the Philistines:

> Then the men of Israel retreated, but he stood his ground and
> struck down the Philistines till his hand grew tired and froze to
> the sword. The LORD brought about a great victory that day.
> (2 Samuel 23:9-10)

Eleazar refused to be ensnared anymore. Everyone else was running from the enemy, but he put his foot down and said, "I've had it with this running. I'm going to fight until I drop dead or until I drop to the field in victorious exhaustion. This is my moment to live or die."

Have you had it with the running? In his early twenties, author and pastor Jack Hayford once sat in his car after a banking transaction with a lovely bank teller and said to himself, "I'm either going to have to purify my mind and consecrate myself unto God, or I'm going to have to masturbate right here." That Jack could say this in front of tens of thousands of men at a Promise Keepers conference was inspirational.

How about you? How long will you allow the Philistines to chase you? Are you motivated instead to fight?

MOTIVATED TO WIN

Here's a story of someone who became very motivated to change. Several weeks prior to his planned wedding, Barry heard me (Fred) give a talk on sexual purity. My words weighed heavily on his heart because he'd been masturbating to R-rated movies since his midteens. He'd been planning to marry Heather with his secret safely tucked away, but now he decided to tell her the truth. Heather recalls her reaction to Barry's confession:

> I was shocked and numbed when we talked in the car that night.
> I just stared straight ahead with no feelings at all. After dropping
> him off, I cried and cried, refusing to talk to him for days. When
> I did agree to see him, he commented to me that I looked pretty.
> I got so mad and repulsed by him that I threw the engagement
> ring in his face and told him to get out of my sight. I felt sick
> and dirty.

As you can see, this topic was an emotional one. Women take it personally when they find out what their boyfriends have been doing in secret.

Heather asked Brenda and me to meet with her, which we did. After much prayer and counseling, Heather gave Barry a deadline of one week to turn his life around.

Then I met with Barry. "Can you help me?" he asked. "I'm absolutely hooked on sexy movies. I expected Heather to understand, but she was horrified and called me a sex addict. Fred, I'm desperate. The invitations have already been sent out, but if I don't get this stopped, I'll have to somehow explain all this to my mother-in-law! You've got to help me!"

Do you suppose Barry was motivated? He surely was. Rarely have I met with someone who wanted to win a war more quickly. In short order, Barry defeated his problem. He became a man of sexual integrity, and today he and Heather have a wonderful marriage.

You can win the war as well—and start winning it now, long before you get engaged.

ALL YOU NEED

As the basis for your victory, God has provided you with everything you need for a life of purity. God's way is far better than a state-of-the-art GPS navigational system.

At Calvary, He purchased for you the freedom and authority to live in purity. That freedom and authority are His gifts to you through the presence of His Spirit, who took up residence within you when you gave your life to Christ. The freedom and authority are wrapped up in our new inner connection to His divine nature, which is the link that gives us His power and the fulfillment of His promises.

> His divine power has given us everything we need for life and godliness through our knowledge of him who called us by his own glory and goodness. Through these he has given us his very great and precious promises, so that through them you may participate in the divine nature and escape the corruption in the world caused by evil desires. (2 Peter 1:3-4)

It's like the situation that Joshua and the people of Israel faced as they prepared to cross the Jordan River and possess the Promised Land. What did God say to Joshua?

> Have I not commanded you? Be strong and courageous! Do not be terrified; do not be discouraged, for the LORD your God will be with you wherever you go. (Joshua 1:9)

He'd given the Israelites all they needed. They merely had to cross the river. Regarding sexual purity, God knows the provision He's made for us. We aren't short on power or authority; what we lack is urgency. We must choose to be strong and courageous in order to walk into purity. In the millisecond it takes to make that choice, the Holy Spirit will start guiding you and walking alongside you during your struggle.

GOD IS WAITING

Each one of us has been manipulated by our sexual culture; each of us has made choices to sin. To varying degrees, each of us became ensnared by these choices, but we can overcome this affliction. Far too often, however, we ignore our own responsibility in this. We complain, "Well, of course I want to be free from impurity! I've been to the altar 433 times about it, haven't I? It just doesn't seem to be God's will to free me."

Not God's will? That's an offense to the character of God. Don't blame God. His will is for you to have sexual purity, and He has made a provision for that purity. Listen to these Scriptures:

> Count yourselves dead to sin but alive to God in Christ Jesus. Therefore do not let sin reign in your mortal body so that you obey its evil desires. Do not offer the parts of your body to sin, as instruments of wickedness, but rather offer yourselves to God, as those who have been brought from death to life; and offer the parts of your body to him as instruments of righteousness. For sin shall not be your master, because you are not under law, but under grace. (Romans 6:11-14)

> You have been set free from sin and have become slaves to righteousness. (Romans 6:18)

God is waiting for you, but He isn't waiting by the altar, hoping you'll drop by and talk for a while. He's waiting for you to rise up and engage in the battle. We have power through the Lord to overcome every level of sexual immorality, but if we don't utilize that power, we'll never break free from the habit.

You see, sexual impurity isn't like a tumor growing out of control inside us. We treat it like a tumor when our prayers focus on deliverance, as we plead for God to come remove it. Actually, sexual impurity is a series of bad decisions on our part—and a by-product of our immature characters—and deliverance won't deliver us into instant maturity. Character work needs to be done.

Holiness isn't some nebulous thing. It's a series of right choices. You needn't wait for some holy cloud to form around you. You'll be holy when you choose not to sin. You're already free from the *power* of sexual immorality—it's just that you aren't yet free from the *habit* of sexual immorality. That is, until you choose to say, "That's enough! I'm choosing to live purely!"

Ready for authenticity? Good. Let's get to it. We'll recount Steve's story in the next chapter and use the rest of the book to offer guidelines for living authentically as a real man.

masturbation

Steve's long slide

When I (Steve) was eleven years old, I was a fairly good kid. I had accepted Jesus as my Savior when I was nine in an exhilarating walk to the altar, and I was living like most Christian boys were supposed to live. Sure, I forgot to take out the trash from time to time and even tossed out a few cuss words on occasion, but that was about as bad as it got. I was one of the happiest kids around. Life was fun, and I felt free in Jesus.

About a year or so after my salvation, I tagged along with my parents to a youth outing about thirty miles away in Curtain, Texas, where we spent an evening roller-skating in an old school gymnasium. That school district was a bit poor, so it raised a little money by allowing groups to come in and destroy the gym floor this way! I suppose by today's standards it was a pretty lame outing, but in a small Texas town back then, it was a lot of fun.

Mixing in with the older kids, I did my best to stay on my wheels and act as grown up as possible. I did neither very well, but at least I was trying. Soon, during an "all skate" moment, I found myself wobbling forward and backward like an unearthed earthworm. Just as I was about to wobble back, down, and out, two soft "angels" swept up beside me and kept my wheels under my feet.

Gabriel and Michael? Nope. They were Nancy Hewitt and Marcia Mallard, the two most gorgeous girls I'd ever seen in my life.

FIRST CONTACT WITH COMPROMISE

While they were eight years older than I was, something happened when I found myself woven into the arms of these two roller-rink goddesses. I hadn't felt anything so intense, so magnificent since I walked down to the front of the church to accept Christ.

Until then, I thought nothing could feel as good as becoming a Christian, but rolling around the rink with those two perfect "10"s was the discovery that there are some things in this world that can make a person feel *really* good. After that night, I decided I wanted to feel really good. And I decided that night to begin a search of all things that felt good. I wanted to experience them all, but it occurred to me that I might have to compromise a little bit to experience them. Sadly, I sensed I was willing to move away from God if it led me to more of these "heavenly" pleasures. Looking back, I guess I can say that becoming a Christian didn't produce instant character in me, and it was the absence of character that paved the road of compromise.

Compromise is a killer that seems so innocent in the beginning. Yet when you compromise and do a small thing you know isn't right, it rarely stays small or ends there. It becomes easier and easier to choose the wrong path the next time around.

Then it feels as if the wrong path begins to choose you.

Alcoholics explain it like this: First a man takes a drink, then the drink takes the drink, and then the drink takes the man. What feels first like liquid medicine eventually poisons. We saw the same process in Fred's slide down the slippery slope of premarital sex. He made a few small wrong choices, and before he knew it, he couldn't choose anything right.

Shoplifters start by giving in to the urge that first time. A piece of two-cent candy becomes a candy bar, and sooner or later, stealing candy becomes a habit, all because of the first compromise. There are guys sitting in prison right now who likely told themselves, "Just this once." But once led to twice, which led to thrice, and now there are too many times to count. If they didn't get caught in the beginning, they continued to steal until they lost the person they were created to be. We're talking total compromise, and the life of compromise is never the life God intends for us.

That was the way it was for me when it came to cheating in school. I was a fairly clever guy in fifth grade, but not clever enough to do right. Everyone in the fifth grade was supposed to learn the fifty states and capitals before moving on to the sixth grade. My problem? By the time I remembered to study, it was too late. The right thing was to study the best I could, accept the grade I received, and accept the responsibility for not starting in time.

I didn't want to do that. A lousy grade wouldn't feel good, and I wanted to feel good. If I had just taken the bad grade I deserved, I would be looking back now with a bit of pride that at least I was man enough to accept the consequences of my procrastination. Instead, I'm writing about it today because I've never forgotten that first time I made the decision to cheat. That's because I figured out a way I could get a perfect grade without learning one state or capital. You see, figuring it out felt good, and I wanted to feel good.

How typical of guys like me! I didn't want the hassle of studying, but I ended up with a much *bigger* hassle for not studying. My procrastination was replaced with guilt, shame, fear, and an unexplainable emptiness. Exchanging study time for worry time turned out to be a poor trade.

Then the worst possible thing happened. I didn't get caught. No one ever knew but me. Well, except God, of course, and now you know as well. Looking back, I can see that what I really needed were consequences; instead, I experienced nothing but pure relief. So, thanks to Satan, I got my reward for compromise. I didn't get a bad grade or a tough talk from my dad. No, I felt as though I had hit some dollar-slot jackpot in Las Vegas.

In that city out in the desert, some men simply gamble away the money they saved for the trip and then return home. Others stay until they've gambled away all the money they brought with them—including gas money to drive home! If you talk to these big-time losers, you often find a common theme. Somewhere along the way, they won big and were rewarded with a huge jackpot prize.

Since that moment, they no longer gamble for the money. They gamble to feel that exhilaration of winning one more time. Surely there's a way to recapture that feeling of invincibility again! If you sit in on a Gamblers Anonymous meeting, you'll hear guys say that the worst thing that ever happened to them was the time when they won, not when they lost.

It was the same with me when I got away with cheating. When I received the good grade that I didn't deserve, it was as if the red light on top of my Las Vegas slot machine started flashing, bells started ringing, and sirens started screaming. I had won big! The sense of power I felt from beating the Brazos Valley school system was enormous.

But I had not beaten God's system. In God's system, when you do the right thing, He protects you from the sorry consequences of merely following your urges, feelings, and desires. Christ loves you and wants to protect you so He can lead you to the best of what He has to offer.

I wasn't thinking that way. I thought I was an exception to the rule and exempt from God's system, but I wasn't. No one is. Sooner or later, you pay the price and experience the consequences of compromise.

DELAYED CONSEQUENCES

Let's say you do something stupid, like stick your hand into a fire. If you leave your hand in the flames long enough, you'll feel the immediate consequences of excruciating pain. An even dumber action, however, would be to think that you're different and stronger than everyone else, believing you can put your hand in a campfire and not be burned. Since everyone knows that fire's consequences are instantaneous, few men play with fire.

Sin has a different timetable, however. You might sin for years and never experience the consequences, but they will come. I wish somebody had told me that the consequences may not appear for many years. I wish somebody had told me that God wanted me to obey Him out of love and faith, not just to avoid immediate pain.

Since there were no *immediate* consequences when I cheated in fifth grade, I figured there were no consequences at all. So the next time I had the choice, I cheated again. I felt pretty good about getting by and moving forward. Yet if you fast-forward ten years of my life, you would find me graduating from college with a degree in a subject that I had no intention of using. I wish I would have graduated with a degree in music, which might have led to a career in opera or musicals on Broadway, but I wasn't able to learn a foreign language, which was a requirement for a degree in music. Having cheated all those years, I'd never learned to study well enough, so I had to drop out of the music school and find another major.

That's not all. I graduated from college with the easiest degree I could find, just to get out. The consequences of compromise landed on me with a crushing thud.

I must stress this important truth. If you base your life on wanting to feel good, any time something feels good, you'll believe it's acceptable. Every time there are no consequences, you'll believe that it's even more acceptable. It's so tempting to live that way! The world is always screaming at you to do what you want *when* you want. If it makes you feel the way you want to feel, then go ahead.

So I never delayed gratification. Feeling good was the ultimate goal of my life, which is why I cheated rather than studied. This proclivity led to a wasted education rather than preparation for a great career in music. Wasting four years of expensive college education was nothing, however, compared to what was in store in the other areas of my life.

That first decision to cheat on the fifty states and their capitals led to a far greater pain outside the classroom than I ever experienced inside a school. As much as I hate to admit it, my unwillingness to delay gratification even led to the death of a child—my unborn boy or girl. It grieves me today to say this, but it took the death of my child for me to learn some hard lessons that I desperately want you to learn so that you don't make the same mistakes I made.

WHAT A FRIEND TAUGHT ME

As I mentioned, I was a good kid with a vibrant faith until I turned eleven and began making up my own rules. When I didn't get caught at cheating, I reckoned that maybe the other things Mom and Dad called "wrong" might not be so wrong after all. Right in the wake of those first decisions to compromise for anything that felt good, I discovered masturbation. A friend taught me how to do it.

I'd heard nothing about this practice before then. My parents never talked about sex, and my two older brothers never told me about it either. I'd never had an orgasm and had no idea what one was, but my buddy seemed to know everything. I remember the night very well. We'd gone next door to his grandmother's house to have some homemade bread covered with generous swaths of butter and molasses.

We took the molasses-soaked bread up to a tree house in his backyard. We ate as we lay on the floor of his small and dark home away from home. After we finished, he told me he'd learned how to do something that felt very good. He said all I had to do was reach inside my pants and rub my penis up and down. If I kept doing that, it would feel even better and better, and then some stuff would come out, and when that happened, it would feel *really* good. But first I had to get my penis hard to get things started.

I thought this all sounded weird and strange but, as usual, I would try anything to make me feel good, so I reached inside my pants. I had to get my penis hard, right? I knew very well how to make that happen. I had some pictures stored in the back of my mind that I instantly called up and viewed as if I were seeing them for the first time. They were pictures of naked women I'd seen tacked up on the walls in my grandfather's machine shop.

Ever since I was four and five years old, I loved walking into that old shop filled with lathes and presses, where Grandpa made tools to retrieve broken oil-well pipes. His office wall was adorned with nude pinups, and I stared at these voluptuous naked women in awe. My favorites were the women wearing hard hats and operating heavy machinery. There was also a drawing of an Indian's face with a hidden picture of a naked woman for those who looked closely enough. I did, and I grew to love seeing the naked form of the opposite sex.

My grandfather thought nothing of having those pictures displayed so boldly; after all, his machine shop was his turf. Meanwhile, I thought plenty about it, although to this day, I still don't understand how my father could have allowed me to go into my grandfather's shop. My father was a nondrinking, nonsmoking Southern Baptist deacon and Sunday school teacher. It made no sense that he would allow my brothers and me to see pictures of naked women, but my grandfather was a strong and stubborn man. Perhaps my father felt too weak to confront him. Who knows? All I know is that those pictures heavily impacted my life and affected the way I came to view women.

Just the fact that a man could put pictures of naked women up on his walls made a huge statement about women. First, since none of these women were his wife, it meant that unclothed women were public property. They were items…things…objects for everyone to look at. Second, those images meant that they were objects that men could use for their pleasure. Those pinups might not have seemed too significant to my grandfather, but they certainly changed the way I viewed women, and I'm talking about *all* women, not just the busty models in those pictures. I began to view women as a little less than human, as if they were just a little less than men.

When it came time in that tree house to recall those pictures, I could do it instantly. All I had to do was transport my mind to my grandfather's machine shop, and that was easy enough. I remember that everything felt good and, just as my friend promised, something happened that felt *very* good, and this stuff came out. I remember thinking that I would never forget that night, and I haven't. I remember wanting to do it again and, before the night was over, I did, although I had this small feeling that what I had done was bad. I knew one thing: I wasn't about to bring it up and talk to anyone else about it. It would just remain a secret between my friend and me.

Everyone has a different story on how they learned about masturbation, but more important than how you learned is what happened *after* you learned about it. When you learned to masturbate, you didn't learn how to commit the unpardonable sin. You didn't engage in some perversion or do what only mentally ill people do. You did what almost everyone learns to do. For a few, the practice is of little consequence, but for many, it becomes a destructive habit or dependency.

It certainly became a problem for me. Almost every day I would go back to the naked picture files of my brain and view the collection while I masturbated. It wasn't long before I got a little tired of the same old pictures, so I added some to the collection. Those were easy to find. The more I added, the more it felt like women weren't real people to me. I didn't see them as fully human; they were just something to give me physical pleasure. All I was concerned about was their physical properties. Psychologists call this the objectification of women. When you do that, you can then feel free to treat them any way you want.

I continued masturbating almost daily until I began dating, which started when I got my driver's license at age fourteen (another reason I loved rural Texas). There were some girls I really liked. There were a few I think I actually loved. I treated those with as much respect as I could and had great times doing fun things. But there were other girls that I just wanted to use.

All I wanted to do was touch them and have them touch me. I wanted to see them like I wanted to see those pictures on my grandfather's wall.

Each time I did, I collected a new image of a new object that I could recall when I engaged in my daily habit. All I wanted to do was to feel good, and I had decided long ago that I was willing to compromise to feel good. While many young women I dated in high school and college were sexually pure and stayed sexually pure while we dated, I was always manipulating and conniving, going for what was forbidden. I wanted to collect new images.

Eventually, however, I wanted more than auto-sex. I wanted the real thing. I eventually tasted the forbidden fruit when I entered the promiscuous period of my life. When I did have premarital sex, it gave me a sense of control and ownership, as if these young women belonged to me. They were objects of my gratification, just like those pictures on the wall of my grandfather's shop.

THE END OF THE ROAD

What started as a discovery in a tree house at age eleven led to a lifestyle of promiscuity and using women. In college, every relationship was a sexual one—at least in my mind. So often I had little to offer a girl, but I wanted everything from her. It didn't register with me that this was someone's future wife, or that she was a real human with real needs that I could meet. Instead, it was all about me and making me feel good. Had I been godly, she could have become *more* because of her relationship with me. Too often, she was *less* because I took from her only what a husband should take. Nothing about any of that feels good today. In fact, it feels horrible.

I was promiscuous, reckless, and looking for anyone who could make me feel good. None of the rules applied to me, especially with a certain girl that I started dating. She couldn't have been more wonderful, except for one flaw—she somehow settled for someone like me to date. She listened as I proclaimed my love for her. In response, she gave me everything she had.

She really seemed like an incredible person to me, until she got pregnant. When she announced the fateful news, I couldn't believe it at first. It was just too horrible. But nothing I could do would change the truth. Then I remembered that there *was* something I could do to change it. I could buy an abortion, the great eraser of our sexual miscues. I could then go on with my life and be rid of the whole thing. After many discussions and a few simple arrangements, I bought her an abortion and went on with my life. Sort of.

The relationship broke up, as is usually the case, but the abortion didn't buy me peace. A simple thought continued to haunt me mercilessly. I hadn't simply purchased an abortion—I had killed my own child! That so-called glob of tissue was bone of my bone and flesh of my flesh. I had it snuffed out.

But that wasn't the worst thing. I hadn't simply paid for the abortion. I had manipulated and pressured my girlfriend into going to the abortion clinic because I made it very clear that I would not be there for her or her baby, even though she wanted us to marry. When I shot down that idea, she said that she wanted to carry the baby to term and put it up for adoption.

I brought every argument to bear in order to stop her. Having a child out of wedlock would have been too humiliating to me. I wasn't going to think of anyone but myself. All I wanted was to get this "situation" behind me.

The result? I never did put it behind me. In fact, the grief and shame of pressuring her to have an abortion literally almost killed me. Eighty ulcers grew in my stomach and intestines, and I'd have bled to death if things had continued the way they were. Not long after that, I hit a car at an intersection and dropped out of school. There was just too much pain to even think of studying.

I had killed more than my baby. I had killed *my* life, and nothing would ever be the same again. In the future, whenever I held someone else's baby, it was awful. Every cry, every squeal of the word "Daddy" brought sorrow and suffering welling up, and the emotional and spiritual scars remain to this day. Sure, I'm forgiven. But I hope these are scars you'll never have to bear. If you make authenticity your priority, you never will.

If you connect the dots of my life—the cheating, the compromise, the masturbation, the early exposure to pornography, the objectification of women, and the promiscuity—you end up with an abortion. Each dot was significant, and masturbation was one large, devastating dot along the way.

Examine the dots in your life. What picture forms behind you as you connect these dots on your walk to your future? What kind of man do you want to become? Are the things you're doing today leading you there? If your dots look anything like mine, please make changes today. Please, for your sake and God's sake, create a very different history from mine.

GOING IN A NEW DIRECTION

In Fred's story, we saw how moving toward sexual purity strengthens your spiritual life. In my story, we see the opposite is also true. No matter how spiritually strong you start out, a life of pornography, masturbation, premarital foreplay, and intercourse will weaken you and leave you distant from God.

So where do we go from here? Before we talk about the direction we're going to take, let me share a story about Fred. Believe it or not, when Fred was in high school, he never attended a rock concert. But he made up for lost time in college when he took a job with Wu Wei Associates, a concert security company that hired Stanford football players and Stanford karate club members to work security at Bay Area concerts.

Fred saw a zillion concerts for free during those four years, including many hot chart-topping acts of the day. But the best concert he ever saw was not free, and the band he saw that night had only two real hits, as he recalls. While Fred bought tickets for the Sanford Townsend Band, the group did something that night that blew the roof off the place.

Almost every concert starts slowly, with the band playing its lesser-known songs from their newest album. The concert then builds to a crescendo as the group plays their best-known songs at the end, leading into a rip-roaring encore. Not on this night. The Sanford Townsend Band stepped out of the shadows, strapped on their instruments, and blasted straight into the hit song that everyone expected to come during the encore! The house went delirious, and the emotional fever didn't break all night long.

So, we're going to take a cue from the Sanford Townsend Band and blast straight into the chapter you've been waiting for—you got it—the one on masturbation.

We'll address the questions that you most want answered:

Is masturbation a sin?

If it is, why can't I stop it?

If it isn't, why do I feel so guilty?

And the biggest question of all: If God didn't want me to masturbate, why did He put my genitals within easy reach of my hands? (On second thought, let's save that one for heaven!)

all about the M word

Let's get right to it, first things first. Masturbation isn't addressed in the Bible, so there's no direct, definitive scripture that says the practice is right or wrong. In other words, the issue of masturbation won't be as cut and dried as say, adultery. But the fact that adultery is a sin helps us out a great deal in defining almost all *marital* masturbation as sin. Jesus said:

> I tell you that anyone who looks at a woman lustfully has already
> committed adultery with her in his heart. (Matthew 5:28)

If Jesus defines simply *looking lustfully* at a woman as adultery for the married man, certainly looking lustfully at a woman *and* masturbating is adultery. This is indisputable. But what about you single guys? While the Bible is unclear about masturbation, this same scripture makes a similarly strong case against lustful looks in single men. If looking lustfully at a woman is the same as going to bed with her for married guys, looking lustfully at a woman is the same as going to bed with her for single guys. We don't see much difference.

Neither does Ed Cole, a pastor with a national speaking platform:

> Not only does pornography encourage its viewers to create an image
> in their minds. It also entices them to fantasize about it. Usually these
> fantasies involve an erotic act that can only be satisfied with someone
> else or by masturbation. Once an image develops in the mind, that

picture creates a stronghold in the mind and becomes a trap. Some people think I'm old-fashioned for preaching this, but I continually encounter men who have lost all sense of balance because of habitual masturbation. One man asked, "How many times a day would you consider habitual?" That's reason enough to teach it!

Some make a case that isolated instances of masturbation to relieve sexual tension are okay, if you're married and focusing on your wife—not some supermodel—during periods of separation or illness. Even if that's true, where does that leave you single guys? Nowhere. You really have no woman you can legitimately lust after.

So unless a guy can figure out how to masturbate without any lustful fantasy, masturbation is technically a sin. But that begs other questions. Let's suppose a man *can* figure out how to masturbate without any fantasy, and he simply does it to relieve sexual tension. Where does that sexual tension come from in the first place? If all of this sexual tension were natural and rooted in his hormonal makeup, that would be one thing. He'd have little direct control over it.

But what if it isn't all natural? That would be another thing entirely. For instance, what if he brought all this frustrating sexual tension upon himself by looking at Internet porn during the last few evenings after work? What about the cumulative effects of renting *Titanic* on Friday night, watching nubile sweat-soaked girls in tight nylon shorts at the track meet on Saturday afternoon, and lightly rubbing your genitals against a girl during the slow dance at the Saturday night social?

Even if this guy *can* masturbate with a clean mind, wasn't the sexual tension caused by his own sin in the first place? If we bring the sexual tension upon ourselves through sin, wouldn't releasing that sexual tension through masturbation also be a sin? Looking at it from another direction, is masturbation the only way to release sexual tension? There may be purer ways. We need to discuss all these questions.

WELCOME TO THE GRAY ZONE

As you can see, since God didn't address masturbation directly in Scripture, the questions can seem endless. Theologians will argue over this until Christ returns, and maybe that's how it should be whenever Scripture is silent. Even we coauthors have found it difficult to decide together what to label masturbation and where to draw the lines of sin.

I (Fred) feel most comfortable simply calling masturbation a "sin" because its effects are exactly like the effects of any other sin in a man's life. If it looks like a duck, walks like a duck, and quacks like a duck, it likely *is* a duck:

- Habitual masturbation consistently creates distance from God.
- Jesus said that lusting after women in your heart is the same as doing it. Since most masturbation involves a lustful fantasy or pornography, we're certain that nearly all instances violate Scripture.
- The pornography and fantasy that surround masturbation change the way we view women, as you saw in Steve's story. How can that be right?
- Habitual masturbation is hard to stop. If you don't believe it, wait till you get married and try to quit masturbating.
- Masturbation is progressive. You're more likely to masturbate the day after you masturbate than you're likely to do it the day after you - didn't. In other words, the pleasurable chemical reactions draw you to repeat the practice more and more. This is bondage, and God hates bondage in His sons.

Another point is that at least 98 percent of all masturbation involves lustful mental fantasies or pornography. Most all of it, then, is a sin. I say, "Why quibble over *whether* to call masturbation a 'sin' when most of it clearly *is* a sin?"

Steve agrees with this in principle. How could he not? Look at what compromising with pornography and fantasy did to his life! He treated women in a demeaning way. He was spiritually weakened. He caused an abortion. Still, Steve says, "Like anything, it's what is in the heart that can produce the sin. Even consensual sex between two married people can involve sin depending on what a person might be thinking at the time. Because of the unwarranted, crushing shame that revolves around masturbation, we need to be careful how we communicate about it. When you masturbate for the first time, you don't commit the unpardonable sin or engage in something that grows hair on your palms or causes you to go blind."

KEEP THE SHAME AWAY

While Steve believes masturbation nearly always involves sin, because of the deep levels of shame often associated with it, he prefers not to focus on the word *sin,* but on the heart. He has seen young men react negatively to harsh preaching about sexual sin, whereas hearing a hopeful message about change and freedom, and honoring God and women, can result in positive change. The shaming approach often makes the problem worse.

In a recent radio broadcast, Steve said,

> When masturbation *is* a sin, it's not an end-of-the-world kind of
> sin that should drive a guy into deeper isolation. I know of young
> men and women who aren't involved with church because they are
> involved with masturbation. They were told this is the worst and
> most horrible thing they could do, so when it happens, they feel
> like total outcasts from God. It is never good to drive young people
> from the church. If masturbation *is* done in a sinful way, it's not
> something that should elicit deep shame. Masturbation is not rare,
> and most have tried it at some point. They just don't admit it or
> talk about it.

In the same conversation, Steve said,

What's so great with men I've worked with, who have been masturbating with pornography since they were teens, is that when they
stop, they find there's a different world out there. They find that
they can handle stress differently. When they go without masturbating for a month, they feel so clean and good about themselves.

We both want to remove deep shame from the equation. We've seen
masturbation used by young men to salve deep insecurity or psychological
pain. Derrick said, "I've been a Christian all my life, and I had no problem
with sexual sin until my parents divorced two years ago when I was seventeen. I was so upset. For some reason, I started up with some mild porn and
masturbation. It felt good, but now it's gotten steadily worse. I don't know
what to do." Pound the sin and shame aspect too hard, and his insecurity
problems get only stronger.

Many other "issues" besides family problems can prompt a young male
to pleasure himself in order to mask the pain felt elsewhere in his life.
Maybe a guy has acne problems or big ears or a lisp. Whatever. The point
is, it doesn't do any good to pile a bucket-load of "You ain't no good" on
top of him. Self-condemnation only sets the cycle of masturbation into a
downward spiral, causing deeper embarrassment and humiliation.

While I (Fred) still call masturbation a "sin" because of the lust and fantasy involved, I agree that deep, false shame has no place in the equation.
God isn't a Father who shames His children. We'll get to that in a moment.

Many leaders are concerned with this shame issue and how it adds fuel
to the fire. In regard to masturbation, you might have been taught to "keep
it to a minimum." The motivation is right. So many young men feel powerless to stop and feel debased when it does happen, and nobody wants
to pile more shame upon them. Maybe Patrick Middleton, a friend and a

brilliant Christian counselor, summed it up best when he said, "I'm very anti-masturbation and see it as a violation of God's design for sexual intimacy. But I'm also very anti-shame and see how this very topic really shames young men harmfully."

CALL IT WHAT YOU WILL…

Steve and I join lockstep with Patrick on that score. We must reduce the level of *false* shame in this discussion, while simultaneously making sure the pendulum doesn't swing too far in the other direction. We must never, ever see masturbation as just "guys being guys."

Take a look at what masturbation caused in my life. I experienced a deep separation and distance from God and, in the end, discovered that I couldn't make a complete connection with my wife. Call masturbation whatever you will, but it was wrong. I couldn't get free, and I felt plenty of the guilt of deception.

The results in Steve's life were no better. What if teaching the "guys will be guys" message causes young men to breathe such a sigh of relief that they freely get into masturbation without concern—only to get totally stuck in sinful cycles of pornography and fantasy from which they can't escape? What if they wreck their relationship with God because the caution flags hang too limply? If so, we need to get the flags flying again.

If there's a "clear-minded" and "clean" form of masturbation (we'll get to this later), the keep-it-to-a-minimum advice would be decent counsel. But clearly, "knock it off" is the only advice for nearly all men because of the pornography and lustful sin involved. Sin binds, and such bondage is devastating. It's like our society's decisions about crack cocaine or methamphetamines. We can change our views and legalize them, thereby removing the shame. But they'll still ensnare us in addictive, binding cycles that isolate us in despair.

So in the last analysis, splitting hairs over what we call masturbation is silly. There are only two questions that matter. If you're in bondage to masturbation, should you try to break free? The answer is yes. Is it possible to break free? We believe it is.

If you're living with a deep sense of shame over masturbation, you need to stop masturbating, but you also need to stop the shame. A good first step is to change your harsh view of God—more precisely, God's view of *you*. Only then can you deal with masturbation as the binding, grinding problem it is, without worrying about any silly false shame that we needn't carry as beloved children of God. We want young men to focus on steps they can take to overcome this habit. Where there's hope, there's a future.

the view from above

I have always loved the story of the prodigal son. What intrigues me most is the father's view of his son, because it mirrors God's view of us. God's eyes are always fixed on the crest of the hill, longing to see us coming from over the horizon and walking closer to Him.

> When he [the son] came to his senses, he said, "How many of my father's hired men have food to spare, and here I am starving to death! I will set out and go back to my father and say to him: Father, I have sinned against heaven and against you. I am no longer worthy to be called your son; make me like one of your hired men." So, he got up and went to his father.
>
> But while he was still a long way off, his father saw him and was filled with compassion for him; he ran to his son, threw his arms around him and kissed him.
>
> The son said to him, "Father, I have sinned against heaven and against you. I am no longer worthy to be called your son." But the father said to his servants, "Quick! Bring the best robe and put it on him. Put a ring on his finger and sandals on his feet. Bring the fattened calf and kill it. Let's have a feast and celebrate."
> (Luke 15:17-23)

God isn't the least bit concerned about whether you're worthy to return to Him, although it's natural for us to think that way. The prodigal son worried about this too. He was certain that his sinful lifestyle made him unworthy to be called his father's son.

But the father in the story quickly brushed that aside. "What's all this talk about worthiness? You're back! That's all that matters!" He slipped a ring on his son's hand and presented him with a clean robe and new shoes. Their relationship was restored instantly.

No paybacks. No shame. No looking back.

STILL FEELING UNWORTHY?

When we masturbate, some of us come to our Father and say, "I've masturbated again, and I'm not worthy to be called Your son." He brushes that aside, saying, "No one but Jesus is *worthy* to be called my Son, but I love you and forgive you." He demonstrates that love by presenting us with a ring, robe, and shoes. Then He says, "In case you forgot, Jesus picked these up at Calvary for you. That makes you worthy enough for Me. Now let's celebrate and enjoy each other!"

When we sin, God doesn't shout, "Hell and damnation on you!" Since we're saved, He knows full well that there's now no more condemnation for us because of Christ. Remember, He personally had the apostles write that into the Bible! Jesus paid it all. Our Father isn't interested in making us pay further by adding shame after another orgasmic failure in cyberspace.

God, your Father, is *for* you. He has plans to prosper you, and plans to give you a hope and a future, as promised in Jeremiah 29. Granted, God doesn't unconditionally approve of your *behavior*, but He *does* unconditionally love you. When you masturbate, He wants you to know you missed the mark of His high calling. He wants you to know that this behavior separates you from Him, and that's why you're finding it hard to get close to Him.

Take a long, careful look at how masturbation affects your relationship with God. This is what God is most concerned with. You're already His son. What He wants now is for you to move back closer to Him. And since we're focusing in this section on how we can fully and authentically love God with all our strength (our bodies), this is our primary interest, as well.

If you've ever masturbated, you know that your heart is often gripped with heavy grief and sorrow afterward. At that moment, it is very clear that you don't deserve all the grace Christ has given you, and you can barely lift your head to look into your Father's eyes. The distance is very real.

But our mistakes and this distance are never the centerpiece of God's focus on us. If you would manage to look again into His eyes and run to the foot of the cross, you'll find that Christ's outstretched arms and His desire to forgive are always the glorious centerpiece to every Christian's story. Every one of us can tell our own story of His amazing grace, stories that He Himself has authored and will perfect and complete, regardless of our sin. This is God's focus. It must also be ours.

Does that mean we shouldn't fear God? Does that mean we should be slack on sin? Heavens no! Look at the destructive stories we've shared with you. The prodigal son ended up in a pigsty, eating pig's food, and was appalled at the destruction in his own life.

GOD VIEWS US ANOTHER WAY

Jesus knows very well the struggle you're in. He lived here as a single man Himself, remember? The Bible says He was tempted in all points as we are. The Holy Spirit knows you through and through. He lives in you, and He was sent to guide you and comfort you.

God is with you, and He knows the struggle is great. He fights with you, side by side. This view of God keeps shame away, but it leaves us room to keep a proper caution toward masturbation.

Think hard about this. Obviously, rejecting pornography and fantasy is a baseline requirement. That must be done, because it's sin. Any sinful form of masturbation must stop as well. If there's a form of masturbation that isn't sinful, keeping it to a minimum is better than driving it to the maximum. Who can argue that?

But we want more for you, and God definitely wants more for you. We believe as you read on that you'll understand the depths of the problem and decide you won't want to masturbate at all. There are those who say it's not possible because of the obstacles, but we feel it's very possible. We hope that thousands of readers of this book will decide to stop pouring gasoline on a hot fire of passion, desire, and lust. We're about to show you how, and we believe that those who take this path will never, ever regret it. We don't expect anyone, after having applied the forthcoming advice, to later declare, "Gee, I just wish I had masturbated more."

While there may be some corners of masturbation that aren't sin, most of what surrounds masturbation *is* sin and binds us to the point of strangling us spiritually and emotionally. We must face that truth like men, rejecting shame and choosing manhood.

Now is as good a time as any to address it as best we can. Is there a corner of masturbation that isn't a sin? Can a man masturbate with a totally clean mind? David, seventeen years old, says,

> Let me say this: it is possible to masturbate with a clean mind and eyes, because I've done it. I have to tell you, however, that it really takes a long time without visual stimulation or fantasizing—even if I'm trying to get it over with quick. It's sometimes so demoralizing that I'll just stop. That isn't good because then my motor is riding the red line, and then the mind gets really difficult to control, and I drop back into sin.
>
> Even when I can do it with a clean mind, there's something else that makes me doubtful about the practice. For the past few months I've been into doing what I call "practicing the presence of God," living in continuous prayer and trying to go through my day talking to God and praising Him. When I masturbate, even with a clean mind,

that connection with God clearly gets messed up. It's still there, and I can still talk to God, but I have this weird sense that even if it's not a sin, then it really isn't pure, either.

Intimacy with God is our whole reason for fighting the battle, isn't it? If it messes up the intimacy, why do it? Besides, even if "clear-minded" masturbation isn't a sin technically, we still sense a bondage in the whole matter, and God hates bondage in His people. Paul said in 1 Corinthians 6:12 that we must "not be mastered by anything." On those grounds, all forms of masturbation seem suspect.

BEING FREE FROM SEXUAL FEVERS

I (Steve) once heard these questions posed on my *New Life* radio broadcast: "Is masturbation moving me closer to where I want to go in my life? In my life with others? In my life with God?"

We can answer that it almost never does.

Young men today are spending much of their spiritual energy fighting off sexual fevers. What if you kept yourself free from this draining fever in the first place, which would free you to expend your spiritual energy on God's kingdom?

It can be done. The world hasn't yet seen what God can do with an army of young men free of sexual fevers. You can remain pure so that you might qualify for such an army. The four requirements necessary to stop masturbating are as follows:

1. Making a strong decision to no longer "stop short" of God's standards.
2. Joining an accountability group that allows for the honest expression of feelings.
3. Continuing an active, ongoing relationship with God that involves worship and prayer.

4. Becoming aware of how various media—magazines, cable TV, videos, Internet, and catalogs—affect your sex drive.

Fulfilling these four requirements will allow you to love your God with all your strength and sexuality. We discussed the first point earlier, so we'll deal with the next three in greater detail ahead.

what are you replacing with masturbation?

We said that the first step in becoming free from sexual impurity is making a firm decision. Next, you need to stay close to God and form relationships with like-minded friends who can support you in your battle. Why is that?

We mentioned earlier that loneliness, insecurity, and broken family relationships are often the steppingstones to masturbation. We replace that lost intimacy with the false intimacy of masturbation. A close relationship with God and our friends will make the false intimacy of masturbation unnecessary. So the first question we must deal with is this: *What intimacy in your relationships are you replacing with masturbation?*

Dennis told us that he grew up in the church, but when his parents got divorced while he was in high school, he became involved in pornography—something that still plagues him today. We heard many stories like Dennis's, and we think we know why: 30 percent of fathers who get divorced never see their kids again. These broken relationships cause great internal anguish and insecurity in the sons, leaving them to seek intimacy wherever they can find it.

Sexual sin flourishes in the wake of bad or broken family relationships. The splintering effects of divorce or parental death shatter our worlds. Teens, rather than feeling accepted and cherished by their parents, feel as though they've been cast aside. They spend their lives searching for love and meaning, when it should have been provided in the home by a mother and a father.

IT HAPPENED TO ME

I'll never forget the day when I (Fred) came home from elementary school, tripping quickly down the school bus steps with my sisters and rushing into the house to eat cookies, then to go outdoors to play army and float boats down the creek. When we entered the house, however, my mother called the three of us into the living room to talk. She *never* did that, so I sensed that something serious had happened, especially after I noticed Dad sitting on the edge of the sofa.

"I have something to tell you," Mom said. She leaned against the dining room table, arms crossed, eyes red, her face puffy and moist. I turned quickly toward Dad, who was sitting eagerly with a bemused smile on his face. (Years later, I found out that just before we arrived, he had declared to Mom that when the kids heard she was filing for divorce, all three of us would turn against her and rush to his side. He couldn't wait for his vindication.) As I surveyed the scene, terror struck deeply. Something was terribly wrong.

"Your father and I are getting a divorce," she said.

I don't remember the rest of her words. They didn't matter. My world crumbled into dust, vaporized instantly. We raced headlong to Mom, wailing and clutching her legs. My father, crushed that his children ran to his wife first, burst into tears and ran out of the house—the first time I'd seen him cry. I hurried to the window and watched him get into his car and drive off. Agony swept my soul at seeing my hero cry. This wasn't just another day, nor would any day be the same again. The sun dimmed over my world and never shone as brightly as before.

To his credit, Dad remained in the area to help raise us, but he was an adulterer and very harsh with me. Furthermore, life became an emotional and financial horror for my mother, my two sisters, and me. The pressures of single parenting nearly leveled Mom, but she tenaciously fought on. She'd come home from her day job as a receptionist, grab a bite to eat, then head out to sell grave plots at night. Mom was easily the bravest person I've ever met. My young heart ached for her as she battled on. To ease her pain, I vowed never do anything that would make her cry. As the only male in the family, I shouldered the mantle of manhood as best I could, while inwardly I seethed at my father for doing this to us.

Mixed emotions, however, served only to confuse me further. On the one hand, I loved Dad, even idolized him. He was a bigger-than-life, charismatic superhero, and I wanted to please him in everything I did. Handsome and tough, Dad had been a national wrestling champion in college and a bulldog in business.

Yet, on another level, I couldn't have cared less about him. While I loved my father, deep down I knew he'd traded his life with me for life with a mistress. That spelled betrayal to me. Until the day he died, he never accepted me as a man or an equal. He even crossed me out of his will on his deathbed, if only to express one last time how unworthy I was to carry his name.

All I could do was shrug my shoulders, because he never really knew who this son of his was when he was alive. I remember the time in high school when I began training with a close buddy. We were serious; that's why neither of us dated much. One night Dad chewed out Mom for allowing me to hang out with this buddy, accusing her of turning me into "a gay." He didn't even know that it was my passion for football that caused me to shun dating, not homosexuality.

Another episode occurred when I was fourteen. Dad called Mom early one week and gave her the following order: "Have Freddie ready for me to pick up Friday night at seven o'clock. I've got a clean prostitute arranged for the evening. It's time for him to learn about love." He didn't understand why my mother and I were repulsed by the bizarre idea. I cannot describe the rage that flooded me after I heard that over-the-top suggestion.

Perhaps you've felt the same type of anger and pain in your family relationships. Such anger often opens a door to pornography and masturbation. The desire to become close to *somebody* can also drive you quickly into the arms of women or one-sided friendships. Rather than turn to God, you truly can begin looking for love in all the wrong places, hoping for something, anything, to take the place of that loss.

This is where our maleness works against us. Remember, men primarily give and receive sexual intimacy prior to and during intercourse. When you bring yourself to orgasm while fantasizing or viewing women on a glossy magazine page, you have a feeling of intimacy.

School adds to the problems at home. The cruelest place on Earth is a high-school campus. If you're not part of the right "clique"—the jocks, the cheerleaders, the ASBers—then you're put down and laughed at mercilessly by your peers. I've told my kids to just hang on during the high school years. "Besides, you won't see 99 percent of these kids ever again," I say. "Why let what they say bother you?" I remind them that in college, people mature and things start returning to normal.

Trouble is, during these trying days of acne and academics, many young men get dreadfully lonely and pummeled. For these guys, masturbation makes them feel good and takes away the loneliness—for a moment.

AN INNER FOCUS—AND MORE ISOLATION

The trouble with this tack is that masturbation is an implosion of sexual pleasure that focuses a guy further and further into himself. However, that genuine need for interpersonal intimacy cannot be met by self-seeking sexual activity. It's like slaking your parched thirst with salt water. A sip can satisfy for a moment, but the eventual results are disastrous. If you masturbate to "fix" your feelings of insecurity and isolation, then the masturbation just adds to your loneliness because you're not receiving true intimacy when you do the act.

It's like watching TV all alone. Have you ever noticed that you feel even more lonely and isolated after a night of solitary TV watching because there was no real human contact? Masturbation is similar. It's not a real sexual encounter. Sure, it feels sexual, but it actually leaves a guy feeling more alone and more ashamed than when he woke up that morning. This is the opposite of what real sexual encounters are supposed to do.

If you expect to stop masturbating, in nearly all cases you must first make a strong decision to stop. But the power of interpersonal relationships is also so important to this process that it can sometimes break the power of the masturbation cycle on its own. Will, a friend of mine who directs a drug treatment center in western Iowa, told me that simply deciding to get out with people broke the masturbation cycle when he was single.

I was always kind of a loner and stuck to myself a lot. Every night after work I'd go home to my apartment all alone, and I'd wind up buried in pornography and masturbation. The experience left me feeling lonelier and more isolated! When friends at the office invited me places after work, or my family called to do things on weekends, I found myself saying no to all of them.

One day, I'd just had it with myself. Putting my foot down, I committed to saying yes to every invitation for the next four weeks, just to see what would happen. That was really hard at first because I felt out of place—like a third wheel. It was as though I had forgotten how to be with people in a casual environment. After a few experiences, however, I started getting comfortable and even loosening up around my friends and family. Believe it or not, midway through the fourth week, I realized I hadn't masturbated in over ten days. A habit that had been with me for years began to fall away naturally as I reached out to other people.

ACCOUNTABILITY GROUPS DO HELP

This is why many young men fighting for sexual purity seek support in a men's Bible study group or a smaller accountability group with one or two other men. Having a safe place to discuss this tough issue often results in an honest exchange, although getting there can be awkward. (Another drawback of being a male is that we don't verbalize our feelings very well.)

Honest sharing must occur in these relationships. Tough questions must be asked, and true answers given. After the first three or four weeks of getting to know each other, powder-puff questions like "How'd you like church last week?" must give way to introspective questions like "How were things different this week from last week?" and "What's changing?"

Otherwise, you don't have an accountability group at all, but merely a sympathy gathering where each person admits his failure again and again, week after week. The wounded merely lean on each other, hoping to be told, "That's all right."

To counteract that, you may prefer a one-on-one, direct accountability partner. This should be a male friend, perhaps someone older and well respected in the church—a person who can encourage you in the heat of battle and ask probing questions like, "What are you feeling when you're most tempted to masturbate?" Such questions bring clear insight. The men's ministry at your church can help you find someone who can ask the tough questions and suggest ways to help you.

Are you wondering how this works? Nathan asked his youth pastor for an accountability partner. Ron, a longtime Christian with experience in this area, was asked to help out Nathan. Ron called Nathan on the phone to chat.

"How's it going at home, Nathan?" Ron asked. They'd previously established that this question refers to masturbation.

"I plead the fifth," said Nathan.

"Uh-oh. Talk to me."

"It's been happening every other day for the past two weeks."

"Are you reading the Bible?" Ron asked.

"Yes."

"Are you praying?"

"Yes."

"Are you really angry with someone?"

"Not really."

"What's the problem then?"

"Too much television," Nathan answered. "Shows on HBO and *Baywatch* reruns."

Following this conversation, Ron began calling Nathan every day. Sometimes Nathan needs to be encouraged. Sometimes he needs to be challenged to do what's right. In the end, though, it came down to whether Nathan had made a decision to win, a decision for purity. Accountability only works when coupled with a firm commitment to win.

Who else might be your accountability partner? Ted uses his father. "God is bringing me through the worse struggle of my life," says Ted. "I've struggled with what I watch on TV for five years, but then last year I became hooked on Internet porn. God has provided a wonderful accountability partner into my own dad. Can you believe it? We talk regularly, and he's been real understanding."

Nearly any committed man can be your accountability partner. Let us caution you, however, from enlisting your girlfriend as one. That's a recipe for getting into more trouble.

FOR INTIMACY: WORSHIP!

While you build real interpersonal intimacy into your life by joining a men's group, talking with your youth pastor, or enlisting an accountability partner, don't forget to place God in the center of the equation. By seeking and asking Him for supernatural help in this battle, you can overcome things that you never thought possible. You'll find yourself hungrier to know Him and you'll experience a greater desire to communicate with Him. As your intimacy with God grows, you'll need less of that false intimacy. You'll find Him to be your best accountability partner.

What helps bring true intimacy with God quickly? Worship. We were created to worship. Worship and praise brings intimacy with the Lord and ushers us quickly into His presence.

I first heard Charles Swindoll mention this on his *Insight for Living* radio broadcast when he said that he never enters prayer without first entering worship. I started there, memorizing a few choruses and hymns and singing them softly to the Lord for about twenty minutes before beginning prayer. So what if I couldn't carry a tune across Merle Hay Road if my life depended upon it?

What kind of songs did I use? Love songs! Songs I can sing *to* Him, that address *Him* directly. I want to tell Him I love Him and build on that intimacy. So I use love songs that I can sing straight to Him. There are many songs expressing love to the Lord that are popular now. One of my recent favorites begins simply, "You're the One that I love." Another starts with, "I will worship You, my Love."

Now this isn't the only way to worship or find intimacy with God. However you seek Him, just make sure you don't wait to stop masturbating before you reach out to Christ in worship and praise. You need that intimacy in your life. His heart of passion longs for you. Worship Him. He's the Creator of the universe, and He's *for* you.

A CLOSING THOUGHT

One of the key components to making it through your teen and young adult years is teamwork. Everyone needs supportive friends or groups. Every young man needs an intimate relationship with God.

Ultimately, men of all ages face the same challenge—asking for help and being honest about emotions and struggles. For most young men, it's a major victory to come to the point of asking for help. Have you done that yet?

your sumo sex drive

If we're to quit masturbating, the last of the four requirements is to understand what cable TV, videos, the Internet, magazines, and fantasy can do to our sex drive.

What are the effects? Simple. They increase your sex drive, which makes it practically impossible to eliminate masturbation. Some would say it's simply impossible to live life as a single male without having intercourse, and that we must choose either genuine sexual intercourse with a girl or false intercourse with our hand or go crazy. Are those really the only options? To answer that, we might ask a better question: Do you require masturbation because of the sex drive God gave you or because you've built it into an even *bigger* sex drive?

IT'S ONLY A SYMPTOM

Let us say it clearly: Masturbation is primarily a symptom of uncontrolled eyes and free-racing thoughts. When you create new habits of guarding your eyes and taking fantasy captive, masturbation can cease. Until then, it probably won't. Masturbation is like the low oil warning light on the dash of your car. If it goes on, the problem is not with the light; the real problem is under the hood.

Brennan feels overmatched in the battle. "But my eyes can't be the only problem! What about my sex drive?" he asked. "Look, I'm sixteen and probably have a stronger sex drive than some rabbits. Since I'm lacking in the wife department, what am I going to do about it? How will I get release?"

My reply was, "Is that your natural sex drive, or have you done something to grow it?"

The size of our sex drive isn't fixed. If we're to eliminate masturbation, we must see that our sex drive has two parts. One part is fixed at birth, but the other part can billow up like a hot-air balloon as we encourage it.

That we have a baseline sex drive, there's no question. Dr. James Dobson stated in *What Wives Wished Their Husbands Knew About Women* that the human male, because of sperm production and other factors, naturally desires a sexual release every seventy-two hours or so. You're probably wondering what can be done about that. Is there a way to release that stuff?

Thankfully, yes. While our body has this natural physical pressure for sexual release, God Himself has provided a built-in "relief valve," something with which you're familiar. Clinically it's called a "nocturnal emission," but long ago in a dank, smelly football locker room, some kid decided to call it a "wet dream," and that name stuck. The good news for teens is that nocturnal emissions *can* work for you in your quest for purity.

Having said that, you might wonder how such dreams can work toward purity since some of these semiconscious flights of fancy can get pretty hot and heavy! But don't forget that those hot and heavy aspects arise from what you've been feeding your mind each day. The same pure eyes and mind that keep you from actively seeking release during the day will limit the impurity that your mind can use in your dreams at night. These dreams will be dramatically purer in scope and content than you now realize.

Nocturnal emissions kick in naturally in response to your normal, natural sperm buildup. This means that the fixed part of your sex drive will more or less be taken care of by God's natural relief valve.

So there's at least some help regarding the *natural* baseline part of your sex drive. This means that you aren't necessarily overmatched in this battle simply because you have no wife. However, you can become overmatched if you're not careful to guard your eyes and mind. We bring most of the sexual pressure onto ourselves through visual sensual stimulation and mental fantasy, which puffs up the variable portion of our sex drives to the point where it's difficult to handle it through nocturnal emissions alone. We'll call this the false sex drive.

WHAT MADE YOU FALL?

Keith, a single youth pastor I recently met in North Carolina, said that when any of his guys fall into masturbation, his standard reply is, "Why did you need release? What were you doing during the day that made you fall that night?"

Added Keith, "Look, I'm single too. I understand what they're going through. But in my experience, if I'm faithful to guard my eyes and keep the fantasies out of my life, that false drive, as you call it, simply dries up. It just isn't there anymore."

Some of Keith's guys claim they don't lust while they masturbate, and they're only doing it to release tension. "So what?" says Keith. "You were fantasizing and watching soft-core shows on cable earlier in the day. That forced your hand, and you know it. If you hadn't been watching those shows, you would have had no sexual tension in the first place." They rarely argue.

When you boil it down, sexual purity is simply a choice. Is holiness important to you or is it not?

Thad is a twenty-three-year-old college student, currently single—no wife, no girlfriend, no nothing. "I know God holds me to a very high standard," said Thad, "but I still have a desire for some kind of sexual satisfaction, even if only mental fantasy. I suspect it's wrong to fulfill this desire at all, but what do I replace it with? I can't just ignore it, or probably more honestly, I don't want to. How do I get God to fill this desire in me?"

The honest answer is that it isn't God's job to fill that desire. Thad created that desire himself through fantasy, but now that the situation has become big and frustrating, Thad wants God to bail him out. In God's opinion, it's Thad's job to take care of it. Thad admitted he doesn't want to train his mind to avoid mental fantasy. Our guess is he'd be even less interested in training his eyes to bounce away. He wants God to do it for him.

Well, in most cases, God isn't going to do it. We'll say it once more. Sooner or later, we all have to fight for our purity. That word *fight* leads us to a helpful word picture.

So Enter the Ring!

Have you ever been channel surfing and seen two Japanese sumo wrestlers going at it inside a small ring? In a sumo wrestling match, two bloated behemoths dressed in loincloth diapers (gross!) grab each other's arms and ram shoulders until one gets knocked out of the ring. Well, picture your battle with masturbation as being like a sumo match. You're on one side of the ring, and your overgrown, bloated opponent—known as Mr. Sex Drive—is on the other. If you knock Mr. Sex Drive out of the ring, you don't have to masturbate. If Mr. Sex Drive knocks you out of the ring, you do have to masturbate.

You're standing just inside the ring, wearing that silly white thong, with your arms crossed and your gritted teeth bared. With piercing eyes, you snarl at Mr. Sex Drive to leave you alone. Mr. Sex Drive, bloated by a billion meals of lust and fantasy, yawns and looks at his watch. Then, appearing quite bored, he waddles over your way. Without bothering to lock arms with you in battle, he merely swings his huge thonged rear and sends you flying against the wall, where you dutifully sit down and masturbate on the spot.

Time and again, you enter the ring, and time and again you fly against the wall, emptying jar after jar of Vaseline. For a while, you keep up your courage by bravely facing up to Mr. Sex Drive again and again. But eventually your bruised and battered spirit gets angry, and you blame it all on God, spitting under your breath, "God put me in this ring with this massive sex drive. If He hadn't given it to me, I wouldn't keep getting knocked out of the ring and have to masturbate. It's His problem, not mine."

You wait and wait, but Mr. Sex Drive just keeps standing there bored as the dickens, waiting for some more lust. Meanwhile, you climb back into the ring for another flying lesson, and then another, and the ache gets deeper as the despair brings tears to your eyes. You decide to leave the arena from time to time to go to church. Your pastor claims it's God's will for you to defeat Mr. Sex Drive. You pray for victory. When church is over, you rise up encouraged, march back to the arena, and declare your victory once more. Standing on your side of the circle, you command Mr. Sex Drive to "Go, in the name of the Lord." Nevertheless, he waddles over and knocks you on your rear.

You hope that a hormone drop will shrink him down to size, but that never materializes. You hope you'll grow in spiritual strength, but that doesn't seem to happen. You feel shame before God, especially after viewing all the empty jars of Vaseline lying around. Finally you say, "I guess it's not God's will that I win this battle."

Not God's will? That's an offense to the character of God.

God turns to you and says, "Get into the ring." So you obey, but Mr. Sex Drive knocks you clean into the wall again.

Turning to God with pleading eyes, you cry, "See God? Save me from this monster! Don't You love me?"

"Of course, I love you," says the Creator of the universe. "Don't you love Me?"

"Lord, you know that I do!"

"Then starve the sumo!"

You see, lying beneath the size and girth of that monstrous Mr. Sex Drive is a genetic makeup of what your sex drive is *supposed* to look like. Really, Mr. Sex Drive is built like a five-foot, three-inch, 110-pound shrimp, but he's just grown huge because you've been feeding him very well over the years. You served him six to ten lusty meals a day until he became big and fat as a barn door.

Once you decide to starve Mr. Sex Drive, however, his weight and heft will shrink. He'll shed pounds overnight. All you have to do is stop feeding him the cable TV, videos, Internet, magazines, and fantasy we mentioned earlier!

Sure, he won't lose two hundred pounds overnight, but Mr. Sex Drive will shed weight rather quickly if you choose not to heap huge helpings of "sexy" food in front of his fat face. Then you'll cut Mr. Sex Drive down in size, and once that happens, you'll start winning some of those battles inside the ring.

You can do it, but you must act with urgency and choose to be strong and courageous before your peers in your quest for purity. In the millisecond it takes to make that choice, the Holy Spirit will start to guide you through the struggle.

Let's talk specifics by considering the movie *Titanic*. How did this movie ever pull down a PG-13 rating? The raw sexuality of the "sketching scene" alone should have qualified this film for an R rating. Frankly, that nude scene was reminiscent of some of the 1970s-era X-rated flicks that I (Fred) watched in the dorms back when I didn't give a fig about Christ's laws. We aren't to have a hint of sexual immorality in our lives; how can the soft-core porn in *Titanic* rest easily with this truth?

How many young men have popped *Titanic* into the VCR and masturbated over this sketching scene? How many Christian parents have unwittingly purchased this video, not knowing their sons can have sex with actress Kate Winslett anytime they choose, day or night?

And what of the days that follow? The alarm goes off, and you lay groggily in the warm softness of your bed as you struggle to consciousness. Soon, the softness of her image seeps into your mind, and in the quiet morning light your mind again fondles her curvaceous fullness. A gentle, come-on smile plays across her lips as your engines churn higher and higher. Helpless before her charms, you're masturbating again.

And it doesn't stop with R and PG-13 movies. The PG-rated *Dead Poet's Society* sports a long closeup of a *Playboy*-style foldout. The PG-rated *Runaway Bride* has no nudity, but the film has plenty of sensual joking that is out of place for Christians in light of Ephesians 5:4. How many sexual fires has Julia Roberts kindled by playfully teasing that she'd already "charmed the one-eyed snake" long before marriage?

Such sensuous food can sumo-size a sex drive faster than you can say, "I'll make mine supersize." If you can't control your sex drive, whose fault is it? Is it God's, for giving you the sex drive? Or is it yours, because you've jumped on the gas pedal and sped past the red line far too often?

You've got a decision to make. You can't visually feed on the same films as your school chums and expect to stay sexually pure. Does this mean I have to give up going to the movies? Of course not. Still, you do have to discern what is right to see. Do you want sexual purity and the deeper intimacy with God that follows, or do you want to be one of the gang, squeezing in purity only when it's convenient?

God's will *is* for you to have sexual purity. We have real power through the Lord to overcome every level of sexual immorality, but if we just keep gorging the sumo while kicking back to enjoy our many orgasms day by day, all bets are off.

God's help for you in this battle is sure. God sent His son to brutally die so that you might gain the freedom to say no to sin. He placed the new life of Christ in you to transform you. He sent His Spirit to comfort and guide you. He fights for you every day, even actively intervening as He did with me in Janet's apartment when I couldn't perform in bed that night.

Without question, God has His job in this battle, but you also have yours—and that's to flee sexual immorality. Starve the sumo!

Those who belong to Christ Jesus have crucified the sinful nature with its passions and desires. (Galatians 5:24)

May I never boast except in the cross of our Lord Jesus Christ, through which the world has been crucified to me, and I to the world. (Galatians 6:14)

Gentlemen, rise up and crucify!

Crucify what? Every hint of sexual immorality. Your sumo match rests on it. If you've always thought Mr. Sex Drive was too big and too strong, wait until you begin withholding "sexy" food from him. You'll cut him down in no time and knock him out of the ring!

setting your defenses

developing
your battle plan

Before we started winning our battles for purity, we experienced a number of setbacks—partially because we hadn't really made a firm, line-in-the-sand decision. We sort of wanted purity, and we sort of didn't. We didn't understand the best approach to take, and besides, the whole business of sexual integrity was mysterious. No one ever told us to starve our sumo.

Satan didn't want us to tell you, either, but now that you know, his greatest attack weapon will be deception. He knows Jesus has already purchased your freedom. He also knows that once you understand how to starve Mr. Sex Drive, you'll probably push the big fellow right out of the ring in short order. So he deceives and confuses. He tricks you into thinking that you're a helpless victim. He tells you that sexual sin is just part of being a man and that there's nothing you can or should do about it. He tells you that you don't need to live a life of obedience because *obedience* is just another word for legalism. He tells you that rules will only weigh you down.

This chapter will remove the mystery surrounding your enemy. First, we'll define your actual objective in practical terms, describing some critical attributes of your sexual sin along the way. Pay close attention to these details, because once you step into the ring, you want to come out victorious. Later we'll lead you through Fred's actual battle plan to show you how he defends against his most bothersome temptations.

YOUR OBJECTIVE

Your goal is sexual purity. Here's a good working definition of it—good because of its simplicity: You're sexually pure when sexual gratification only comes from your wife.

Wait a minute. I'm not married! We know that, but sexual purity has the same definition whether you're married or single. When you're sexually pure, it means you're not seeking sexual gratification. Sexual gratification feeds the sumo. So how do you get to that point?

For teens and young adults, sexual gratification comes from three places: the eyes, the mind, and the body. Therefore, as in any war, you must blockade the "shipping lanes" of the eyes and mind that drive you toward sexual sin and that keep your enemy strong. Beyond that, you must also make sure that you have healthy, positive affections and attitudes in your relationships with girls. In other words, you want your heart to be right and your boundaries clear. To accomplish this, you need to build three perimeters of defense into your life:

1. You need to build a line of defense with your *eyes*.
2. You need to build a line of defense in your *mind*.
3. You need to build a line of defense in your *heart*.

Think of the first line of defense—your eyes—as a wall with "Keep Out" signs around it. That sign defends your eyes by being a covenant like the one Job set up: "I made a covenant with my eyes not to look lustfully at a girl." You defend your eyes by training them to "bounce" from anything sensual. (We'll talk about it a bit in this chapter, then thoroughly explain how to do it in chapter 18.)

The second line of defense is your mind. With the mind, you don't necessarily block out the objects of lust, but you do evaluate and capture them. A key support verse is 2 Corinthians 10:5: "We take captive every thought to make it obedient to Christ." You must train your mind to take thoughts captive, something your mind hasn't been inclined to do. (You'll learn more about this in chapter 19.)

Your third line of defense (which we'll describe further in chapter 20) is your heart. This innermost defense perimeter is built by strengthening the authenticity of your Christian love for the girls you date, as well as increasing your commitment to becoming a blessing to others. You want to honor and cherish every young woman you date, just as you hope that the guy dating your future wife is honoring and cherishing her.

So there's your battle plan. That's it—nothing more, nothing less. As soon as you set up the perimeters, you'll have freedom from sexual impurity. This attack plan may seem too simple to be effective, but disregard that thought. As you study the attributes of your enemy, you'll realize that simplicity is more than sufficient.

Before we move on to build the first of the three lines of defense, let's remove the mystery surrounding sexual sin by gaining a better understanding of the enemy so that we might not be deceived.

IMPURITY IS A HABIT

Some may think impurity is genetic, like the color of our eyes. *I'm male, so that's why I have impure eyes and an impure mind.* But we can't blame our roving eyes on genetics, even though we men are definitely more visually oriented than women. The problem is that some men excuse themselves as *victims* of impure eyes and thoughts, as if that absolves them from all responsibility.

Do you want to know the truth? Impurity is a habit. It lives and acts like a habit. When some hot-looking babe in a French bikini walks by your beach towel, your eyes have the habit of locking on her, sliding up and down. When the cheerleader with the biggest breasts walks past you in the hall, your eyes run away with her. When the *Sports Illustrated* swimsuit issue arrives in your mailbox every February, you fantasize over the curves and crevices, imagining what it would feel like if you could touch her there.

You do these things because you're in the *habit* of doing them. Haven't you been doing them since you discovered girls back in sixth grade? Since checking out the "goods" is only a habit and not some victimizing spell, it can be changed. And we believe it can be done in as little as six weeks.

So how do you break the bad habit of locking on to every rack and tush that swivels your way? You simply replace it with a new and better habit. Sure, it will take some practice. But if you can commit to doing this for the next four to six weeks, the old habit that seemed so strong will become unnatural.

IMPURITY WORKS LIKE A HABIT

Your life is full of routine. If you're still in school, then the alarm clock rings precisely at 6:38. You slowly take your time waking up, jumping into the shower, getting dressed, and eating your favorite bowl of cereal—Wheaties—in a rush to leave the house at 7:35. Each morning, you don't even have to think about what to do next. It's like *Groundhog Day* all over again.

You've also developed similar habits in the sexual arena, especially in the way you look at young women. That's the bad news. The good news is that while sexual impurity works like a bad habit, sexual *purity* can work like a *good* habit.

This should be encouraging news for you. As you enter the fight against impurity, you may see nothing but exhausting battle after exhausting battle waiting on the horizon. You might be saying to yourself, "I can't work this hard at purity for the rest of my life." But if you can just hang in there a little longer, that good habit of purity will gain a foothold. Then you'll be engaged in a fight that requires much less effort.

Currently, you sin without even thinking; your eyes gravitate toward any bouncing breasts that mosey by. Without thinking, your bad habits start kicking in. But with the habit of purity in place, when the shapely cheerleader walks down the hall toward you, you'll look away without even thinking. If you want to peek, you'll have to force your eyes to do so.

IMPURITY FIGHTS LIKE AN ADDICTION

Impurity of the eyes and mind lives like a habit but fights like an addiction. Many habits are addictive. Smokers have the urge to smoke. Drug users "get a jones." Alcoholics need an "eyeopener" to start the day.

In overcoming some addictions, the addictive source can be gradually reduced. For others, the best method is cold turkey. What works best with sexual impurity? Answer: going cold turkey. You cannot just taper down. We tried, and it didn't work because we found our minds and eyes were too tricky and deceitful. With tapering, whatever impurity you do allow seems to multiply in its impact, and the habit won't break. Besides, tapering down also brings with it the possibility of sexual binges that might go on for days.

Binges crush your spirit. "I used to try to stop my sexual sin without really understanding what I was fighting," said Cliff. "I might grit my teeth and do well for a while, but then suddenly, maybe because of some chick-flick or some lustful thoughts that just got carried away, I would masturbate. Then I would say to myself, 'Well, since I failed, I might as well fail big.' I would masturbate two, three times a day for the next week or two before I could regain the strength to fight again. I can't tell you how many times I've binged like this."

So cold turkey is the way to go. You shut off the spigot by totally starving your eyes of all things sensual. Starving the eyes will also help you overcome the desire for premarital sex with the women you date. You'll begin to see your date as a person and not an object.

Now don't expect the habits to die too easily. You can expect an inner "urge to fail" since you're accustomed to grabbing sexual gratification through your eyes, anytime and anywhere you please. Remember, these bring chemical highs, and your body will fight for these highs. This sexual gratification has served to gradually increase your sex drive since puberty. Cutting this source of gratification through the eyes works to decrease your sex drive and make purity easier.

But remember: It will always be a fight to some degree. While there may not be spiritual oppression involved in your battle, there'll always be spiritual opposition. The enemy constantly whispers in your ear. He doesn't want you to win this fight, and he knows the lies that break down a young man's confidence and will to win. You can expect to hear lies and plenty of them. Here's a list of some of the all-time favorites. (After each lie, we'll state the actual truth.)

Satan: "You're the only one dealing with this problem. If anyone ever finds out, you'll be the laughingstock of the youth group!"

The truth: Most young men are dealing with this problem, so no one will laugh.

Satan: "You failed again. You'll never be able to train your eyes. It's impossible."

The truth: It isn't impossible. Didn't Job train his eyes? He was a man just like you.

Satan: "You're being so legalistic! You're splitting hairs."

The truth: God still has standards of behavior for us, and it's still a good idea to live purely by His standards.

Satan: "Oh, c'mon! Don't be such a moron. This 'habit-changing' plan will never work."

The truth: The plan will work, because for most men the problem of sexual impurity is nothing more than bad choices evolving into bad habits.

Satan: "Why fight it? Sex is fun and doesn't hurt anybody."

The truth: You can't always see them, but the costs of your sin are greater than you think.

As you can see, the opposition is vicious and merciless. To set up your first line of defense, start with your eyes. You want to train them to "bounce." If you can bounce your eyes for six weeks, you can win this war.

BOUNCING THE EYES

In the past, your eyes have always bounced *toward* the sexual and not *away* from it. To combat years and years of this reflexive action, you need to train your eyes to immediately bounce away when it comes upon a sexy image—much like the way you jerk your hand away from a hot stove. Here it is in a nutshell:

> When your eyes bounce toward a woman's attributes, they must bounce away immediately.

But why must the bounce be immediate? One might argue that a glance is just a glance. A glance doesn't linger.

Granted, a glance is different from staring open-mouthed until drool pools at your feet, but a glance can be more than enough "eye juice" to give you that little chemical high, that little pop. In our experience, bouncing away immediately is clean and easy for the mind to understand and doesn't give the mind wiggle room to "lock and load."

Watch out! As we've just said, when you start bouncing your eyes, your body will fight you in peculiar, unexpected ways. Since sexual sin has an addictive nature, your body will not give up on its pleasures without a fight. You'll have to creatively look for ways to stay visually pure, and you do that through these two logical steps:

1. Study yourself. How and where are you attacked the most?
2. Design your defense for each of the greatest enemies you've identified.

Your first step is listing your own "greatest enemies." What are the most obvious and prolific sources of sensual images coming your way? Where do you look most often? Where are you weakest?

In choosing them, remember that they must be areas from which you visually draw sexual satisfaction. Don't make the mistake of choosing non-visual weaknesses for this list, which Justin did. Here's what this college-age student jotted as his three big areas of weakness:

1. showers
2. being home alone
3. studying late

We can all understand why these can be troublesome. In the shower, you're nude with warm water cascading down your body. That can be sensual. When you're home alone, no one's around to discover you if you're looking at things you shouldn't or decide to masturbate. When you're studying late, you feel sorry for yourself and need "comfort."

But such weak spots needn't be targeted if you train your eyes to bounce and eliminate the visual stimuli. With no food for the mental fantasies, the sexual fevers that draw your mind to sin will dissipate. These situations will lose their power naturally.

DEFENDING ON ALL FRONTS

I (Fred) had no problem coming up with a list of my six biggest areas of weakness. Let me share how I dealt with them. Granted, I was a bit older than you and married at the time, but these weaknesses are fairly universal. Besides, I can't give you as much detail on the inner fight if I use someone else's story. Just incorporate what you learn from these details in dealing with your own weaknesses. In the next chapters, we'll share some of the unique obstacles faced in this battle by other young men like yourself through telling their stories as well.

1. Defending Against Those Lingerie Ads

Lingerie advertisements were my worst enemy and remained difficult to control for quite some time. I know—newspaper ads of women in their bras and panties wouldn't appear to hold a candle to the total nudity you see in *Hustler*, but I would let my imagination fill in the gaps. That was almost just as fun. From time to time, I hit the mother lode: a swimsuit feature or an exercise feature illustrated with bun-fitting spandex all around.

I had to train my eyes to bounce away when I came upon these images in the newspaper, right? That turned out to be too difficult, at least in the beginning, so I established a number of rules to keep these images out of my hands before my eyes had a chance to take them in.

Rule 1: When my hand reached for the department store ad insert (where the bra and panty ads were), I forfeited the right to pick it up if I sensed in the slightest that my underlying motive was to see something sensual.

To be honest, this approach didn't work well at first. Although sensing my motive was easy, forfeiting my right to pick it up was not. My flesh simply ignored what was happening. My mind screamed, "Shut up! I want this, and I'll have it!" My flesh won continually, but as I began to succeed elsewhere in blocking my eyes, my hatred for the sin grew and my will and discipline grew stronger. I never gave up, and there came a day when the lingerie ads finally failed to ensnare me.

Rule 2: If a magazine had an overtly sensual babe on the cover, I tore off the cover and threw it away. Mail-order clothing catalogs or magazines with sensual cover pictures can hang around a house for a long time, drawing your eyes all month long. Now I ask you this: What if a full-breasted woman in a teensy-weensy bikini came to your room and sat down on your desk and said, "I'll just sit here awhile, but I promise to leave by the end of the month"? Would you let her stay to catch your eye every time you walked into the room? I don't think so. So why do you leave her there in picture form?

Rule 3: Regarding department store inserts, I would allow myself to pick one up if I was genuinely looking for sale prices on computer equipment or auto parts, but I forced myself to start looking from the back.

Don't ask me how I found out, but the lingerie ads were usually placed on pages two and three. The camping, automotive, and computer ads were relegated to the back half of the insert. By opening the insert from the rear, I avoided seeing the young, nubile models entirely. As time moved on, if I happened to come upon a sensual image where I didn't expect it (lurking in the local news section, for instance), I kept the normal covenant to bounce my eyes immediately.

2. Un-Fixating on Female Joggers

Whenever I approached a roadside jogger while driving, my eyes fixed on her like heat-seeking missiles. I had to move quickly—or I would soon pass her! But trying to look away from a jogger created a problem: I couldn't drive safely if I was concentrating on *not* looking out for her. That could be dangerous, even on the country roads of Iowa. After all, I didn't want to run over anyone.

Studying the situation, I found a solution. Rather than look completely away, I turned my gaze to the opposite side of the road and kept the jogger at the edge of my peripheral vision. She wasn't completely out of sight, but she was out of mind.

My body began to fight back in some interesting ways. First, my brain argued fiercely with me: *If you keep this up, you'll cause a wreck or run over somebody.* I considered this argument then answered, *You know and I know that's highly unlikely. Believe me, I can handle a car.*

My body's second attempt to stop me was very peculiar. Whenever I saw a jogger and reflexively looked away, my mind tricked me into believing I recognized the individual, prompting a second look. My mind was so nimble that nearly every female jogger reminded me of someone I knew. Talk about irritating! It took awhile for me to stop falling for that ruse.

My brain tried one last trick. As I passed the jogger without a direct look, I would momentarily relax. In the same moment, my brain took advantage of my lowered guard by ordering my eyes to glance into the rearview mirror for a more direct look. Depending on whether she was coming or going, I scored on that one. But then I caught on to what was happening, and that really burned me up! I had to learn not to drop my guard after passing her, and in time that trick faded away as well.

Whenever I fell for one of those tricks, I'd bark to myself, "You've made a covenant with your eyes! You can't do that anymore." In the first two weeks, I must have said that a million times, but the repeated confession of truth eventually worked a transformation in me.

3. Bouncing the Billboards

Those big signboards along the highway are notorious for featuring some long, tall, slinky, sexy woman lying across a car hood. She whispers, "C'mon, big boy, buy this muscle car and you'll get me, too!" I know of one giant billboard for a rock radio station that showed a closeup of bikini-clad breasts with this tag line: "What a pair!"

My defense mechanism, of course, was to bounce my eyes. But I took it a step further by remembering where the sensual billboards were placed along my commute. You should do the same on your route to school or work. Out of sight, out of mind, right?

When designing my defense against billboards, I thought of my teenage experience in driving a hotel van. We had a contract with the airlines to drive the pilots and flight attendants from the airport to the hotel. The contract required that we complete the trip within ten minutes. Only one route from the airport was short enough to make the time limit— an unpaved road with a billion potholes. I painfully learned of the direct correlation between the number of potholes I hit and the size of my tip, so I memorized every pothole on that road along with the driving angles necessary to miss most of them. Eventually, I became proficient enough to drive that road blindfolded and hit very few of those teeth-rattling craters.

With the billboards, it's easier to memorize their locations and avoid visual contact entirely than it is to look and then bounce the eyes.

4. Saying Bye-Bye to Beer-and-Bikini Commercials

No red-blooded American male can watch a major sporting event these days without being assaulted by temptation. That's because the sports shows come packaged with commercials showing the typical bunch of half-naked women cavorting on some beach with some beer-soaked yahoos. What's a young man to do?

The answer is to maintain command of the remote control and zap those commercials! When you're armed with a remote, you can do anything! *Phasers set to kill, Worf.* All sexy babes get zapped by the clicker as you hit on ESPN or Fox News during the commercial break. (If your father hogs the clicker, as fathers love to do, have him read this section of the book. He should zap the beer-and-bikini commercials for himself too.)

5. Staying Motivated at the Movies Too

Teens and young men are in a tough spot when it comes to the latest movie releases from Hollywood. That's because the studios have painted a big bull's-eye right on your chest (or elsewhere). It's no secret that today's new releases are targeted toward the biggest ticket-buying audience, which happens to be you young people. To sell more tickets and make more money, the Hollywood crowd has found that "pushing the envelope" can pack them in on Friday and Saturday evenings—"date night."

This is where you need to educate yourself about what's playing. Hollywood releases "horny teen" movies with regularity, and they're filled with sexual innuendo, girls taking their tops off, simulated sex acts, and tons of randy behavior.

This is an area that's up to you, because many teens live with parents who don't care what they see at the local cineplex or when they're home alone. For you young men living on your own, nothing is keeping you from buying a ticket. The question is this: Are you going to be authentic? A Christian lives like a Christian when no one else is around.

I didn't have trouble with "horny teen" movies since I was married and had a family when I began my new ways. But cable movies on the road caused me to get weak in the knees. My job involved regular overnight travel, so I'd check into a hotel when the business day was over. That left me with *hours* with nothing to do in the hotel room. I was obviously vulnerable to watching cable movies, and I fell for them again and again.

I tried a variation of my "motive rule" with magazine advertisements to beat these sexually charged movies. When I reached for the clicker to turn it on, I would check my motives. If they were clean, I would allow myself to turn on the TV, usually sticking with the news or ESPN. The trouble was, I would get bored and, without thinking, start channel surfing.

The "motive rule" worked better with magazine ads, because once I forfeited the right to look at them, I could get up and go elsewhere and find something else to do. Not so with the hotel TV; I still had hours alone in the room with the blank screen staring back at me, saying, "Come on over, Big Boy!"

Let me tell you—it was hard grounding myself from hotel TV. But that's what I did, deciding that I'd lost my privileges and wasn't allowed to turn it on for a while. Sound drastic? I've had some traveling salesmen tell me that they put blankets over their TVs to keep them out of sight. Others call the front desk and ask them to "block" the pay-per-view soft-core movies.

Whatever you have to do, do it.

If you live alone, you'll have the same problem with your TV, especially if you subscribe to a premium movie channel like HBO. You might want to rethink that subscription. If you're still living with parents and siblings, then only watch TV when you have some company. If you're home alone, be careful.

6. Respecting Receptionists—Promptly!

Sometimes when I enter office buildings, the receptionist is standing. When I tell her my name, she'll typically bend over to use the phone to announce my arrival. Often her loose-fitting, silky blouse falls open to reveal everything.

It had never occurred to me to turn away from this display; I simply figured it was my lucky day. But when I began my search for purity, I realized this had to stop. The defense was simple. Before, when I came in and saw the receptionist standing, I knew what might happen, and I looked for it. Now I use this same knowledge to my advantage. When I see her standing, I avert my eyes even before she bends over. Or, if I see her walking toward a file cabinet, I avert my eyes before she bends over for that file. Of all the weaknesses, this one was addressed most easily. I now naturally turn away.

You probably don't meet that many receptionists, but there are clothing store clerks, ticket takers, waitresses…maybe a few teachers…tons of sexy-looking women out there you might run into as you go through life. Remember to bounce those eyes away promptly!

So there you have a practical example of a useful battle plan. Have you developed some personalized strategies for yourself? More to the heart of the matter: *Have you finally made your decision for sexual purity?* If so, great! You now understand why failing to eliminate every hint of sexual immorality from your life can be dangerous. You understand how the visual sensuality of immodest dress, racy movies, over-the-top commercials, and all the rest feeds your eyes and ignites you sexually. You understand how the brain gets pleasure from the chemical high it experiences when arousal happens.

We're simply saying that to break through to the other side, you must start by cutting off the sensual images reaching your mind through your eyes. In other words, go cold turkey on the chemical highs. It's time.

Taking on Technological Temptations

I want to touch on three stories I've run across since *Every Young Man's Battle* first released in 2002.

First, consider Brady, who'd been dealing with lust and pornography for some time until he read our book. He'd learned to begin treating women respectfully with his eyes and mind and to see them as people instead of as hot collections of interesting body parts. "I was doing great, and I wasn't even thinking about girls in that way, at least until the day I was in a chat room online and the chat turned sexy. Then I noticed the Web cam that my dad had purchased. The next thing I knew, I was broadcasting myself to five girls while masturbating. When I was done, I felt so bad that I cried my eyes out, but the next day, I did the very same thing. By now it's like I'm addicted to doing that stuff. I hate what I do, but somehow I can't seem to stop it."

Next, there's Craig, who met nineteen-year-old Clara over the Internet. Because Craig was a twenty-seven-year-old single missionary, Clara immediately put 100 percent stock in his character. Their cell-phone conversations lingered until the early hours of the morning. For many weeks their talks centered on spiritual matters such as, "When is Jesus returning?" and, "What will heaven be like?" But after those conversations grew stale, the topics turned more personal: "What would we do if we were alone together right now?" or, "What turns you on most?"

One night Craig, feeling relatively sure that Clara wouldn't deny his request, asked her to use her cell phone to make a video clip of herself masturbating. Clara thought it was the least she could do to satisfy them both what with all the miles separating them. But after that deed was done, they were eaten up with guilty consciences. They vowed not to do it again—a promise that lasted all of two weeks. Even as "technical virgins," they were both hooked on phone sex... until Clara's mom found her phone and the most recent videos sent. But those consequences were minimal compared to what happened to Jared.

Jared, twenty-four, and Tessa, twenty-one, started dating in July while attending the University of Georgia. The relationship was a whirlwind: soon after discovering each other on Facebook and hooking up, they moved in together and, according to Jared, bought a Great Dane and exchanged promise rings. But their union unraveled just as quickly as it had begun, and they broke up by January. Then things really went wrong. Police say that when Tessa began dating another guy that spring, Jared posted nude photos of her on his Facebook page. He was arrested soon after the pictures appeared online.

The term *revenge porn*—uploading homemade porn to humiliate an ex after a vicious breakup—didn't exist when *Every Young Man's Battle* was released. In fact, all three of these stories would've been inconceivable only a few years ago. Advancing technology continually changes our battle's landscape.

I share these stories with you because there's a common thread: these people compromised their sexual integrity and, as a result, were publicly humiliated. But it's not the Web cams or cell phones or Facebook pages that are at fault; it's how these people were behaving in the first place that got them into trouble. To avoid similar problems, consider these eight guidelines:

1. Hot conversation, whether by phone or by text or by computer, gets your mind racing and puts your body

in the lead. Since this talk takes you from one level of arousal to the next, it's not "sophisticated" or just "harmless fun." It's foreplay, and it works on the pleasure centers of the brain exactly like porn. Why else would 1-900 numbers be so profitable?

2. When the next new technology comes along and you wonder if what you're doing is right, ask these questions: *Does it drive me from one level of arousal to the next? Am I driven to do it again and again?* If so, call it what it is—sex outside of marriage. Remember, you don't have to be with someone to have sex. We call it phone sex because we get the same kick and the same high as other forms of sex, whether we're in her presence or not.

3. What turns her on is none of your business unless you've entered a covenant relationship with her in marriage. Ever.

4. When it comes to any form of text messages (cell phones, e-mails, Facebook, and so on), don't type anything that you wouldn't want someone—like your parents or your pastor—to read or hear you say in person.

5. The fastest way to put a stop to text messages with inappropriate language or innuendos is to simply not respond. Let the other person eat static. If she follows up with a "why aren't you answering?" message, then you can reply with something like, "I don't play that game. Talk to me respectfully or don't talk to me at all."

6. Don't post photos of anyone on the Internet without that person's permission.

7. Keep in mind that the purpose of social networking sites such as Facebook and MySpace is to connect people. Using these sites to reach out and befriend others is fine, but avoid using them to attack other people and destroy reputations.

8. An urge for revenge is a reflection of your character, not hers, and it reveals that you never really loved her in the first place. You were only using her body for selfish sexual desires, and you should be seeking repentance, not revenge.

When you consider how you use technology, remember these three stories. Remember, too, that a picture is worth a thousand words. Never, ever create sexual photos, videos, e-mails, text messages, or anything else that someone could keep and share in the future. Think of revenge porn or any of these possible disasters the way you think of an STD: something that can only happen when you mix sex with irresponsibility.

your sword
and your shield

You'll need to develop your own strategies for bouncing your eyes, as your weaknesses are different from ours. After all, your school is likely swarming with girls wearing spaghetti-strap tops, low-cut dresses, and underwear as outerwear. You've got access to X-rated sites on the Internet that weren't there when you were in junior high. When your friends head to the beach or water park, every girl you know sports a bikini.

While we face different obstacles, the principles are the same, and the strategies will be similar. But it's important to remember one thing: Our strategies for bouncing the eyes may sound rather simple, and maybe even easy to do, but they aren't. Satan fights you with lies while your body fights you with the desires and strength of deeply entrenched bad habits. To win, you'll also need a sword and a shield. Of all the parts of your battle plan, this is likely the most important.

TAKE UP YOUR SWORD AND SHIELD

You'll need a good Bible verse to use as a sword and rallying point.

Just one? It may be useful to memorize several verses of Scripture about purity since they work to eventually transform and wash the mind. But in the cold-turkey, day-to-day fight against impurity, having several memory verses might be as cumbersome as strapping on a hundred-pound backpack to engage in hand-to-hand combat. You aren't agile enough to maneuver quickly.

That's why we recommend a single "attack verse," and it better be quick. We suggest the opening line of Job 31:

I have made a covenant with my eyes.

When you fail and linger over some hot babe, say sharply, "No, I've made a covenant with my eyes. I can't do that!" When you look at a busty billboard, say, "No, I've made a covenant with my eyes. I can't do that!" This action will be a quick dagger to the heart of your enemy.

Your shield—a single "protective verse" that you can reflect on and draw strength from even when you aren't in the direct line of fire—may be even more important than your sword because it places temptation out of earshot. We suggest selecting this verse as your shield:

Flee from sexual immorality.... You are not your own; you were
bought at a price. Therefore honor God with your body.
(1 Corinthians 6:18-20)

We've distilled this shield verse to its core kernel and repeated it in the face of many tempting situations when facing sensual images or thoughts:

I have no right to look at that or think about it. I haven't the
authority.

A shield such as this will help you think rightly about the real issues involved as you face temptation in your fight for purity. Satan's power of temptation lies in your supposed right to make decisions regarding your own behavior. If you didn't believe you had this right, no tempting power could touch you.

Consider a specific example. I (Fred) recall once walking down a hotel hallway to the ice machine. On top of the machine lay a *Playboy* magazine. Believing I had a right to choose my behavior, I asked myself this question: Should I look at this *Playboy* or not?

The moment I asked that question, I opened myself to counsel. I began talking pros and cons to myself. But far worse, I opened myself to Satan's counsel. He wanted to be heard on this issue.

He cajoled and lied, keeping my mind focused on the conversation so I didn't even notice my body slipping down the slope of lust. By the time he finished, the only answer I wanted to hear was "Yes, you can look at it. Just make sure to read the articles."

Therein lies the power of temptation. You may fear that temptation will be too strong for you in this battle, but temptations honestly have no power at all without our own arrogant questions.

Put yourself in my situation. You take a seat in the back of the library, and on the chair is the latest issue of *Playboy* magazine. This is when your shield verse—the words from 1 Corinthians 6—should come to mind:

I have no right to even consider looking at it. I haven't the authority.

That conviction leaves no room for pros and cons to drift deceitfully into your brain. And as for Satan, since you asked no questions, no conversation with him transpires—a conversation in which he could try to get you to change your mind.

FOR THE MIND AS WELL AS THE EYES

Your sword and shield will help strengthen you, not only in controlling your eyes, but also in establishing a defense perimeter with your mind (which we'll explore thoroughly a little later).

Here's an example. You're minding your own business as you do some homework. Then you go online to do some research. You decide to check your e-mail. It becomes apparent that you've received some spam from an X-rated site. What's your reaction? Note the great difference in perspective between the following two possible responses:

1. Should I open this e-mail right now?
2. I don't even have the *right* to ask such a *question,* because I don't have the *authority* to make that *decision.*

The first response implies that you have the authority and the right to make that decision. The second implies that the question itself is moot. You not only *won't* consider it, you *can't* consider it. You're not your own. You have no right.

We call this second response "living within our rights." If we submit always and live within our rights, God's laws of reaping and sowing protect us. Once we step beyond our rights, the sowing and reaping laws work against us. We're in mutiny, having stolen authority from our Captain. Do that, and we're back within earshot of Satan.

Derrick was confused about his rights. "My girlfriend, Janice, and I had a big fight the other day," he said. "We were walking along, and I saw some pretty hot babes and gave a low, little whistle. She got angry and said I shouldn't be looking at other women. Well, I think it's okay to scope them out. Sure, I love Janice and plan on dating her a long time. I'm not going to hop into bed with them or anything, but like my dad always says, 'Just because I can't order doesn't mean I can't look at the menu.'"

Our response: First of all, we don't think any man has the biblical right to scope out anyone lustfully. But if a girlfriend says she's bothered by it, all rights surely vanish. That's unloving. Derrick stepped outside his rights when he thought he could look at other women like an epicure regarding the menu of a fine restaurant. He opened himself up to Satan's confusing counsel. Here's what the Deceiver may have whispered:

1. "God made them beautiful on purpose. Of course you should look. He intended that for you!"

2. "It won't hurt anything…you're only looking."

3. "Life is unbearable if you're going to live by such tight standards. God couldn't possibly have intended that for you. Go ahead and look. He loves you and wants you to live life more abundantly."

4. "So what if your girlfriend is bothered when you look at other women? She's immature. She has the problem, not you!"

Stepping outside his rights, with his shield down, Derrick was nodding his head to all four statements.

But it didn't have to happen. Shield yourself from the power of temptation by submitting to God's definition of your rights.

HERE'S WHAT TO EXPECT

Okay, you've made a covenant with your eyes to starve them and to train them to bounce. Maybe you've defined your weak areas, creating a custom defense for each one, and you've picked up your sword and shield. What can you expect to happen over the next few weeks and months? Here's a bit of the timeline that unfolded for me (Fred) as my defense perimeters went up.

- *Short-Term Results:* The first two weeks were largely failure after failure for me. My eyes simply wouldn't fall in line and bounce away from the sexual. My shields from Satan's lies were weak, but I kept plodding ahead in faith, knowing that God was with me.

During the third and fourth weeks, hope dawned as I began to win about as often as I failed. I can't overemphasize how dramatic and surprising this change was for me. God's blessings and gifts truly go beyond what we can ask or think, for when we sow righteousness, only the mind of God can conceive of the blessings we'll reap. For instance, I couldn't believe how much I now lived to please Brenda. And I couldn't believe how intimate I began to feel with the Lord. The veil between us was disintegrating.

During the fifth and sixth weeks, my eyes found a consistency in bouncing away from the sensual. The spiritual oppression lifted, and the veil of distance from God vanished. Though I still wasn't perfect, the rest was downhill.

For you, it needn't take long to raise the defense perimeter of your eyes. If you really want to do it, you'll see that progress comes quickly. More than once, guys have said to me, "Fred, this is amazing, but it happened just like you said! Right about the sixth week, it all came together!" But six weeks is surely no hard-and-fast rule. It may take less time or perhaps more, depending on your strongholds and your commitment to the task at hand.

• *Long-Term Results:* As you continue to live purely, the hedge of protection from temptation grows thicker around you. If you're diligent, it becomes a much longer throw for Satan to lob temptation grenades into your living quarters.

In the long term, do you still have to monitor your eyes? Yes, because the natural bent of your eyes is to sin, and you'll return to bad habits if you're careless. But with only the slightest effort, you'll make good habits permanent. (On a practical note, if you live in a four-season region, you may find that late spring and early summer call for a fresh dose of diligence as warmer temperatures allow women to wear less clothing. Plan to heighten your defenses at those times.)

After a year or so—though it may take longer—nearly all major skirmishes will stop. Bouncing your eyes will become deeply entrenched. Your brain, now policing itself tightly, will rarely slip, having given up long ago on its chances to return to the old days of pornographic pleasure highs.

ARE WE CRAZY?

Looking back at the details of our plan, even we will admit that it all sounds slightly crazy. Defenses, brain tricks, bouncing your eyes, forfeiting rights. Man! We wonder if even Job would be a bit startled.

On the other hand, maybe we should expect a sound plan to look this way. Consider all the men who are called to purity, yet so few seem to know how to do it. How many of the guys in your youth group are sexually pure?

Yeah. That's what we thought.

What's the bottom line? It took all our resources and creativity to destroy the old habits and every inch of freedom in Christ to walk free from sin. We'd been owned by these habits for years, taking whatever women we desired with our eyes, whenever we wanted.

Freedom from sin is worth dying for, according to Jesus. Take it from us—it's also worth living for!

what might
slow you down?

Will you move along the same timeline to success that we outlined in the previous chapter? In some ways yes, but in other significant ways no. For instance, it will take a couple of weeks to get the hang of bouncing the eyes, and then a number of weeks to solidify the new, good habit. But there's another consideration that you single guys must keep in mind.

When I went cold turkey with my eyes, I was married. I didn't have to go cold turkey on intercourse simultaneously. After cutting off those addictive pleasure highs through my eyes, my wife could serve as a kind of cool methadone while I adjusted to my new life of purity.

You don't have that option, so the battle is going to be tougher, especially if you're going cold turkey on sexual intercourse with your girlfriend or the false intercourse of oral sex and masturbation.

Eric is a college-aged single guy with a Web-based design business that he runs out of his apartment. Eric's story paints the picture pretty well:

> Porn leaves a big hole of emptiness, but I cannot get myself to turn
> away from it when I'm the only one in my lonely apartment. I've
> tried bouncing my eyes, but that's as far as I can go. What happens

after that is that I cannot concentrate on my work. I can't get anything done because sex constantly floods my preoccupations and thoughts.

What's going on here? The best way to describe what's happening is to compare it to withdrawal. Eric's body had gotten accustomed to getting the chemical highs from the "visual pops" stemming from porn. This isn't unusual. Many of us have had similar experiences outside the sexual arena. Richard told me, "You guys don't seem to drink much Dr Pepper in Iowa, but where I come from in Texas, Dr Pepper is *the* soft drink of choice. Everyone drinks Dr Pepper, and I used to have one for breakfast, lunch, supper, and in between. If I went too long without a Dr Pepper, I'd actually get grumpy. My body demanded one."

I (Steve) became real addicted to the sugar high from cookies once, and when I tried to pull back, I got headaches! Going without afternoon cookies even affected my work. We see the same thing with caffeine, alcohol, and other drugs. An aspect of this is kicking in when you go cold turkey with your sexuality.

But it's also more than that if you're constantly masturbating. An orgasm releases a flood of "feel good" brain chemicals—endorphins—into the bloodstream, and the act gives you a bigger kick than anything that comes through the eyes. Your body wants that feeling again, and that's why some guys masturbate three, four, even five times a day, even though this goes far beyond the demands of any natural sex drive.

If you're getting regular orgasms through masturbation, oral sex, mutual masturbation, or whatever, and if you're living in a constant state of visual foreplay, then the crest of your sex drive has risen to a height where it's flooding every dike and riverbank that God put in place for you. In other words, you're out of control. You have a flood on your hands, and that flood has to settle back into its banks. This means your sex drive has to "dry up" to normal levels as a "drought" of images and orgasms has their natural effect. That will take some time—probably more than three weeks.

DEALING WITH STRONG SEXUAL URGES

What else can be done about the head-throbbing sexual pressure of withdrawals? Hopefully, nocturnal emissions will kick in quickly to take the edge off while the river dries up. But not always right away, it seems. Listen to this story from Marc:

> I finished reading *Every Man's Battle* and began bouncing my eyes.
> I had success for about a week and then fell to the temptation as the
> sexual urges got stronger. I've been so used to focusing on attractive
> babes that this was a tougher habit for me to break than I thought
> it would be. Plus, I'd been masturbating quite a bit. *Every Man's
> Battle* was written to married men, so it assumed that the reader had
> a wife for release when the sexual urges got strong. I figure married
> guys must get release once a week, at worse. But you also mentioned
> that the single person has nocturnal emissions to relieve the sexual
> tension. I don't recall the last time I had a nocturnal emission. How
> am I going to abstain from masturbation without those?

Marc's problem is simple. He hasn't ridden it out yet. He needs to hang in there and be patient. As for Marc's stating that he'd experienced no nocturnal emissions, let's talk about it. Nocturnal emissions are there to release a buildup of sperm in the sperm banks. But those banks may never get filled because of "overuse." Some guys have never had a nocturnal emission simply because their regular masturbation and promiscuity keeps the banks from filling up and demanding release.

Maybe you've never had one for the same reason, and you wonder whether they'll really help you at all. It may take some time for your body to adjust to this new scenario. Besides, nocturnal emissions aren't exactly science and don't work on the clock, so they can't be expected to happen every third evening on the dot. They're there to release the sexual pressure that comes from "sperm production," not the sexual pressure that comes from impurity. This means that it may take some time to get in balance.

Along these lines, I (Fred) have a great story for you from a young reader of *Every Man's Battle* whom I've come to appreciate through a series of e-mail interchanges. I think you will too. His name is David:

> My whole life I've gone to church and lived in a Christian home
> where my dad's a deacon and my mom plays the piano for the choir.
> Anyway, I had some problems to deal with, being seventeen. Like
> porn, porn, porn. Dirty chat rooms. Videos. You name it. It took a
> while to become honest with my youth pastor, but we are extremely
> close, so I finally got it out and we discussed it. I'd been trying to do
> different things to get over it before reading your book.
>
> I found *Every Man's Battle* to be very entertaining reading, and I
> learned the techniques of bouncing the eyes and taking thoughts cap-
> tive. I'd been struggling with random dirty thoughts and glances at
> close friends of mine, and the book was very helpful. I feel so liberated!
>
> But I have a few comments. I'm not married, so does this mean
> I'm just supposed to wait for nocturnal emissions? But in the three or
> four years since puberty, I have *never* had one. Not once. Never, ever,
> ever. And it wasn't because I never went seventy-two hours without a
> release, either. At times in the past, I have made bets with friends to
> see who could "last the longest" without release, and I've made many,
> many seventy-two-hour sets in a row.
>
> I know that *Every Man's Battle* was written for the perspective
> of married guys, but you left us single guys hanging out to dry. I'm

sorry, but telling a man he should go at his wife with great gusto and then telling the single guy to wait for a nocturnal emission is insane!

So here we arrive at the topic of masturbation. Right now, I'm well past seventy-two hours and I am kinda frustrated…if you know what I mean. Since I'm "emission deficient," I'm going crazy!

I corresponded with David, and we got a dialogue going. Then I heard this from him:

It had been a number of days since I last masturbated, and I don't know why, but IT WAS BAD! I always thought the term "blue balls" was made up, but I actually ached! I have no idea why. I've gone weeks before on bets, and it had only been a couple of days. I was pretty confused. It was bad, I'm telling you!

Well, after a couple of more days I took matters into my own hands again—literally. I did it earlier in the day. I tell you that because I want you to know that when I went to bed that night, I was not really still thinking about sex.

So that night, guess what happened? Yep, a nocturnal emission. The first time it's ever happened in my life. I think God was saying, "Ha, ha" to me or something, maybe implying that if I'd have just waited, He'd have taken care of it for me. He must be a joker!

What can we say? As you move into purity, the physical side of your sexuality should begin to rebalance, and we're confident that it will fall in line with God's natural intent. Even if you never have a nocturnal emission, be advised that some guys don't ever have them, and that's okay because God provided a second natural mechanism in which the body simply reabsorbs the excess sperm. It may take a while for the physical processes to kick in and the sex drive to become manageable, but it should happen.

Coping with "Mind Lag"

What else might slow up your timeline to victory? It may also take a while for your mental processes to kick in. Kind of a jet lag of the pure mind. Remember, you've likely been using the false intimacy of masturbation to replace the real intimacy you were missing in your family or school. That doesn't change overnight, so there may be a number of false starts early on.

You don't form intimacy with God overnight, either. That will take some time. You also won't build intimacy with new friends or accountability partners overnight, either. Since these needs for intimacy are very real, you must be diligent in finding friends to fill those needs. Eric said,

> Even if I *could* get past three weeks on bouncing my eyes and staying
> away from the Internet, I wonder if there would still be an emptiness
> that would drag me down? It seems I need to fill a void in my life
> that the porn now fills. Can I really expect my legitimate needs for
> companionship to suddenly disappear?

On the one hand, we can say no. On the other hand, we urge you to be as diligent about building up friendships and finding companionship as you need to be about bouncing your eyes. This is a critical component in your battle for sexual purity. Without it, the struggle may be merciless.

Growing Into a Healthy Discipline

Another reason the process may slow down is that your commitment and discipline to this process of purity may take some time to kick in. Our society doesn't glorify discipline all that much, especially in high school. This means it may take you some time to learn a disciplined lifestyle.

The apostle Paul said we're to be like Olympic athletes, beating our bodies and running so as to win. Most of us haven't disciplined our bodies to that extent, certainly not in the sexual arena. But the truth is clear. We're to crucify the flesh. Part of that process is learning not to put yourself in the same old situations that lead to sin.

For instance, an alcoholic shouldn't hang out at a sports bar on Friday nights watching the ball game. Similarly, renting *American Pie,* or feasting on the visual sensuality of Lara Croft in *Tomb Raider,* drags us away from God's best, even though we may not notice it on the surface. In fact, we're amazed at how many guys can watch raunchy movies and think that the sexy stuff doesn't affect them.

Did you see Tom Hanks in *Forrest Gump*? If so, you probably remember the scene at the beginning where Sally Field had sex with the principal to get her son into the "right" school. You'll remember the bare breasts at the New Year's party and the nude on-stage guitar performance. You'll never forget how Forrest's girlfriend let him touch her breast, which set off an orgasm. Or the time she climbed on top of him in bed—which led to her conceiving a child out of wedlock.

Seeing this type of stuff causes your mind to race in all kinds of directions. At night and in bed, you wonder what it would be like to touch her breast like Forrest did. You fantasize about your girl making you grunt and pant like Sally Field did with the principal. Finally, you masturbate just to make all the thoughts go away.

Some may think that objecting to *Forrest Gump* is minor, legalistic meddling. But such subtle influences, added to hundreds of others over time, provide more than a hint of sexual immorality in our lives. Soon, the effect isn't so subtle anymore, because it builds that false sex drive into a permanent low-grade sexual fever that isn't fun to deal with at all. Before long, your conscience dims until you can't quite tell what's right or wrong anymore. You're watching movies like this without even noticing the sexuality. But it's there just the same, turbocharging your desires.

While we're talking about discipline, let's go beyond our concern for our eyes. We must also be concerned with where we place ourselves in other ways. For example, Tim told us that he never takes a shower without playing Christian music at the same time. Otherwise, the warm shower water tempts a fantasy. Mike told us he chooses to do his homework every night in the living room instead of his bedroom, even though he studies better in the quiet of his room. "I don't want to spend so much time alone where my thoughts and eyes can go crazy on me," he said. Dave told us that he and his girlfriend have a rule that they can't be alone in either home if the parents are away. And Josh said to us, "Kissing isn't wrong, but when a girl decides to kiss me on the first date, I find it hard to believe she cares much about her purity. That's dangerous, because if she doesn't care much about hers, she won't care so much about mine. So I have a rule not to date them a second time."

These guys are smart. To be bold here, it's obvious that if you want to stay in control, lying on your bed without any clothes on wouldn't be a smart move. Limit the times you're alone and in a highly excitable situation. Do things with friends of both sexes. Go on group dates. Limit the amount of touching *and* the amount of kissing. Whatever your defenses, set your rules and then be disciplined.

Walk in truth.

keep focusing on the goal

What happens if you don't win this battle in six weeks? We don't know, but in some sense, we're not sure how much that matters. Sure, you're anxious to win. Sure, you want to put this stuff behind you. But it's not as important to focus on some self-imposed deadline as it to *focus on where you're headed.* This is going to be a battle—a battle that will demand your patience and time.

What should be our focus? Actually, there are two primary areas of focus: (1) getting closer to God and (2) integrating our sexuality into our Christian lives. Let's take a close look at each of these before Steve shares some thoughts about starting with less while moving to none.

GETTING CLOSER TO GOD

It's so important to remember that God once looked upon His only begotten Son in Gethsemane as He struggled to submit in the biggest battle of His life. Jesus' submission was precious to the Father. Now this same Father is looking down from heaven upon you, His adopted son, as you struggle to submit in *your* battle for sexual purity. Sure, He wants victory, but He doesn't look only at the wins and losses. He looks at the heart. The very fact that you've entered the fray is precious to Him. From the foundation of the world, He's longed for you to call His name and reach for His heart. He's pumped!

Like the father in the prodigal son story, your heavenly Father is thrilled just to see you at the crest of the hill walking toward Him. If you stumble a bit as you come home, it won't change the fact that He is eagerly waiting for you to arrive. Just get up and get walking again. Reject discouragement and fall into His arms.

Victory is more than stopping masturbation, after all. It's starting to experience God in those moments that would have been dedicated to sex. It's finding God and His help in the midst of every struggle and even every failure. It's not about extinguishing masturbation as much as it's about igniting a new passion for God, with sexuality integrated into your life in a balanced way.

Rather than say yes to masturbation, say yes to intimacy with God. Replace moments that left you with regret and shame with moments of fulfillment and devotion to Him. Rather than just saying no to looking at the body parts of a woman, say yes to getting to know the incredible human beings that God has hidden behind those fantastic body parts. When you say yes to this kind of life and attitude, you more than replace the momentary relief that masturbation brings.

INTEGRATING YOUR SEXUALITY

One of the most difficult assignments you'll ever have is to integrate the sexual person you are with the emotional, spiritual, social, and relational person you can and will be. *Don't view your sexuality as something shamefully separate and distinct from the rest of you.* Instead, develop every advantage possible so you can win the battle for sexual integrity. First Peter 5:8 warns us all to "be self-controlled and alert. Your enemy the devil prowls around like a roaring lion looking for someone to devour."

With no defenses and no understanding, you're an easy target for this roaring lion of a devil who wants nothing more than to ensnare you sexually and to destroy your life. But by reading this book, applying the principles, and reaching out to talk to God and others, the enemy can't win, even if you stumble from time to time. Your defenses keep him at bay.

Let these verses from Scripture encourage you:

He does not treat us as our sins deserve or repay us according to our iniquities. For as high as the heavens are above the earth, so great is his love for those who fear him.… As a father has compassion on his children, so the LORD has compassion on those who fear him; *for he knows how we are formed, he remembers that we are dust.* (Psalm 103:10-11,13-14)

That last line is the greatest source of encouragement. He knows what we're made of, and nothing surprises Him! He knew about "blue balls" long before we ever coined the phrase, and He also knew that the struggle for purity would be overbearing at times.

Don't worry if total victory doesn't come by next Tuesday. Rejoice in what you *do* have. Do you remember Dave's story? Dave couldn't escape masturbation immediately, but the random dirty thoughts and glances at close friends fell away as he practiced bouncing the eyes. His sex drive began to dry up. Do you remember what he said? "I feel so liberated!" He was rejoicing! And so was God.

So, too, should you. Move out. Grab sexual territory and integrate it. Rejoice with the Lord over victories. Proclaim His power. Where you lose, don't hang your head in shame. Rise up, pray, and hit it again. Never quit. With each victory, your spiritual, emotional, and physical sides will align further.

Eventually, total victory will be yours.

MOVING TO NONE

For me (Steve) the most difficult part of this book is providing a standard for you that doesn't inflict needless shame but instead guides you toward a life of meaningful relationships and lays a foundation for your sexuality being fully integrated into your marriage relationship.

Bouncing the eyes can be done by everyone right away. Taking thoughts captive can be learned by everyone. But stopping masturbation? That may—or may not—take a while.

Am I advocating two standards? No. The standard is no masturbation. But just because you may fail for even a long time doesn't mean it shouldn't be the standard to claim. Believe us, the standard is achievable. I say that knowing that I certainly didn't achieve it—but that's because I never even *tried* to. I didn't even know that not masturbating was a reasonable standard. But it is, and many can achieve it.

Actually, exploring the topic of masturbation has revealed some weird surprises to me. A friend of mine told me he'd never masturbated until *after* he was married. Imagine! He enjoyed twenty years of celibacy after puberty without masturbating, but then he fell into it *after* marriage. Now he's stopped the practice, and so have many other men.

If you really want to prepare your heart for your future wife, then place masturbation on the altar and sacrifice it for her. If you're not convinced it's the right thing to do, then try not masturbating for three months. See what happens during those three months. See whether your relationship with females is better and your feelings about yourself are better. We know they will be.

Truth is truth, so there aren't two standards. But there may also be more than one way to get there. Some of you may be able to get victory over masturbation right away. Some of you, however, may not get to "none" unless you first achieve the standard of less masturbation than you're practicing now. The standard of less may help you bring your habit under control until the real standard of none becomes achievable.

Wait a minute. I know you might not think this is the right approach (since we've already advocated "cold turkey"), but let me use an example of tithing to illustrate.

In my early years, I was quite financially irresponsible and deeply in debt. My father had taught me to tithe, but he hadn't taught me to manage money. So each time a paycheck came, I would write out a check for 10 percent to the church. I wouldn't drop it into the collection plate, however; otherwise, I wouldn't be able to pay my bills. I was so far underwater in debt that all I could see was darkness.

Each month I would write that check and keep it right there in the checkbook, absolutely sure that I would drop it in the collection just as soon as God provided a miracle. That never happened, so after I'd accumulated a few checks, I would tear them all up, feel horrible about what I did, then start over with the practice of going through the motions of tithing *but giving nothing* to the church.

I really believe that the standard of giving is a 10-percent tithe. Many people, however, indicate that tithing was an Old Testament standard, and we're free from it. Even if that were true, it just makes sense to me that a tenth isn't much to sacrifice if we believe God has given us everything we have. Thus I knew what the standard was, but I was in a situation that prevented me from ever achieving it.

So this is what I did. I decided that I couldn't give 10 percent, but I could give 1 percent. I began to give 1 percent to God's church, and I felt great. I was now a giver.

Some might criticize a faith that was so puny that I could only give 1 percent. Some might say that if my faith had been stronger I could have given 10 percent from the very beginning. But the reality was that I didn't have the faith or desire to turn in even one of those 10-percent checks, but I did when it came to writing out a check for 1 percent. Result? I wasn't there yet, but I was headed toward God's best. I asked God to help me find a way to double my 1 percent, and before long I was at 2 percent.

It just got better and better. Two percent became 4 percent as I continued to double my gifts to God. And it wasn't long before 4 percent became 8 percent, and later I was *exceeding* 10 percent!

Now let me clarify something. I wasn't just committed to giving 1 percent for only the first time I dropped one of those checks into the offering. No, I was committed to 1 percent *for the rest of my life*. Each new level became a lifetime commitment. I can't tell you what joy it has been to give back what has been given to me. These days, I love to give. I make money in order to give. I look forward to writing as big a check as possible whenever I can, but I don't think I would ever have gotten there if I hadn't started somewhere.

The same principle, I believe, applies to masturbation. If the idea of never masturbating again produces so much anxiety in you that you're compelled to do it just to prove that it's still an option, then don't tell yourself that you can't do it ever again. You'll be just like me, tearing up those checks.

If you're one of those who have the habit so deeply embedded into your life that you depend on it, then begin with a 1-percent standard of less. Determine that you're going to do it less. Commit to putting less material into your mind that would lead you down that road. Commit your eyes to purity so that your mind and body can achieve it. After you've done that, determine that just for today, you'll say no to masturbation. If it's too much to consider going a whole day without it, then pick half a day. Commit that you won't collect the images in your mind that fuel your sex drive and lead you to masturbate.

Then see how many of those half-days and whole days you can string together. If it's just one, then desire to go two days. Believe that it's possible. After that, try going from two to four days, and from four days to eight days, and after that, eight days to sixteen days.

Once you get some momentum going in the right direction, you'll notice how much better you feel about yourself on those victorious days. You'll notice how much more connected to God and others you're feeling. You'll also notice such a radical difference in the way you feel and look at life that you discover it's actually a better feeling than the feeling you get from masturbation. It's a feeling that's certainly going to last longer. In fact, "less" may become so seldom that you achieve what we believe is the ultimate standard of "none." And when that happens, we believe you'll like the standard and you'll like yourself and women a whole lot more.

Again, if you don't think you can go without masturbating for the rest of your life, just decide to go one day without masturbating. If that one day is all you ever experience without masturbating, then you're better off to have experienced that one day. But don't forget that God will give you the power to do what you cannot do on your own. Ephesians 5:2-3 lays out the standard God has for all of us, single or married, young or old. It's very difficult to misinterpret the message of this passage:

> Live a life of love, just as Christ loved us and gave himself up for us
> as a fragrant offering and sacrifice to God.…
>
> Among you there must not be even a hint of sexual immorality,
> or of any kind of impurity, or of greed, because these are improper
> for God's holy people.

God's way really is clear. Clean up the hints of sexual immorality. Wipe out the things that destroy sexual purity. Be satisfied with God and the sex He has planned for you in the future. Commit today to His standard, and you'll be surprised at how many of those days you can string together to create a life that honors God.

what will you gain?

Every battle in life is hard, but with victory comes the spoils. So what are the "spoils" if you construct that perimeter around your eyes? Well, you're going to feel great about yourself, about your life, and about your future.

I (Fred) remember the time Garrett's mother yanked on my sweater when I was at her church one Sunday morning. "My son just finished reading *Every Man's Battle*," she gushed. "And is he ever inspired! He's changed, too. He called from college the other night and said, 'Mom, since I've stopped doing the old "up-downs" with my eyes, my love for Tracy [his fiancée] has just flown off the scale.'"

"That's great," I said, as people streamed past us in the church foyer.

"And that's not all," she continued. "Garrett said that since he's not noticing other girls in that way anymore, he's gotten more attentive and protective of Tracy, as well. Tracy read your book and liked it too."

Whenever I hear stories like that, I like to get it straight from the horse's mouth. So a few months later, I invited Garrett over to my house to chat...

STORY OF A "WAKE-UP CALL"

Garrett began his story by noting that he was raised in the church, but by the time he was a senior in high school, he was drinking heavily, keeping a case of Bud longnecks iced up in a cooler that he kept in his trunk. He and his buddies drank a beer before school, then downed one at lunch, and kept right on going after school. According to Garrett, "We mostly did it just to see how long we could go before we got caught."

He was also smoking heavily and getting high, but the highs he liked the most came from the porn magazines and videos that he stashed away in his bedroom and car. Eventually, he wanted to see the real thing in action, so midway through his senior year, he began dropping by Big Earl's Gold Mine, a strip joint on the northeast side of Des Moines.

One night Garrett was hopping around from friend's place to friend's place, partying pretty heavily. While on the interstate to the next spot, he noticed a mass of lights and sirens in the distance. He exited the freeway to check things out, only to find Big Earl's club engulfed in flames. Garrett stared at the scene, mesmerized while remembering his nights in the Gold Mine. Then a disturbing thought pierced him between the eyes: "That's my sin going up in flames. And that's where this life of mine is leading—right into flames!"

Garrett didn't heed this first wake-up call, but then came his arrest for shoplifting. What did he steal? Robitussin—an over-the-counter cough medicine. "You probably don't know it, Fred, but there's a chemical in one type of Robitussin that gets you high if you drink enough of it."

"But why'd you steal it? It couldn't cost that much," I replied.

He grinned wryly. "Think about it," he said. "Why would an eighteen-year-old in perfect health walk into a pharmacy to buy four bottles of Robitussin in the middle of summer? We figured that would make any clerk suspicious, and we were afraid we'd get caught. So we stole it but got caught anyway."

He was released right away that evening, but he'd heard that second wake-up call. Things weren't going well.

Amazingly, the next morning he was scheduled to sing in a youth choir. With his eyes still bugged out a bit from the effects of the Robitussin he'd finished off before the shoplifting attempt, he sang and sang. When the final chords and notes drifted into silence, he found himself overcome by emotion. He knelt right there and returned his full heart to Christ. "I dropped the sin and turned to Christ that day, including walking away from pornography. But the temptation was still there, and I felt I needed protection. I decided I'd better head for a Christian college because I knew that would keep me out of trouble."

A decent athlete, Garrett turned to intramural sports, making friends and adjusting to college life fairly well. Soon, he was growing deeply in the Lord.

Early in his sophomore year he met Tracy. "Tracy and I started getting pretty close, and I got to thinking that this could end up in marriage. Simultaneously, I also started thinking that I really might be able to do a little better than her physically. She was cute enough, but certainly no knockout. I'd always dreamed I'd marry a real babe."

I motioned for him to continue his story.

"Well, I was just a few days away from breaking up with her when my mom called me about *Every Man's Battle*. Wow! I'd stopped the pornography the day I sang in church…but not the rest of it. My eyes roamed over every girl I saw. Looking back, that's probably why Tracy didn't look so good to me.

"Honestly, I'd never really guarded my eyes before or even thought about it. I watched any movies I wanted, and I looked way too long at the girls at school, but I really didn't think these things affected my life. But after my mom read your book and told me about it, I began to wonder. So I paid more attention to my eyes over the next day or so, and I found that they were collecting more sexual gratification than I'd thought.

"I read *Every Man's Battle* and started bouncing my eyes. You can probably guess what happened. Tracy started looking incredible to me. I even started getting offended when other guys looked at her, like a big brother protecting his little sister. I know this sounds trite, but when I stopped lusting over Tracy, I really did start seeing more of what was inside her heart instead of what was outside her, and I really liked what I saw. I never thought about breaking up with her again."

Garrett didn't say it, but he was getting exactly what we can expect when we follow God.

A RELATIONSHIP CHANGES

Earlier in the book we discussed how women become sex objects when we view porn or lust over them in our minds. It even happens with girlfriends. Clearly, Garrett had seen Tracy as an object, and he was ready to exchange her for a prettier one.

One of the spoils of this victory was how God reversed the way Garrett had objectified women. When He did, Garrett's relationship with Tracy changed. But there's more.

"When Tracy read *Every Man's Battle,* she was blown away," said Garrett. "She had no idea how men's eyes work, and she was surprised to learn what Christian girls like her were doing to their Christian brothers with the clothes they wear.

"She has become the best help to me. When we're watching TV together and something bad comes on, she covers my eyes and we both giggle together. She's also real careful not to bend over in front of me, and things like that. She's just so sweet, and we're so close now. You can see that our spiritual walk has real teamwork now. I'm beginning to understand for the first time what the Bible means when it says two people become one flesh in marriage. She even calls out her friends when they're wearing skimpy things around. She's quite the little evangelist on that score!"

Even though I've lived through this kind of restoration myself, I was enthralled by Garrett's story. I had to know more, so I asked, "What about God? What happened there?"

"You wouldn't believe it!" he exclaimed. "I'd been in ministerial studies for a year and a half already, so you have to know that I was reading my Bible plenty. I was praying a lot too.

"But when I started bouncing my eyes, and the lust rolled away, it was as if the Bible opened up like a blue sky before me after a really dark night. Bouncing my eyes really helped me read my Bible better.

"And I've noticed an interesting thing: When I read my Bible less and don't stay close to the Word, it's harder to bounce my eyes. They really go hand in hand, and one can't be done very well without the other.

"As for my prayer times—my, oh my. I used to get lustful thoughts popping up all the time during prayer. But now that my eyes are protected, it doesn't happen, so prayer has become so much deeper and uninterrupted. Worshiping God is better as well. Now I feel free to express my heart to God. Before, I didn't have the freedom to express my love to God, probably because I was too involved in impure thoughts and stuff."

NEW LIGHT AND LIGHTNESS

When I (Fred) made that covenant with my eyes, before long I felt a new light and lightness in my soul. My sexual sin had brought a darkness so deep and smothering that when it vanished, the difference was so real I could practically touch it. I felt loved and approved by God.

And that can happen to you as well. Tyler, a college freshman, said,

I don't like masturbation. Every time I did it, I felt guilty about it. Yet I kept on doing it because it felt good. I had the problem for about two years, until I finally put my foot down and said I wouldn't do it anymore. For about five years or so, I haven't. I am so thankful God has delivered me from this. I love God with all my heart, and I do my best to show it at all times, even in this way. I've found there's nothing better than the love God gives us. It fulfills all my needs.

Some say God's standards aren't fair, but I think His standards are plenty fair. You are allowed to have godly relationships with girls, and then at some point in your life you can get married. What's unfair about that? Besides, it shouldn't really matter whether it's fair or not, because these are God's standards we're talking about here. God is awesome!

Well said, Tyler. Rock on, warrior!

your mustang mind

As you may recall, we not only have to guard our eyes, but we also need a defense perimeter in our mind. You'll find that the perimeter of the eyes goes up much faster than the perimeter of the mind. Why?

First, your mind is far more crafty than your eyes and more difficult to corral. Second, you really can't rein in the mind effectively until the defense perimeter of the eyes is in place. Knowing this, you shouldn't be discouraged if your mind responds more slowly than your eyes.

The great news is that the defense perimeter of the eyes works with you to build the perimeter of the mind. The mind needs an object for its lust, so when the eyes view sexual images the mind has plenty to dance with. Without those images, the mind has an empty dance card. By starving the eyes, you starve the mind as well.

Although this alone isn't enough—the mind can still create its own lust objects using memories of videos or by generating fantasies about girl-friends or busty schoolmates—at least with your eyes under control you won't be overwhelmed by a continuing flood of fresh lust objects as you struggle to learn to control your mind.

YOUR MIND COMING CLEAN

Currently, your brain moves nimbly to lust and to the little pleasure-high it brings. Your brain's "worldview" has always included lustful thinking.

Double entendres, daydreams, and other creative forms of sexual thinking are approved pathways, so your mind feels free to run on these paths to pleasure.

But your mind is orderly, and your worldview colors what comes through it. The mind will allow these impure thoughts only if they "fit" the way you look at the world. As you set up the perimeter of defense for your mind, your brain's worldview will be transformed by a new matrix of allowed thoughts, or what we call "allowables."

Within the old matrix of your thinking, lust fits perfectly and in that sense was "orderly." But with a new, purer matrix firmly in place, lustful thoughts will bring disorder. Your brain, acting as a responsible policeman, will nab these lustful thoughts even before they rise to consciousness. Essentially the brain begins cleaning itself like a hard drive, so elusive enemies like double entendres and daydreams, which are hard to control on the conscious level, simply vanish on their own.

This transformation of the mind takes some time as you wait for the old sexual pollution to be washed away. It's much like living near a creek that becomes polluted when a sewer main breaks upstream. After repair crews replace the cracked sewage pipe, it will still take some time for the water downstream to clear.

In transforming your mind, you'll be taking an active, conscious role in capturing rogue thoughts, but in the long run, the mind will wash itself and will begin to work naturally for you and your purity by capturing such thoughts. With the eyes bouncing away from sexual images, and the mind policing itself, your defenses will grow incredibly strong.

LURKING AT THE DOOR

With that confidence, you'll want to be doing all you can to push along your mental transformation. A helpful concept here is the scriptural imagery of "lurking at the door." Job mentioned it. Just a few verses after we read about the covenant he made with his eyes, we hear Job saying this:

> If my heart has been enticed by a woman, or if I have lurked at my
> neighbor's door, then may my wife grind another man's grain, and
> may other men sleep with her. For that would have been shameful,
> a sin to be judged. (Job 31:9-11)

Have you "lurked at your neighbor's door"? Of course, this verse is clearly talking about Job's own life as a married man, but this can easily refer to you as a young, single male. Lurking could mean stealing glances at her rack and rear. Lurking could mean roaming in areas you shouldn't be accessing on the World Wide Web.

When I (Fred) was a freshman in high school, a certain girl sat near me in French class. She had long, straight, dishwater blonde hair, wore a jean jacket every day, and had a cute little face that never smiled. She had a rebellious air, which made her a bit scary to me—and attractive. I stole glances at her a lot, but mostly at her upper thighs where her tight jeans came together. I had weeks of intense, wild wet dreams in the aftermath. I was lurking big-time.

WILD THINKING

What am I supposed to do? you ask. *Those thoughts come on their own. I can't help them.* That certainly seems true, since controlling the mind can seem bizarre. As we've seen, sexy daydreams can happen in church. Where do these thoughts come from? The mind is like a wild mustang, running free, one thought triggering another in no real order. Still, the Bible says we must control not just our eyes, but our whole bodies:

You are not your own; you were bought at a price. Therefore honor
God with your body. (1 Corinthians 6:19-20)

And not just our bodies, but our minds as well. The Holy Spirit,
through Paul, is clear on this:

We demolish arguments and every pretension that sets itself up
against the knowledge of God, and we take captive every thought to
make it obedient to Christ. (2 Corinthians 10:5)

This is a jarring verse. Reading it, it's easy to wonder, "Take every
thought captive? Is that really possible?"

YOUR MENTAL CUSTOMS STATION

All impure thoughts generate from processing both visual and live attractions through your senses. Gazing at girls on the beach. Flirting with the
new girl in math class. Remembering an old girlfriend and those hot Saturday nights. During improper processing, our minds can get carried away
in impurity, and our engines can really get charging. However, by properly
processing these attractions, we can capture or eliminate impure thoughts.

We've already discussed one form of proper processing called bouncing
the eyes. It processes visual attractions by training the eyes to bounce
and then starving them. When it's effectively established, your defense
perimeter of the eyes has the nature of the old Berlin Wall. No visual entry
visas are ever granted, for any reason.

But the defense perimeter of the mind is less like a wall and more like a
customs area in an international airport. Customs departments are filters,
preventing dangerous elements from entering a country. The U.S. Customs
Service attempts to filter out drugs, Mediterranean fruit flies, terrorists, and

other harmful agents. Similarly, the defense perimeter of the mind properly processes attractive babes into your "country," allowing them in but filtering out the alien, impure thoughts that you're tempted with as they enter. This perimeter stops the lurking.

LOST IN THE ATTRACTIONS

What happens at our mental customs station? Say you're starting a new school year, with a brand-new slate of classes and classmates. On the first day, Rachel walks around the corner, starts talking, and…*wham!* You're attracted. From this point, she can either be processed properly in your mind without generating impure thoughts, or you can mishandle the situation.

What happens next is critical to the purity of your mind. Let's say that you continue interacting with Rachel over time. The early interactions feed the attractions, and at first you get lost in them. For instance, Rachel might return your attraction signals. Or her sense of humor may match yours. Maybe she loves your favorite pizza, or she's simply mad about football. Rachel is refreshing and fascinating, so you love to think about her. At this point, improper processing carries you away into sensual thoughts or other impure practices, like sensual flirting, suggestive teasing, or even masturbation back home.

LEARNING THE RIGHT MENTAL PROCESSING

There's nothing wrong with our attractions. Many of us have been lost in our attractions. You may be lost in one right now. I (Fred) got lost in high school with Julie.

I noticed her early in my senior year, when Julie was a junior. You talk about hitting attraction buttons! I was carried away into a land of silly dreaminess whenever I thought about her. I thought about what I would say and how we would love each other and where we would go, my mind filling in billions of blanks since I knew nothing about Julie except her name and her grade level.

All year long I dreamily longed for her, watching her bounce merrily by, hoping for the day we could speak. I yearned to ask her for a date, but I lacked the courage. Even though I was the superstud athlete of the year, my heart turned to raspberry Jell-O when it came to girls.

As the year wound down, one chance remained: the senior prom. Struggling fiercely, I dialed her phone number. After some meaningless small talk, I stammered out my request. She actually said yes! Her melodious voice affirmed my existence, and you can imagine what my mind did with that.

After the prom dance, I found the perfect place to take her—the Ironmen Inn. While the traditional site for after-prom dinners was the Highlander, I decided that I couldn't give my newfound love something so trite and dreary. In the secluded, curtained booths at the Ironmen, we could sit transfixed and not be interrupted on that glorious first night of the rest of our lives together. After being escorted to our booth, we bantered lightly, my heart pounding deeply within me. My attraction grew with each passing moment.

Quietly secluded at the Ironmen, we had the hostess romantically draw the curtains. Julie's ravishing face glowed, and her lovely, full lips parted to speak. Enchanted, I listened dreamily, only to hear her say, "You know, I don't know how to say this, but I really, really wanted to go to the Highlander. Do you mind if we go over there?"

Clunk.

Although my attraction for her shuddered wildly, chivalry and honor carried the day. Mustering an air of nonchalance, I responded, "Sure, I guess so," though I knew this wasn't good for our date.

At the Highlander, as we stood waiting to be seated, Julie brazenly asked, "Do you mind if I go over to Ritchie's table for a while?"

I didn't know what to say, so I said nothing. She left me and spent the rest of the night with him.

I ate alone with my thoughts, musing, *This is why I like football better than girls.*

Later she graciously threw me a bone, allowing me the honor of driving her highness home. She confided that she'd hoped all along to find a way to be with Ritchie that night since he hadn't asked her to the prom as she'd expected.

My attraction to Julie died that night. Now there was nothing wrong with that attraction. True, I wasted a big part of my senior year being an idiot. But I never lusted over her, and I certainly never masturbated over her.

But when we lurk and go beyond that, we sin. Sean told me, "Erica just blows me away. She sits right in front of me in science class, and I can't keep my eyes off her. She's so full-bodied, and the guys in the locker room have told me she's kind of loose about what she'll do with you. I know she'd never pay any attention to me, but I found this picture of her in her tight volleyball shorts in the yearbook, and I've masturbated over that picture a million times."

Sean has rocketed well past attraction, splashing down squarely in a big, scummy pond of lust.

A CORRAL FOR YOUR MUSTANG MIND

We said earlier that our minds are like wild mustangs running free. Mustangs have two characteristics that resemble male brains. First, the mustang runs where he wills. Second, the mustang mates where he wants to and with whom he chooses. There are mares everywhere! And if a mustang doesn't happen to see one nearby, he'll sniff the wind and, sensing a mare over the horizon, run over there and mate.

This trait is similar to the wild donkey that God talked about through the prophet Jeremiah:

A wild donkey accustomed to the desert, sniffing the wind in her crav-
ing—in her heat who can restrain her? Any males that pursue her need
not tire themselves; at mating time they will find her. (Jeremiah 2:24)

Can you control the mustang? Can you run him down on foot or
simply wag your finger and admonish him? No, of course not. Then how
do you keep him from running and mating where he wills?

With a corral.

Currently, your mind runs like a mustang. What's more, your mind
"mates" where it wills with attractive, sensual girls. They're everywhere. With
a mustang mind, how do you stop the running and the mating? With a
corral around your mind.

Let's expand a bit on this metaphor to help you better understand our
goal of reining in our roving minds.

Once, you were a proud mustang, wild and free. Sleek and rippling,
you ranged the hills and valleys, running and mating where you willed,
master of your destiny. God, owner of a large local ranch, noticed you from
a distance as He worked His herd. Though you took no notice of Him, He
loved you and desired to make you His own. He sought you in many ways,
but you ran from Him again and again.

One day He found you trapped in a deep, dark canyon, with no way
out. With the lariat of salvation, He gently drew you near, and you became
one of His own. He desired to break you, that you might be useful to Him
and bring Him further joy. But knowing your natural ways and how you
loved to run free with the mares, He set a fence around you. This corral was
the perimeter of the eyes. It stopped the running and kept you from sniffing the winds and running wildly over the horizon.

While the corral stopped the running, it hasn't yet stopped the mating.
You mate in your mind, through attractions, thoughts, and fantasy, flirting and neighing lustily at the mares inside or near your corral. You must be
broken.

CLOSER AND CLOSER

There are many girls who aren't attractive to you and don't generate impure thoughts. They can include your friends, stepsisters, classmates, and church gal pals. Your friend Joe may notice someone and say, "Wow, look at her! She's hot!" You respond in mild surprise, saying, "I guess so. I've known her so long I don't even think of her in those terms. She's just a friend."

But there are young women you know who hit every attraction key on your keyboard—like Rachel, that new student, or maybe the new girl in the worship band who makes you breathless every time she gets up and sings. You neigh, drawing them toward your corral, but only in your mind. Among those may be an old girlfriend to whom you're still deeply attached because of your past sexual sins. You mate easily with her in your mind because of your many trysts together. Mentally, she's still right next to you. Because of your former intimacy, she may seem yours for the taking in your mind. You remember the thrills, so you feel free to play with your thoughts.

But you must lead her out of your corral and stop lurking. The perimeter of the mind processes the live attractions that canter up over the horizon and pass our corrals. By starving the attractions, these young women retreat to safety zones of "friendship" or "acquaintance," where they no longer threaten your purity.

Most girls won't hit all your attraction buttons, of course. But sometimes it seems you can find something attractive in nearly every girl that walks by. Tight jeans and Wonderbras. Sweet-smelling hair. Happy, lilting giggles and voices. You want to open the gate to every one of them.

Don't you owe it to the Lord to put up a mental defense perimeter? If not, you'll have a sad story to tell, like the one we heard from Jake. He was the student leader of a youth group, along with four others, including Gina. He was standing strong and respected throughout the church. He had no mental defense perimeter, however, because he blissfully thought he didn't need one. As a result he allowed Gina to come too close to his corral:

Gina and I led the youth group together, and we were both involved in the Wednesday night meetings. Because of our leadership positions, we were involved in many activities together. We also had some pretty intimate prayer times, just the two of us. I found I spent a lot of time thinking about her, fantasizing and wondering what she'd think if I grabbed her and kissed her. I figured those thoughts were harmless. She was pure and from a strict family. I didn't think she'd see anything in me anyway.

But I thought about it all the time, how I would reach out, how I would take her in my arms. It was almost as if we'd done it many times already. One night we were the last two to leave after cleaning up on a Wednesday night, and we were standing in the parking lot. That's when my mental games became a reality. Before I knew it, we were in the back of my mom's van, naked and scared, wondering what we'd just done.

Since then, we've been having intercourse constantly for about six months, leading worship and prayer times like always, but living in such hypocrisy. I can't imagine we have any real leadership or power in the Spirit realm. I feel like a fool and a failure, but how can I stop? We can't figure out how.

You need a defense, my friend. You need to stop the lurking. For example, there are the mares who immediately fire up your hormones at first sight. And there are the ones who immediately like what *they* see when they glance your way too.

WOMEN YOU FIND ATTRACTIVE

If you find someone attractive in an obsessive, sexual way, your first line of defense is a proper mind-set, which is this: *This attraction threatens my intimacy with Christ.* It may not appear threatening early in the attraction, when everything seems innocent. You're just having fun, exploring things in your mind, and goofing around. But remember, the mind is strong, and like it did with Jake and Gina, an attraction can grow quickly out of control and destroy your spiritual relationships.

Your second line of defense is to declare, *I have no right to think these sexual things.* State this to yourself clearly, decisively, and often. You don't even know this girl! Who are you to essentially rape her in your mind?

The third line of defense is to *heighten your alert.* Consider the *Star Trek* television series. What did Captain Picard do when danger approached? He cried out, "Red alert! Shields up!" In a similar vein, when an attractive woman approaches your corral, your defense perimeter must immediately respond: Red alert! Shields up!

Bounce your eyes. You saw her passing your corral, and you were physically attracted to her. Starve this lustful part of the attraction by bouncing your eyes. Don't dwell on her beauty by stealing glances or by lying in bed fantasizing. You have no right to that. That clearly is sexual sin, and it represents more than a hint of sexual immorality in your life.

To summarize: If you're attracted to a young woman, it doesn't mean you can't have any sort of relationship or friendship with her. It only means you must enact your defense perimeters against lust and lurking. Once you've starved your mind of that, you can have a proper relationship, one that's honoring to her and to the Lord.

WOMEN WHO FIND YOU ATTRACTIVE

No matter what our age, we're still capable of saying preposterous things like, "Finally, here's a young woman who clearly has good taste and knows 'handsome' when she sees it. I simply must get to know her better."

Brian is a sophomore wrestler in college. He's also a virgin. Do you know what he told me? "I was pretty popular in school because I was a state qualifier, among other things. I don't know how, but everyone seemed to know I was a virgin. I still can't believe it, but I had six different girls come up to me in my senior year and ask whether they could be 'my first one.' "

While most of us will never experience anything close to that, even one girl that pushes our boundaries hard can threaten our intimacy with Christ. If she's a non-Christian, she's even more dangerous since she has no moral reason not to go to bed with you. With such girls, it's best stopping her by returning no attraction signals.

Don't dawdle about getting your shields up. In one movie from the *Star Trek* series, the enemy had captured a Federation starship and was approaching Captain Kirk and the starship *Enterprise* (the good guys). The enemy commander didn't respond to any calls from Captain Kirk. As the Captain hailed him repeatedly, the enemy commander simply sneered, "Let them eat static."

Captain Kirk found this lack of response peculiar. Confused and unsure of the intentions of the approaching ship, he dawdled. He didn't put up his shields. Finally, when close enough, the enemy blasted away, severely disabling the *Enterprise*. Kirk paid a dear price for dawdling, losing his best friend to death in the ensuing interchanges.

Get your shields up and ask questions later. Implement at least one of these strategies—

• *Flee from her*. First, prepare with a few "war game" simulations. What will you say if she drops by your house after school, when she knows your mom isn't home? What will you do if she starts unbuttoning her blouse? Josh McDowell tells teens to decide what they'll do in the backseat of the car *before* they ever get to the backseat of the car. Otherwise passion rules, and reasoning isn't clear. Second, send absolutely no return attraction signals. Don't answer the call. Let them eat static!

- *When you're in her company, play the dweeb.* You can be just like Dweebman, who steps into a nearby public restroom and emerges as the polyester-clad enemy of all things flirtatious and hip. Dull, mild-mannered, and nerdy Dweebman—pocket protector shielding his heart, with hair slightly askew—wages his quiet, thankless war of boring interchange. Our once-threatening Amazon withdraws to undefended sectors, leaving Dweebman victorious again in his never-ending good fight to stave off the hip and the impure in his galactic empire!

Okay, there's not much glory in playing the dweeb. There are no comic book deals, no endorsement contracts, and no *20/20* interviews with Barbara Walters.

But you'll be a hero to our Lord.

A dweeb is the opposite of a player. In relationships, players send and receive social signals smoothly. Dweebs do not. When a player wants to send attraction signals, there are certain things he'll do. He'll flirt. He'll banter. He'll smile with a knowing look. He'll talk about hip things. In short, he'll be cool. Sometimes it seems that four years of high school is spent learning how to be a player to some degree or another, so in seeking sexual purity, a little social suicide is often very much in order.

Always play the dweeb if a girl is pushing too hard. If a girl smiles at you with a knowing look, learn to smile with a slightly confused look. If she talks about hip things, talk about things that are unhip to her, like your car engine or your grades. She'll find you pleasant enough but rather bland and uninteresting. *Perfect.*

sexual honor

love for her father

As a father, I (Fred) carry my daughter's baton. I remember when Laura was born and the times I cradled her when her fever was so high her eyes rolled up into her head. I remember the time she broke her finger in the car door, and I held her close. I remember the time she won a part in the school play, and I practiced her lines with her again and again. I remember reviewing math flashcards before her big tests.

When the volleyball was spiked at her feet three times in a row at the family reunion, I held Laura close so she could hide her tears in my chest as she sobbed, "They all think I'm no good." I stayed close to her for the rest of the day, defending her honor and brazenly daring another spike against my "Peanut."

I talked with her about junior high and how she was on the cusp of adolescence, and now that she's in high school, we've talked about dating and college and growing up. I've felt deep pride when she began leading Bible studies before school during the last two years, and I've felt indignant rage and sorrow when some of her "Christian sisters" from that same study told her, "Your high standards are what give Christians a bad name."

Raising Laura in purity and holiness has been one of my highest callings in life. We've walked and talked, laughed and cried. I know her through and through. But what about you, young man? Who are you? What are you like? How long have you prayed for her? All I know is that I carry the torch for my daughter, and no hip haircut, fast car, or sweet smile will trick it out of my hand. My investment is too great.

CAN YOU HONOR ME?

I know you're my Christian brother, and I want to count on you to stand shoulder to shoulder with me in this call I have from God. Yes, I'm in my early forties and you may be in your teens or early twenties, but I'm as much your brother as your buddies are, and I'm counting on you not to lay your hands on my daughter just as much as your best friend is counting on you not to lay your hands on his girlfriend. Honor me in this.

Every father you'll ever meet has been seventeen before, but not one of you has been forty-four years old with a teenage daughter. So guess what? First, you can't understand how I'm feeling and won't naturally treat my concerns with enough care. Second, and maybe far worse for the both of us, I know what *you're* thinking.

My young friend Tyson, from my youth group, tells it exactly like it is. He recently declared to me, "It's no secret. Most guys just want to have sex or get some kind of action. They don't care about the relationship part of things, like the girls do. Guys like to see girls with little or nothing on, that's the bottom line. Even us Christian guys."

Even us Christians. Hmm. No surprise there. As a guy coming out of the world later in life, I may have a different perspective on the term "Christian" than you do, and it doesn't matter if you're Catholic or Protestant, evangelical or charismatic. If you were to ask me what surprises me most about Christianity, it would be that so few Christians live any differently than anyone else.

So that leaves us in an interesting position, doesn't it? I know that many Christians don't walk the talk and their word isn't worth the air they breath in order to say it. And yet one of the biggest calls God has placed on *my* life is depending upon *your* character if you're alone with my Laura. That should make me uneasy, and it does.

After all, I don't know you, but I have to put my trust entirely in you, my Christian brother, to stand with me in my call during those moments when she's with you. Don't you owe me some faithfulness and honor? Don't you owe me a few good defenses against your own passions?

This may sound funny to you, as it would have to me at your age, but do you want to know the truth? Until you've proven to me that you have honor, I don't even think you have the right to *talk* to my daughter, let alone hold her hand in the park. You may think you're already an honorable guy. Maybe you are, but let's see how you stack up against one of the most honorable men in the Bible.

CHECK OUT THIS GREAT EXAMPLE

In 1 Chronicles 11, we learn that a man named Uriah is listed as one of David's "mighty men"—the men who "gave his kingship strong support to extend it over the whole land, as the LORD had promised" (11:10).

Uriah was clearly consumed with the purposes of his king, David. He was also consumed with the purposes of God. Uriah was by David's side in the caves when Saul hounded their heels. He cried with David as their homes burned at Ziklag. He cheered himself hoarse at David's coronation, and he fearlessly fought to extend David's kingdom over the whole land. Swearing his life to the purposes of God, Uriah stood in harm's way on behalf of David's throne.

Uriah's faithfulness was complete, but alas, David's faithfulness wasn't. He went to bed with Bathsheba, Uriah's wife. When she became pregnant, David had a mess on his hands. As always, Uriah was out fighting David's battles. Bathsheba's pregnancy could mean only one thing: David—not Uriah—was the father.

David addressed the situation by fabricating a ruse. He ordered Uriah back from the front lines. David's plan was to send Uriah quickly home for a warm, cuddly night with Bathsheba. She would be particularly amorous that night. If Uriah did his part, people would naturally assume the unborn child was his.

Tragically, Uriah's faithfulness to the king was so complete that David's plan didn't work:

> David said to Uriah, "Go down to your house and wash your feet."
> So Uriah left the palace, and a gift from the king was sent after him.
> But Uriah slept at the entrance to the palace with all his master's
> servants and did not go down to his house.
>
> When David was told, "Uriah did not go home," he asked him,
> "Haven't you just come from a distance? Why didn't you go home?"
>
> Uriah said to David, "The ark and Israel and Judah are staying in
> tents, and my master Joab and my lord's men are camped in the open
> fields. How could I go to my house to eat and drink and lie with my
> wife? As surely as you live, I will not do such a thing!"
>
> Then David said to him, "Stay here one more day, and tomor-
> row I will send you back." So Uriah remained in Jerusalem that day
> and the next. At David's invitation, he ate and drank with him,
> and David made him drunk. But in the evening Uriah went out
> to sleep on his mat among his master's servants; he did not go
> home. (2 Samuel 11:8-13)

Look at Uriah! He was so consumed by the purposes of God that he refused to go to his house even to wash his feet. His faithfulness and honor were so strong that, even when drunk, he didn't waver and wander on home for a little sack time with his own wife!

Do you honor God's purposes like that? I wonder if you could stay out of bed if given such an open invitation to jump in. I know that God's purposes regarding my daughter, Laura, are that she be raised in purity and holiness. God's purposes and mine, therefore, are the same. You must defend my purposes for Laura like I do, with the faithfulness of Uriah, without wavering...even if drunk, heaven forbid. Could you stack up against Uriah, one of David's "mighty men"?

Or are you a sissy like Zedekiah, whom we read about earlier? In that story, God, through Jeremiah, asked the king to surrender, to do something very difficult, something that made no sense. Zedekiah failed to obey. The right thing to do was too illogical, too costly. The results for him, his family, and his nation were tragic.

You've been asked to do something that makes no sense and is costly. You, a sexual being, are being asked to live purely with pretty girls all around you. As for my Laura, if you failed to obey like Zedekiah, the results to my daughter and my family would be tragic.

That's why I need you to act with honor. You need real defenses, not stupid ones. My roommate in college told me that in order to avoid sex with his dream girl back home, he would masturbate before picking her up on dates. That's neither pure nor honorable.

DEFENSES ARE THE KEY

Danny is the kind of guy who loves and honors a father. "My first defense was to date only Christians," he said. "But the biggest problem with most guys is they stop at this one defense. What a mistake, since we can all make mistakes, given the right situation. So I set up some rules to keep me out of such situations as best I could.

"In practice, this meant that I was not to be alone with the person I was dating. Obviously, I didn't take this to the extreme. I *could* ride in a car with her, for instance. On the other hand, if we were sitting in the car talking, it had to be in a place like her parents' driveway—not some lover's lane. I also made it a rule that I couldn't be alone in a house with the girl I was dating.

"I kept these standards when I moved away from my parents because I felt it was wise and very honorable to God. Of course, it was much easier when I was living at home. I could say, 'I can't do it because my parents won't let me.' Now I had to keep those same standards as my own. But what a great standard! I've just gotten married, and you better believe that I'm so glad that I stood strong, especially when Lisa and I were engaged. I can think of several occasions when, without this standard living strong in our lives, it would have been easy to lose the purity in our relationship.

"Before we got married, Lisa and I allowed ourselves to sit in the car and talk many times in my parents' driveway. (While I no longer lived there, we often visited.) The neighbors would always peek out their kitchen curtains at us. We always waved at them, but we never got a wave in return! God bless those neighbors...they were definitely a part of our accountability, whether we liked it or not. I'm sure my mom was doing the same thing, but at least she was never obvious about it!

"Another defense was to tell everyone I knew about my standards. After that, the standards were never hard to follow because most people knew what they were. If I messed up, every guy in town seemed to know about it, and they would bash me for it. When God places a conviction on your heart, that standard becomes just as important as the ones He wrote out clearly in the Bible. This is what can set apart the 'average' Christian dating couple from the ones who want God's perfect will.

"I remember the time shortly after I met Lisa. I was driving her home after doing some group dating things. We were trying to think of something we could do because it was still pretty early. Lisa turned to me and said, 'Do you want to come back to my place? We could make some dessert and play some board games.' You have to know that Lisa was living on her own at the time, and I could feel the lump in my throat and the knot in my stomach in a split second. Thoughts flooded my mind and heart... Lisa did have a roommate, but I wasn't sure she'd be there or how long she might stay. I knew we weren't yet 'technically dating,' but I was sure starting to like this girl.

"How do I explain to this nice girl that I couldn't go back to her house to simply play games? Should I say that I needed to go home because I was tired? But if I did, she'd know that I was avoiding telling her something because it was still early. I decided to face it head on, knowing full well that she could laugh and tell me how silly I was. I urgently thought, *Lord, help me!* It felt like an eternity before I could get any words out. I nervously said, 'You might think this sounds a little funny, but I have a rule for myself that I don't spend time alone with a girl in her home. I just don't put myself in those situations.' The moment those words left my mouth, I felt a huge weight lifted off my chest. I was so proud, yet at the same time, I was scared to hear Lisa's response. To my shock, she quickly said, 'Don't worry about it. We'll find something else to do.'

"I seriously can't remember what she suggested we could do that evening, but at that moment, I felt like the Lord rewarded me for taking a stand for Him. Even though I didn't know at that time that Lisa would be my future wife, the Lord knew."

Danny and Uriah are cut from the same cloth. Young men like Danny have real honor, courage, and love.

GO AHEAD, ASK FOR HER HAND

Honoring the father means that you ask his permission when it comes time to marry. When I asked my father-in-law for Brenda's hand in marriage, he was on his deathbed. Although he strengthened from time to time, we both knew his time on earth was nearly over. I entered his hospital room, much stronger than he but far more frightened. I knew how much he loved his daughter. I knew how he once held her and let her cry when she came home with a squirrel-cut instead of a haircut. I knew how he proudly gave her a used, red Chevy Nova as a gift. I knew how he used to swim way out into the ocean and let her sit on him like a raft, floating merrily. I knew how he had diligently raised her in purity, keeping her in church and away from ribald influences on her life.

When I asked for her hand, he said something to me that has remained engraved indelibly in my memory over the years. "Though I don't know you well," he began, "I know you're the kind of man who will do what you say. I know you'll take care of her." Never in my life had a man believed in me so, trusting my manhood and entrusting me with something so valuable. He gave his cherished only daughter to me, even while knowing he could never step back in to defend her if I didn't keep my word, that he would never be there to remind me of my promises, that he would never be there to put that sparkle back in her eye if I ever made it disappear.

I owed him because he trusted me, both while Brenda and I were dating and right now, as he lies in his grave. I owed him because he provided such a wonderful daughter to me. I owed him because of his great investment in her. When I see him again in heaven, I won't have to avert my eyes sheepishly in shame. He gave me the baton, and I ran well with it.

That's love and honor. That's authenticity.

what do girls think?

We thought it would be interesting for you to hear from your counterparts—young women. What do they think about all this? What type of pressures are they feeling? What are they looking for in a guy?

Before we go much deeper, you should know that many young women today are growing up without a male presence in the home. An estimated 30 percent of girls and young women don't know what it's like to have a full-time dad, to feel the warmth of his embrace and to watch how he treats her mother. You can blame the high divorce rate and the quarter-century rise in single parenting for this development.

Furthermore, there's the sad phenomenon of abuse, including inappropriate sexual behavior. Countless girls are fondled and raped by cousins, uncles, and their mother's boyfriends—as many as one out of three, if we're to believe the statistics. Our culture has left many young women so hurting, lonely, and insecure that they're willing to trade their bodies just for a chance to hold someone close and look deeply into another person's eyes. Now, keeping all of this in mind, what did the girls have to say?

LET'S JUST ASK 'EM!

I interviewed three young women for this chapter: Amber, Brynna, and Cassie. Amber started the conversation by saying, "I know that most of us girls fall short of God's standards in the way we conduct ourselves. We need to feel accepted, and when we don't understand the value we have from being a daughter of the King or even our own fathers, we search hard for acceptance. Sometimes it seems like a fair trade to lower our standards to meet those needs within us."

Guys, they said, have a way of finding emotionally needy young women. Amber said, "Many girls are insecure, so they let the guys do what they want, even if it disagrees with them, just so they can have that relationship with him. If she stops his advances, she fears he'll break up with her, and then she'll no longer have that identity with him. I see that happen to my friends all the time."

But remember, guys—we're called to be like Christ. That means treating her like *we* would like to be treated. This means that we aren't to bruise the broken reed. This means leaving the girls you date better for having known you. I (Fred) can't think of a single girl I dated that I left better than when I met her, which is a pretty sad indictment of where my head was at. And what about Steve? Do you think the abortion left his girlfriend better off? Of course not.

And yet, being better off for having known you is exactly what women want. If you provide it, you'll be their hero. I once heard a teenage girl say wistfully, "You know, I really missed the boat when I let Bill slip away. He was truly kind, and he never hurt me once."

"Girls desire to be loved and cherished for the person they are," Brynna commented. "We like to be told we're beautiful with no hidden agendas."

Added Amber: "Guys, you need to let them know you care more about their heart than the way they dress."

Cassie simply stated, "Please be a leader."

Yet too often the only leadership we take is to charge across her sexual boundaries. "Girls want guys to take the lead in the relationship," said Cassie. "Yet often it's the guys who are pushing the boundaries. When that has happened to me, I felt very resentful. I know that it makes girls just feel used. We neither feel validated in who we are nor in what we stand for as women. I remember the time when a guy I really liked tried some things that made me uncomfortable. I asked him to stop, but he persisted. Finally, he just wore me down and I eventually gave in. He had weakened my defenses."

Understand what's being said here. There's nothing manly about pushing past your girlfriend's sexual boundaries, especially when their pain or their desire for acceptance weakens their defenses. Besides, sex isn't so much a physical act as it's an emotional act for women—much different from the male perspective.

You may be saying, *Wait a minute, Fred. The girls I know sure look like they're all about sex.* One guy put it this way: "Girls in my youth group definitely have caused me to stumble. It's really hard for a guy to worship God when they're standing right in front of you with a sleeveless shirt and tight, tight shorts. I'm joking, of course, but sometimes I feel as though I have to repent for having gone to church!"

We don't deny this, nor are we saying that girls are never tempted by sex, or that they hate every minute of it. Amber said she knew she'd done some things that were wrong sexually, things that should be reserved for marriage. "But I didn't lower my standards just because the guy was pushing for it," she said. "I wanted to be touched just as much as he wanted to touch me. It has happened often, and each time in the middle of it I would be thinking, *This isn't right, but it isn't that wrong. We're not having intercourse, and we're not taking our clothes off.* Plus, it just felt so good that it was hard to stop."

Yes, it's even possible for a girl to race across *your* borders once in a while, so you have to be prepared for that too. Remember, young women are just as influenced by our sensual culture as you are. One of our pastors told me, "I'm starting to think that our girls are just as horny as the guys."

But don't get the idea that young women think like you do about sex. They don't. They aren't visually oriented like you. Amber said, "It's honestly inconceivable to me that just by looking at something sensual a guy can get so turned on that he has to masturbate! I can't comprehend that at all."

LET'S REMEMBER A CRUCIAL DIFFERENCE

Amber's statement ought to remind us: The biggest difference is that sex is not a girl's top priority in the relationship, and you need to understand this very clearly. Maybe it can most simply be said this way:

- Guys give emotions so they can get sex.
- Girls give sex so they can get the emotions.

Guys, girls want a relationship with you, but they should not have to give sex to get it.

"What can a guy do to make me feel cherished?" asked Amber. "By showing that he desires to spend quality time with me, telling me why he loves me, and trusting me with his thoughts and feelings. He can't be afraid to tell me the truth, even if it hurts. He has to honor my family and respect my body by not compromising our boundaries. He needs to keep his promises and be a man of his word by looking out for *my* protection and best interests."

As you can see, sex has little priority with Amber, which is the same story for Brynna. "If you want to know what turns me on, then it's when he remembers what I tell him or gives me an unexpected gift of something I had mentioned in passing. It's when he sends me a card for no reason, gives me hugs or a little kiss, holds my hand in public, and grants me independence with my friends. Oh yes, and showing me respect and praising me in front of others."

Not much sex there. Let's try Cassie. "I want him to be attentive and appreciate who I am and what I like," she began. "I want him to care for me, not just give advice or fix everything before we even talk about it. I want him to do special, thoughtful things for me out of the blue, like presenting me with flowers, gifts, and notes. I want him to open doors and pay for our dates. I want him to act like a gentleman and be proud of me."

No sexual priorities there, either. These young ladies aren't looking for a little action. They are looking for a little relationship along with some spiritual and physical leadership from you. Cassie said, "I often feel that I care more about my purity than my boyfriend, Kevin, does, although he's a great spiritual leader in many areas. We sometimes fast for special needs and for our future together. But this leadership doesn't show up in our physical relationship. We've decided together on boundaries, but he often pushes hard at them. When I resist, he pouts or asks why I don't desire him physically. I hate making him feel bad and having the blame pushed back on me, so sometimes I've given in. Kevin's happy and loving after that, but I get very resentful. Once we even broke up for a number of months."

Whatever kind of leadership that is, it smells bad from here—and it certainly isn't spiritual leadership! If you're going to love your girlfriend as yourself, you're going to have to give her what she wants, and that includes strong spiritual leadership. Sex doesn't fit into the mix at all.

What will strong spiritual leadership look like? For starters, we might ask God, "Where are the boundaries? How far can a Christian go?" Too often we avoid asking God this question, preferring to ask our peers instead.

But remember this: It's not the act of defining sexual boundaries that makes you a spiritual leader. It's the act of defending them. It wasn't that Kevin was ignorant of God's ways. He knew them well enough to help Cassie define proper sexual boundaries for their relationship together. But whenever he neared them he simply kicked out the markers a bit farther so he could stray over them at will.

For Kevin, Bible studies, prayer, and fasting camouflaged his relentless raids across Cassie's sexual borders. In the confusion, she described Kevin as a great spiritual leader on the one hand while pointing out that he has been a painful stumbling block to her sexual purity on the other. How weird. How common.

LET'S BE AUTHENTIC

If there's anywhere we need to be authentic, it's in our relationships with girls. You must leave her better than when you met her. So are you going to do that?

A young lady named Maggie told us that she had a huge problem with her boyfriend:

> When we started dating fourteen months ago, everything was per-
> fect. I felt I'd finally met a great Christian guy who loved my family
> and agreed with my morals. But six months ago, we slept together.
> We were both virgins and, to tell you the truth, I didn't want to do
> it. I had struggled through many relationships before and had re-
> mained pure. I was so wanting to wait for my wedding night, but
> I also wanted to make him happy, so I let it go too far.
>
> Since then, life has been terrible. I knew that getting it on was a
> mistake and a sin before I even did it, but the experience really hit
> him hard too. Now every other area of his life has been impacted.
> He doesn't think looking at pornography is wrong, he doesn't think
> cursing is wrong, he doesn't think premarital sex is wrong, and he
> doesn't honor his parents or mine anymore. We were thinking about
> getting married after college, but now I don't know what to do.
> He views everything I say as "nagging." I just want the same godly
> man back that I grew to love. I guess I don't want to face the fact
> that this man that I gave myself to is not the one who God has
> planned for me to marry.

Maggie didn't do anything to deserve this fate. Sure, she yielded, but that's what she did—she yielded. Her boyfriend should have been a leader. He should have acted as if it was *his* responsibility not only to set the bound-aries but also to keep them. That's what guys are called to do.

I (Fred) have a little motto I live by: "Never, ever bring shame on the name of Christ." There's no quicker way to bring shame on the name of Christ than to slip your hand under her bra or kiss her until she can't resist your advances anymore.

Then how far *can* we go? The Bible defines the outer boundaries quite well—all foreplay is out of bounds. What is foreplay? We defined it earlier, but we'll do it again here: Foreplay is anything that has as its natural result either sexual intercourse or the false intercourse of masturbation. For instance, oral sex, mutual masturbation, heavy petting, and kissing around the neck are in foul territory.

We might loosely paint this picture another way—anything you do with her that causes an erection is out of bounds. An erection is your body's way of preparing for sexual intercourse. Anything she does that prepares your body for intercourse is foreplay.

Author Josh Harris once asked his fiancée, Shannon, to take a nap in the hammock with him. What could be more innocent than a nap in a hammock? It's a far cry from foreplay, right? Listen up:

> As soon as I suggested it, I knew it was a bad idea. My ulterior motive was to get as close to Shannon's body as possible. My conscience was incensed. "Take a nap in a hammock?!" he screamed. "Are you nuts? That's not fleeing temptation—that's inviting it!"

The story continued…

> "Stop looking at her legs, Josh," my conscience said. "Your half-open eyelids don't fool me."
>
> I'm just admiring them.
>
> "You're lusting."
>
> Well, she is going to be my wife in four months.
>
> "Well, she's not your wife today."

God does not want to stifle my sexuality!

"Stifle, no. Control for the sake of righteousness, yes."

Josh, a true leader, soon excused himself and rolled out of the hammock. While a nap may be well within God's outer borders technically, it wasn't the right place for Josh to play. For instance, Josh admits that during his engagement he often struggled with sexual thoughts about Shannon in the morning, right after he woke up.

"If I allowed myself to lie in bed for an extra five minutes and dream about how one day I'd be waking up next to her," he said, "lust often got the better of me—if not at the moment, then later in how I treated her when we were together."

Seeking the boundaries of purity is important, but it's better to seek the center of purity. For instance, kissing is not technically foreplay. I've kissed Mom, my sisters, and even my Aunt Nadine with no sexual overtones at all. Kissing may be fine for you and your girlfriend. We have no problem with that in general.

But when I (Fred) look back, I'm not at all certain that kissing was best for Brenda and me during our courtship. Kissing ignited sensual infernos in my mind and made it only harder for us to remain pure together, while it did little to strengthen our relationship or ensure the success of our pending marriage. All pain, no gain.

Marking out general boundaries like "kissing the lips is okay" but "kissing the neck is not okay" can be useful, no question. But in my relationship with Brenda, splitting hairs on this issue missed the point entirely. Kissing Brenda took my mind into dark, lustful corners where it had no business going.

Maybe you can handle the kissing—fine. But what if it lights her fires, leaving her struggling to stay inbounds? Make a stand for her purity.

The point of this book is not to hammer God's rules into you. True, there are physical characteristics built into our mind and eyes that easily draw sexual gratification from those around us, and if we don't follow God's rules, we'll be ensnared. In light of this, the disciplines of "bouncing the eyes" and "starving the sumo" demand our focus.

But the ultimate point of this book is your intimacy with God. Is what you're doing with her resulting in a closer relationship with Him? Does it glorify Him? Are you satisfied with Him alone, or must you have a taste of her body as well? God is most glorified in us when we are most satisfied in Him alone.

"Please tell your readers to be leaders," said Cassie. "Help them to set high standards and encourage them to stick to them. Don't make girls constantly have to be the strong ones when temptation hits, because girls don't want to be pressured into doing something they don't really want to do. We want a man we can trust and deeply respect."

You're called to lead spiritually, and if you do, you'll go through life without regrets. That's a great place to start as you begin to live on your own, marry, and have a family.

are you ready
for the challenge?

When I told our youth pastor I was writing this book, I asked him whether there was anything he felt was absolutely critical to include. He pleaded, "Fred, they know they're going to fail. They don't have the spiritual strength to say no, and they know it. Show them how to have that strength!"

Amber is a twenty-year-old single woman at a Bible college. When I told her that I was writing this book and asked her the same question, she said, "I wish I would have been told more specifically what 'sexual purity' really meant when I was growing up in the church. I was always taught that sexual purity meant 'no sexual intercourse,' but then I loved the definition given in *Every Man's Battle*. 'Sexual purity is receiving no sexual gratification from anything or anyone outside of your husband or wife.' That's a black-and-white definition that young people need to be taught. If you don't do anything else, please stress this definition."

We *have* stressed this definition throughout *Every Young Man's Battle*, and now that you've been good students, we'd like to leave you with this challenge: We challenge you to live without premarital sex. We challenge you to live without masturbation. We challenge you to clean up what you're watching and the thoughts you're thinking.

We challenge you to stop ridiculing your friends who are trying to walk closer to God. We challenge you to let the girls in your life know that you care more about their hearts than their bodies. As Amber says, "Guys, please don't wait until you're twenty-two and ready to get married to grow up. Start appreciating girls right now—girls who place value on the right things, like character and loving God."

YOUR CHOICE: INTENSITY OR INTIMACY!

These are special days—a time when the idea of sexual purity seems radical. These days are a lot like the days of Ezekiel:

> Her priests do violence to my law and profane my holy things;
> they do not distinguish between the holy and the common; they
> teach that there is no difference between the unclean and the clean.
> (Ezekiel 22:26)

Today, the sexual lines have been so blurred that no one knows what's right or wrong, holy or profane. To put it bluntly, you're living in the era of masturbation. There's more masturbation today and more things to masturbate over than ever before. There are entire industries centered on the practice of masturbation. The porn industry wants you to masturbate compulsively so it can sell you products. *Playboy* succeeds because guys want to look at pictures of naked women and masturbate with them. *Playboy* has always been about masturbation, though they'll never say it out loud. The porn industry will rent out seven hundred million videos a year. They'll release eleven thousand "adult" movies this year so that men can become aroused and masturbate in the privacy of their own homes. These folks want you as a customer.

Porn-related Web sites are also an amazing success. While the dotcom industry is in a shambles with all sorts of Web sites going out of business, seventy thousand adult pay-for-porn sites are flourishing. Clearly, men want to masturbate, so businesses have sprung up to meet that need. For the rest of your life, you'll be bombarded with sensual television shows, horny movies, bra-and-panty ads in newspapers and magazines, and neighborhood strip joints. All of this is waiting out there for you *because men have sought out intensity rather than intimacy in their sexuality.*

The good news is that God is looking for special people in these special times. His eyes are looking throughout the whole earth for young men on whose behalf He can show His power—just like He did in the days of wicked king Ahab, when He needed someone with a steel spine to stand up to the evil man. God found that man in Elijah, who was ready to stand up for God before the king.

How many of us are like Elijah? I don't have an answer, but I do know this: God wants to use you to change these days.

We'll leave you with an inspirational story of a unique young man named Aaron, a person whom God is using in these special days. This is Aaron's story:

I'm now twenty-seven years old, but you have to go back fourteen
years to the start of my story. I was introduced to pornography while
baby-sitting at a neighbor's house when I was only thirteen years old.
Late at night, I'd just sit in the bathroom and look at the magazines.
I even broke into their house on several occasions when no one was
home. I moved into a whole new level of pornography when I turned
fifteen and found I could buy any type of pornography at a local
7-Eleven.

Whenever I had the money, I'd buy magazines. Not just *Playboy*
and *Penthouse,* but the really hard-core mags. When I was bored
with a magazine, I could sell it to a friend for a small profit. After
several months of doing this, I earned the title of "Porn King"
around school. A year later, as my high school years were coming
to a close, my parents found out about my "business." They kicked

me out of the house to protect the rest of the family from the "pervert."

This rejection only fueled my passion for pornography. I looked at porn whenever I was lonely or sad. I could be the stud, the king of my own little world, at least for the moment. My parents moved me back home after a few months, but I continued to look. I just found better hiding places. I had a new job at McDonald's, which provided me with the ready cash to buy magazines whenever I wanted. It was at McDonald's where I met a beautiful girl named Tina.

Tina introduced me to Jesus Christ, and I became a Christian. I gave up so much for Him! I quit swearing, stopped drinking, and never smoked pot again. But the pornography stuck with me. I just couldn't shake it. I *begged* Jesus for help, but nothing worked. I'd buy magazines, look at them, and then masturbate while driving home. Then I'd take the magazine straight to the trash and promise myself that I'd never do it again.

I married Tina when I was twenty. I thought that maybe this would break my pornography habit. I did okay at first, but then I found the Internet. The Internet turned out to be my "crack cocaine." I could look at anything I wanted, and it was virtually free. Plus I no longer had to face the store clerks again.

Tina could always tell when I was looking, since I'd withdraw from her. Before long, we hardly ever had sex, and when we did there was never any true intimacy. At times I would open up and tell her about my struggle. I always told her just enough so that she'd know what was wrong, but I would never tell her how much I looked or how it truly affected me.

In April one year, my brother and I came up with this crazy idea. We were going to start our own pornography company. I wanted to make videos and start my own Internet site. I asked my wife what she thought, and she said, "I really don't care anymore." So my brother and I went to work. After a few weeks, however, Tina threatened to leave me. I told her I'd quit, but deep inside I was mad that she made me quit my business.

My anger grew, but that didn't stop me from looking at Internet porn every chance I got. Tina and I grew apart, and she started seeing another man and was thinking of leaving me. After two months, I found out about their relationship, and I was never more scared in my life. I really didn't want to lose Tina and my two children. We went to counseling, but I still looked at Internet porn. Can you believe it? Even in all this mess, I was still drawn to my sin.

A few months later, I purchased a copy of *Every Man's Battle,* and I began to put the ideas into practice. I memorized Job 31:1. I starved my eyes and began having a daily prayer time. I focused on being obedient to Christ. My mind started to clear, and I no longer heard the double sexual meanings in so many simple statements. I can remember the first time someone said something that had a double meaning and laughed. I asked, "Why are you laughing?" When they told me, I praised God because I didn't get the joke until they told me. My mind was thinking purely for the very first time.

I've maintained the habit of bouncing the eyes. When I get really tempted, I look for what it is in my life that is not right. I've begun filling my needs in a healthy, God-pleasing way, and it's turned my marriage around. In fact, it's better than it has ever been. Tina says she's never been happier, and that the marriage is what she always dreamed of.

I later attended an Every Man's Battle Conference, where I met men just like me who'd been struggling. For some reason, I always thought I was all alone in this battle. I began to talk more about the topic, and when I did, I found out that six out of my seven brothers have the same problem. I'm going to share my story with each one to show them they don't have to live in bondage anymore.

The ironic thing about all this is that I've used my Web experience to start a site to *help* struggling men free themselves from pornography. Now isn't that something?

Thanks, Aaron, for sharing your incredible story. You decided that it was time, and you slew that monster of pornography. You changed the direction of your life, saved your marriage, and became a godly parent to your children. Now that's what we call a turnaround.

What about you?

Isn't it time?

when your feelings are for other guys

We've been talking about sexual attraction to women. But as you read *Every Young Man's Battle* you may have been thinking of how its themes might apply to your feelings for men. If that's true, we're fairly confident there haven't been many people for you to talk to regarding this same-sex attraction. And the fear of being discovered or rejected has no doubt kept you silent.

But the attraction is there. You didn't choose to be attracted to men, but you are. You may have been molested when you were younger, and that started the feelings. Even though it was abuse, you couldn't figure out why it made you feel the way it did. And when it came to anything related to church, perhaps all you heard was condemnation.

There are many theories about why you have the feelings you do. Some of them seem to make sense, and some don't. But let us share with you what we believe makes the most sense. We want to help you understand why you feel the way you do and provide some hope for you.

WHEN A FOUNDATION IS LAID

From the time you were born, your development unfolded in relationship to your mom and dad. Even if one of them wasn't there, that fact was part of your developmental process. When childhood development occurs in a healthy home, where a young boy feels balanced love flowing from a father and a mother, the foundation is laid for heterosexuality. If your father was there for you and acted as role model while expressing his love for you, then that gave you a sense of security in your manhood and total identity.

As far as maleness goes, then, you felt complete. The area in which you felt incompleteness would be in femaleness. In a mode of experiencing completeness, you would be attracted to the thing you didn't have, the thing that would complete you—and that would be someone of the opposite sex. This is an oversimplification, of course, but an accurate explanation of male attraction to females.

If you were raised by an emotionally distant father, or a male who was cruel, abusive, or absent, you might have developed a different sense of who you are. You may not have experienced a secure sense of identity and manhood. If no other man in your life was able to provide that, such as an uncle or a grandfather or a coach, then you were left with a sense of incompleteness that you probably didn't even know was there. The result was for you to be attracted to what would provide that sense of completeness, and that was another male.

The reactions of other boys may have complicated this sense of "lacking" for you. For example, if you weren't into competitive sports and preferred art and drama, you may have felt as though you were an outcast. Boys your age may not have connected with you, and in fact they may have rejected you in order to secure their own sense of manhood.

Some boys like to play with dolls rather than army men. If that was you, it was a setup for experiencing rejection by other boys and later by men. So it was only natural that you would long for what you didn't have, which is a feeling of maleness and a connection to other men. If someone who was experienced in homosexual behavior came along and seduced you, then you probably felt at least some of the acceptance and connection that you'd been longing for.

Attraction to men can also be intensified by a repulsion to women. If you had a mother or other female caretaker who was unhealthy and either smothered you out of her own selfishness or was cruel to you out of her own depravity, it would interrupt the development of an attraction to women. The last thing you would want to have would be a relationship with anyone who was anything like the woman you despised. Your comfort level with women would be minimal. That foundation made you an easy target if you were approached by another man.

If these things ring true in your life, you're one of thousands of confused and searching men who long to know what's normal and how to experience it. This is where your choices come in, because there's much hope for you, if you choose it.

CHANGE IS POSSIBLE

The world will tell you that you must act on your feelings—sexualize them—and only then will you feel whole. They'll tell you that while your family or church will reject you, you'll find completion in a world where homosexual sex is good and the attention you've always craved is available. You can listen to the world, or you can hear another voice that appears fainter but grows stronger everyday.

In the 1970s the growing gay movement, along with liberal psychiatry establishments, was part of a major shift in the thinking about homosexuality. They were successful in having homosexuality deleted from the American Psychological Society's list of mental disorders. Dr. Robert Spitzer helped lead that campaign, which made him a hero of the homosexual community at the time. Recently, however, Spitzer has published the results of his latest research—results that have made him less than popular with those who used to praise him.

"Contrary to conventional wisdom," he wrote, "some highly motivated individuals, using a variety of change efforts, can make substantial change in multiple indicators of sexual orientation." Essentially Spitzer wrote that if you have feelings for the same sex, and you're highly motivated to change, you really do have a choice in who you are, who you become, and how you feel about yourself. His conclusions are based on interviews with two hundred men and women who shifted from homosexual to heterosexual attraction and stayed straight for five years. The reasons they were motivated to change were due to being burned out over a highly promiscuous lifestyle, unstable relationships, the desire to marry, and matters of their faith. Three-fourths of the men and half the women were married after giving up a life of homosexual relationships.[1]

CHOOSE YOUR ACTIONS

What this should mean to you is that while you didn't choose to have the feelings you have, you can choose what you do with them. While many voices in the world tell you there's no choice in the matter, there's plenty of evidence that you *do* have a choice and you can make changes in how you feel about yourself and others. So if your dreams consist of sexual interludes with men, if you fantasize about having sex with men, and if you long to be with and lust after a man, you can change all of that, just as a man lusting after a woman can change his mind and his heart. It won't be easy, but it can be done.

Our thoughts on this topic aren't very popular. But neither are many of the other ideas we've presented here and in the original book, *Every Man's Battle*. In that book, we published our e-mail addresses, just as we've done in this book. Why? Because we wanted to know whether men were doing what we suggested. We wanted to know whether they were successful in experiencing victory over sexual sin.

We would have never been asked to write this book for younger single men if the results of publishing *Every Man's Battle* hadn't been so profound.

---

1. Robert Spitzer, "A Matter of Choice," *World,* 19 May 2001, 8.

Every day we're reading e-mails from men, young adults, and teenagers who have struggled for years and found hope for the first time—heterosexual *and* homosexual. Gays and straights are doing the things we suggested, and they're finding a victory that had escaped them before.

You can trust us when we tell you there's a way out. You do have a choice, and that choice will lead you to what God wants for you and to the relationships He has prepared for you.

The path you choose is your decision, and we hope that this book's content will motivate you. You can do what many other men with the same feelings as you have done. You can change and be successful in developing a new life.

If you would like further information and support with regard to your feelings, please call Exodus International toll-free at 1-888-264-0877 or visit their Web site at www.exodus-international.org.

the rest of the story

FROM FRED

Ten years. I can scarcely believe it's been that long since *Every Man's Battle* first hit the presses. As I look back over all that God's done this decade, it's scary to consider how close I came to snuffing out the Every Man series before it even began.

Mike Yorkey had just informed me that it was too financially risky for him to help me edit and prepare the manuscript for a publisher. Since he was the only connection I had to the publishing industry, his words rolled like granite boulders over my chest. After politely thanking him for his time, I hung up the phone and slumped broken to the floor, my heart shattered.

"My dream's dead!" I moaned to Brenda in desperate tears. "Mike said the manuscript isn't ready to show to a publisher, but he can't help me fix it, and I don't know how to fix it myself. After all this work, it's over!"

With nowhere to turn but up, I headed to the altar at church two days later and stretched facedown across the carpet to pray. The moment I hit the floor, the Lord spoke into my heart. He said, *I want your book!*

I was appalled by His request. "Lord, I can't just give you my book. You know how hard I've worked on it. I can *share* it with You, but I can't just *give* it to You." I knew that once God took over, I'd have no further say in any of the decisions.

Yes, but I want your book. There was a smile in His voice, as if He'd expected my ridiculous response and was amused because He knew me so well.

"This doesn't make sense. Lord, I'm not even sure this is You talking to me. The God I know is a giver. He doesn't just take things like this."

Yes, but I want your book, He responded brightly. He seemed to relish this wrestling match and was completely unruffled by my stubbornness. Not me. As the match stretched past ten minutes and toward the twenty-minute mark, an overwhelming agitation swelled inside me as the inevitable grew more and more obvious. I was going down, and there would be nothing I could do about it. Though hopeless, I grappled on valiantly until I couldn't take it any longer.

"Okay, Lord. You win," I blurted, bursting into submissive tears. "You can have the book, no strings attached. Only use it for Your glory."

His next words took my breath away: *Because you've given me this book, I'm going to take its message around the world.*

My dream wasn't over. God proceeded to prove it to me. Within two days, Mike called me back and said simply, "I was praying today, and the Lord told me to help you out." Within two months of the book's release, I received e-mails from readers in Chile, Malaysia, Ireland, Albania, and Hong Kong, as if the Lord was going out of His way to prove He was keeping His word.

Within two years, with the release of *Every Man's Marriage* and *Every Young Man's Battle,* Every Man had become a series. Today we're celebrating the tenth anniversary of a book that's still traveling the world, declaring its message of freedom in more than twenty languages.

It's still hard to believe.

THE POWER OF A TESTIMONY

I nearly blew it! In my blindness I tried hard to wrestle my destiny out of God's hands, but (I'm so grateful) He wouldn't be denied. You see, the Lord wanted that manuscript for its testimony to His grace, and for good reason. Freedom is His game, and when it comes to setting people free, testimonies are powerful things, as Scripture reminds us: "Worship God! For the testimony of Jesus is the spirit of prophecy" (Revelation 19:10).

A testimony reveals what's possible in our lives. The original language for the word *testimony* can be translated "to do again," and that's where its power lies. The moment you read or hear a testimony, the Holy Spirit shifts the spiritual atmosphere. Faith explodes in your heart, and hope swirls throughout your soul: *If God can do this in that guy's life, then God can do it in mine!* The power of testimony lies in that stirring of faith, and the Holy Spirit needs only a little faith to duplicate the testimony in you and work victory throughout your life.

I've heard from thousands of guys how our testimonies in *Every Man's Battle* and *Every Young Man's Battle* charged their faith, and today these courageous guys have their own testimonies to share. This has been the most gratifying aspect to coauthoring these books, and I have no doubt that God can do it again in your life, just like He did in mine and just like He's doing in the lives of my sons.

Take a look at my oldest, Jasen, for instance. When I was twenty-three, I was sleeping regularly with three different girls and essentially engaged to marry two of them. When Jasen was twenty-three, I watched him take his newly minted wife in his arms at the wedding altar and kiss a girl for the very first time, ever.

What's more, he never got hooked on porn and masturbation along the way, and he never left a girl worse off for having known him while dating. (He shares how he managed this in his book *Hero,* which we wrote together.) His life, in high school, in college, and now in marriage, is a testament to God's faithfulness for every young man out there who still wonders whether sexual purity is really possible in today's sex-soaked culture. Others are also finding that purity is possible, like Ben:

Tomorrow will be my ten-month anniversary of purity. I never would've thought I'd be talking about ten months without seeing some form of nudity, but here I am living it out, and I love it. The best part is how this freedom has impacted my spiritual life. I have replaced all those wasted hours spent feeding my lust with the pursuit of Jesus and a more intimate relationship with my Lord.

I've had new opportunities in ministry. My brother and I just finished leading an eight-week class on sexual integrity with twelve married and single men from our church, which was absolutely awesome. I've also begun dating a wonderful girl, and I'm intent on leading our relationship in a way that will make God smile. We've been together three months now, and it's neat to see the results of doing a relationship the right way.

A choice for purity will impact you and everyone around you, as Robby relates:

When I finished *Every Young Man's Battle* a few months ago, I decided to make major changes in my life. The atmosphere at college is hedonistic, and I'll admit I've compromised my values in this environment. Given the many temptations surrounding me, I've been fortunate to avoid sexual intercourse, but I've done things with girls here that I will regret for the rest of my life.

Reading your book changed everything. I've not looked at porn or masturbated in over two months, and at this point I'm not tempted by it much. It's as if I really don't care about having that feeling anymore.

I play football here, so I hear sexual comments and stories of conquests all the time. Sometimes they press me about my own sexual experiences, and it feels great to tell them, "I don't live the way you guys live." I realize I haven't always lived up to God's standards with my eyes or in the way I've treated girls, but I've changed, and by now most of the football team knows about it. Many tell me they admire the way I live, but they say they could never have that kind of discipline themselves. I tell them that anyone can do it, but you have to want to change. You can't make a commitment like this one with a halfway attitude.

Perhaps the best point you make in your book is how free you feel once bondage to sensuality is gone. Something else always seemed to be controlling my mind and my life, but not anymore. I can stand face to face with those temptations and spit in their eyes, and the effects of my purity carry over into many areas of my life.

For instance, ever since I stopped the looking and lusting, I'm playing football with greater intensity and with a physical strength I haven't known before. I'm a sophomore running back, and there's a junior ahead of me who's started since he was a freshman. When the season began, I had little hope I could beat him out, but this last weekend I earned my first start. This may seem silly to you, but I am thoroughly convinced that God gave me this new strength because of my new way of living.

Sexual purity will bring a cascade of blessings into your life, but that doesn't mean you won't have to fight to get there. Bouncing the eyes at school or quitting the porn at home may seem impossible at first, but don't be thrown off. After all, these aren't just bad brutal habits. They're addictions, and I don't just use that term for shock value.

Psychiatrist Jeffrey Satinover testified [at a U.S. Senate hearing] regarding pornography's effect on brain chemistry.... "[Porn] is a very carefully designed delivery system for evoking a tremendous flood within the brain of endogenous opioids. Modern science allows us to understand that the underlying nature of an addiction to pornography is chemically nearly identical to a heroin addiction." (*Tactics*, page 39)

It's no wonder that some guys experience withdrawal symptoms as part of the battle. Kyle admitted, "I had a really hard time stopping because I'd been viewing porn and masturbating five or six times a day! Finally I quit the habit, but I had a very nasty withdrawal. There wasn't much to do but hang on and fight through the urges, but I guess that's okay. Everything's subsided now, and I haven't masturbated in eight months."

Some addiction experts claim that there's a common withdrawal wall at the three-week mark—no matter what addiction you're trying to quit— and you'll either tough it out and break through that wall to freedom, or you'll give in to the increasing urges and remain trapped inside. With sexual sin, some guys give up at the wall, thinking, *Well, I have to masturbate to release my sexual tension,* or, *I will just have to learn how to masturbate with a clean mind so I can still do it without sinning.*

Not everyone hits the wall, but if you do, push through the urges and put the addiction to death like Kyle did, or at least put it to sleep, like Andy did:

While there's still some natural physical pressure for release from time to time, I found that once I broke through that wall, the cycle of desire went to sleep or dried up. I've found that if I keep living cleanly, the pressure dissipates. I've also found that emotionally, intellectually, and spiritually intimate relationships with other men can provide the support I need to be faithful in my relationship with God. Ultimately my sexuality is a matter of faithfulness to God— not just obeying His commands but also honoring my relationship with Him.

Ways of Winning

The second book of my trilogy for single guys, *Tactics,* will help you with this part of the battle. It does this by strengthening your view of God as your Father and teaching you how to win through prayer, worship, and forming deeper connections with other guys. *Tactics* was helpful to Travis and Ian in this way:

> I think *Tactics* is even more powerful than your earlier books, which is saying something. I learned so much about my physical and mental makeup, but the one thing I loved most was learning how you worship the Lord in song before praying. I've had much better conversations with God lately as a result. Through this one book, you've taught me more about having devotional times with God than anybody else I know.

> You've impacted me so deeply. I've read *Every Young Man's Battle* and am currently reading *Tactics.* I can't put the book down! I've never met you, but I feel like I know you well, and I really want to give you a big "daddy hug" because you are giving me the straight uncensored talk I always wanted from my father.
>
> My parents divorced when I was very young, and though my mother remarried when I was eight, it's only been recently that my stepdad and I have developed a closer relationship—and I'm going on twenty-one. All my life I've wanted to be fathered the way you were a father to your sons in *Tactics,* but through those stories, I feel like I'm being fathered by you now too. Thanks for all of your transparency and honesty.

And that's the whole point of sexual purity, isn't it? It's not only about guarding your eyes and starving your mind; it's about deepening your connection with God. It's about forging your identity as a man and being everything your Christian label promises you'll be.

Part of that is integrating your sexuality effectively with the rest of your spiritual life, so you'll become your girlfriend's hero, not her nightmare. Some guys never seem to get there, which Tara found out the hard way:

> My Christian boyfriend was frustrated and struggling with my
> sexual boundaries, so he ended the relationship. I hadn't expected
> to face that kind of challenge in a Christian relationship, but he had
> been sexually active in the past, and he used that to his advantage. I
> was surprised how well he'd learned to twist God's truth to justify
> his sexual choices and to manipulate me. Just before we broke up,
> I picked up *Every Young Man's Battle* to get a male perspective on
> the temptations men face sexually. After my experiences with this
> boyfriend, it was very inspiring to read about young men really
> *being* men, as God desires, and it was also inspiring to see you stand
> up for the kind of pure dating relationships that God wants all of us
> to have.

Dating *does* put unique pressure upon your purity, but Jasen's and my new book, *Hero,* will help you keep your passions in check. God wants you to put your sexuality in its place so you'll inspire the hearts of your girlfriends, not crush them. Daniel certainly needed to put his sexual desires in their place:

> Like many guys, I had a porn problem, and I also looked at the
> women around me constantly, even though my fiancée, Kristina,
> tried her best to keep my attention. Once after we ate out, she told
> me I'd been looking at our waitress's breasts the whole evening.
> Embarrassed, I apologized, and I immediately promised to go out
> the next day to practice not looking at women.

I tried, but it felt unnatural and practically impossible to look away from the curves in the women around me. A gulf came between Kristina and me, and I began wondering if this (along with my porn) was also causing my disconnection with God. I didn't like that distance from Him and, besides, it no longer felt right to be constantly masturbating anymore. It seemed like I was aroused 24/7, and I was just disgusted with it.

I began praying about this two months ago, and within a week I was given a copy of *Every Young Man's Battle*. The bondage began to lift that very day. I began noticing all the little things in my life that aroused me. Years of bottled pain and stress were washed away, and a new intoxicating joy filled me. For the first time in my life, I felt I could go all the way forward with God in everything, and I didn't feel dirty anymore.

I can't explain what's happened in my life since then. For years, my genitals were swollen all of the time because of what I looked at throughout my day. Not anymore. For the past month, I haven't been aroused like that, and I'm experiencing an amazing, new kind of physical relaxation. On top of that, I'm respecting women as human beings, not seeing them as objects of sexual satisfaction. My fiancée says I'm more relaxing to be around, as if a dark cloud has left me completely, and she now finds me completely and irresistibly attractive. I love these changes, and I will never go down that old road again.

Finally, consider one more amazing story from Jon:

I was seven when my brother and I began modeling with a Christian agency whose goal was to place missionaries in the advertising world. After high school, I won an elite contest, signed with a New York City agency, and began to travel extensively. At nineteen I was continually surrounded by nudity on the set and in our coed changing rooms. The sensual photo shoots kept my mind racing, and one-night stands became the norm for me. My view of sex and relationships was quickly warped.

Before long I became a promoter in the club scene in Manhattan, creating buzz and filling clubs with hip pretty people. I did it well, setting them up with whatever they wanted but basically pimping them for my gain. As a kid I'd been trained to know God, but I couldn't see what I'd become. I was certainly no missionary.

Through something of a miracle, on a trip home I found *Every Man's Battle* lying on my nightstand. I was frozen by the words and instantly knew they were all true. While I wasn't following the Lord at the time, I felt compelled to apply the principles. That began a cascade of change in my heart that continues to this day.

Soon I was bouncing my eyes from billboards, turning the other way while changing clothes with girls, getting photographers to change racy shoots, and avoiding magazine racks, even walking past them backward. I didn't care anymore how I looked—I was committed to keeping my eyes pure.

After talking with two guys at a YWAM conference, God convinced me I needed to quit modeling. It felt crazy, but I knew it was my only way to complete freedom. It was also time to learn to do relationships the right way. I cut off communication with the women in my past, and I haven't touched or kissed a woman in a sensual way since.

God also showed me I needed a community of believers. I joined a Christian study program called Transit and was soon asked to go to Southeast Asia with a small team to rescue women from human trafficking. I prayed about it and asked a friend for advice. "Did God tell you don't go?" he asked. "No." "Is your heart broken over what's happening there?" "Yes." "Then that's your answer."

So I went. In Cambodia my transformed heart, its natural heroism springing to life and now emboldened by the trust God gave me with this special mission, burned to help the prostitutes and sex slaves. In Bangkok we went to an open-air market called the night bazaar, a two-lane street lined by strip clubs three to five stories high, with bars at street level and sex rooms above. Women and girls pole danced inside. The streets were filled with middle-aged Western men with twentysomething Thai women on their arms and teenagers walking slowly back and forth, peeking into the clubs. I felt over-whelming rage and nearly vomited from disgust. Tourists of all ages and nationalities strolled the streets while promoters tried to lure them into the bars. I wanted to punch them, until the Lord reminded me of New York. Except for God, I was no different from these guys.

I'd never sensed such wretched oppression anywhere, and never had prayer seemed so crucial to me. My friend and I teamed up each night to prayer-walk the red-light district while the women on our team went into the clubs to talk with the girls. We prayed out loud the whole way, looking like a couple tourists talking together. During the days, we heard from teams and met the women rescued the night before. It was beyond amazing. Rather than using God's daughters, I was now defending them, and I'd finally become that missionary God dreamed I'd be.

Daniel and Jon responded to God's call. What will you do?

A little more than ten years ago, God implored, *I want your book!* To-day, He's turning His eyes on you, imploring, *I want your life, starting with your sexuality!*

Will you keep wrestling Him off as I once did, or will you finally give up and let Him write a testimony with your life, one He can take around the world to inspire faith and freedom in those close to you?

Consider the testimonies you've just read, my friend. Isn't it time you allow God to do it again in your life?

workbook

questions you may have about this workbook

What will the *Every Young Man's Battle Workbook* do for me?

First, this workbook will assure you that *you are not alone.* In fact, a large majority of Christian men struggle with various degrees of sexual impurity. You'll find that the authors are refreshingly honest about their own battles as they share what God has taught them about standing strong in the face of sexual temptation. Second, you'll be encouraged by a *circle of caring, praying friends standing alongside you* as you study God's incredible design for human sexuality and learn practical ways to live successfully according to God's plan. Third, you'll *grow in spiritual strength* as you learn to rely on the power of the Holy Spirit to help you live in spiritual and sexual integrity, honoring women (and God) in your thoughts, attitudes, and actions.

Is this workbook enough or do I also need the book *Every Young Man's Battle*?

Included in each weekly study you'll find a number of excerpts from the book *Every Young Man's Battle,* each one marked at the beginning and end by this symbol: 📖. Nevertheless, several study questions refer to more extensive portions of the book, so you'll derive the greatest personal benefit by reading *Every Young Man's Battle* as you go through this companion workbook. You'll find the appropriate chapters to read listed at the beginning of each weekly study.

The lessons look long. Do I need to work through everything in each?
This workbook is designed to promote your thorough exploration of all the material, but you may find it best to focus your time and discussion on some sections and questions more than others.

To help your pacing, we've designed the workbook so it can most easily be used in either an eight-week or twelve-week approach.

- *For the eight-week track,* simply follow the basic organization already set up with the eight different weekly lessons.
- *For the twelve-week track,* the lessons labeled Weeks Two, Five, Six, and Seven can be divided into two parts (you'll see the dividing place marked in the text).

(In addition, of course, you may decide to follow at an even slower pace—whether you're going through the workbook individually or as part of a group.)

Above all, keep in mind that the purpose of this workbook is to help guide you in specific life-applications of the biblical truths taught in *Every Young Man's Battle.* The wide range of questions included in each weekly study is meant to help you approach this practical application from different angles with personal reflection and self-examination. Allowing adequate time to prayerfully reflect on each question will be much more valuable to you than rushing through this workbook.

How do I bring together a small group to go through this workbook?
You'll get far more out of this workbook if you're able to go through it with a small group of like-minded guys. And what do you do if you don't know of a group that's going through the workbook? Start a group of your own!

If you show the book *Every Young Man's Battle* and a copy of this companion workbook to young Christian men you know, you'll be surprised at how many indicate interest in joining you to explore this topic together. And it doesn't require a long commitment. The workbook is clearly set up so you can complete one lesson per week and finish in only eight weeks—or if you'd like to proceed at a slower pace, you can follow the instructions provided for covering the content in a twelve-week track.

Your once-per-week meeting could happen in the early morning before school, on a weekday evening, or even on a Saturday morning. You could meet in the basement or den of one of the guys' homes or at the home of your youth leader, in a church classroom, or a college dorm room. Choose a location where your discussion won't be overheard by others, so the guys are comfortable in sharing candidly and freely.

This workbook follows a simple design that's easy to use. First, each guy in the group completes a week's lesson on his own. Then, when you come together that week, you discuss together the group questions provided under the "Every Young Man's TALK" heading. You might want to show the *Every Young Man's Battle Video* the first week to help open up the guys. Of course, if you have time, you can also discuss at length any of the other questions or topics in that week's lesson; we guarantee the guys in your group will find these worth exploring. They're also likely to have plenty of their own related questions for discussion.

It's best if one person is designated as the group's facilitator. If your group is made up of teens, consider asking an older brother or youth group associate to take this role. This person is not a teacher, but simply has the responsibility to keep the discussion moving and to ensure that each guy in the group has an opportunity to fully join in. If you're all in your twenties, it's likely that one guy in the group will be mature enough to lead.

At the beginning, and several times throughout the course, remind the guys of the simple ground rule that *anything shared in the group stays in the group*—everything's confidential, especially considering the sensitive topics addressed in this study. This will help participants feel safer about sharing honestly and openly in an environment of trust.

Finally, we encourage you to allow time for prayer in each meeting—

conversational, short-sentence prayers expressed in honesty before God. Be sensitive to the fact that many guys don't feel comfortable praying aloud in front of others; over time and without pressure, as you come to trust one another, this barrier to praying aloud can be overcome.

where are we?

This week's reading assignment:

introduction, chapters 1–2 of *Every Young Man's Battle*

There's a time-honored code that almost every male I've known has followed. I'm positive that my father and my brothers followed what I call the "Sexual Code of Silence." The code states that it's okay to joke about sex or even lie about it, but other than that, it's your solemn duty—as a male—to keep silent whenever a serious discussion about sex takes place.

—Steve Arterburn, from the introduction to *Every Young Man's Battle*

📖 EVERY YOUNG MAN'S TRUTH
(Your Personal Journey into God's Word)

As you begin this first study, take some time to read and meditate upon the Bible passages below, which have to do with God's awesome love for you. Realize that no matter what your relationship to sexual lust and pornography in the past, it has not changed God's attitude toward you. You are His precious adopted child, loved unconditionally and completely. Your perfect acceptance in the Lord is the key fact to focus on, day by day, as you rely on Him to guide you through every temptation.

When I consider your heavens,
     the work of your fingers,
the moon and the stars,
     which you have set in place,
what is man that you are mindful of him,
     the son of man that you care for him?
You made him a little lower than the heavenly beings
     and crowned him with glory and honor. (Psalm 8:3-5)

See that you do not look down on one of these little ones.
For I tell you that their angels in heaven always see the face
of my Father in heaven.

    What do you think? If a man owns a hundred sheep, and
one of them wanders away, will he not leave the ninety-nine
on the hills and go to look for the one that wandered off?
And if he finds it, I tell you the truth, he is happier about
that one sheep than about the ninety-nine that did not
wander off. In the same way your Father in heaven is not
willing that any of these little ones should be lost. (Matthew
18:10-14)

Who shall separate us from the love of Christ? Shall trouble
or hardship or persecution or famine or nakedness or danger
or sword? As it is written:

    "For your sake we face death all day long;
        we are considered as sheep to be slaughtered."

    No, in all these things we are more than conquerors
through him who loved us. For I am convinced that neither

death nor life, neither angels nor demons, neither the present
nor the future, nor any powers, neither height nor depth,
nor anything else in all creation, will be able to separate us
from the love of God that is in Christ Jesus our Lord.
(Romans 8:35-39)

1. The psalmist tells us how God views his human creatures. What phrase
   shows you how much God values you—just for being a human being?
2. When Jesus was on earth, He demonstrated His love and gentleness
   toward children. Have you ever seen yourself as a "little one" in His
   eyes? When? How could you begin to develop more of a sense of
   childlike dependence on Jesus?
3. According to the apostle Paul (author of the letter to the Romans),
   how strong is the love of Christ for you? What modern-day invention
   or image do you think might symbolize the strength of this love
   for you?
4. Can your sexual sins separate you from the love of God? Why or
   why not?
5. Name the most encouraging truth that comes through to you in the
   scripture passages above. How will you remind yourself of that truth
   during the coming week?

☑ EVERY YOUNG MAN'S CHOICE
(Questions for Personal Reflection and Examination)

> 📖 Since everyone is determined not to talk about this, or
> maybe is embarrassed to do so, you probably don't have a
> clear picture of what healthy sex is all about. In fact, you're
> probably thinking that some very wonderful things are not
> normal and that some very normal things are pretty weird. 📖

   📖 Like any red-blooded football player, however, I had more than a passing interest in sex. I'd been hooked on *Playboy* centerfolds ever since I found a stack of the magazines beneath my dad's bed when I was in first grade. I also discovered copies of *From Sex to Sexty,* a publication filled with naughty jokes and sexy comic strips. 📖

6. How have you learned about sex so far? Do you believe you have a healthy view of sex? Why or why not?

7. What is your own experience with pornography? Can you relate to Fred's stories about his early exposure to porn? How was your experience like or unlike his? How do you think exposure to pornography influences a young boy's early perspective on sexuality? How do you think continued exposure to pornography influences a young man's perspective?

8. What is your basic attitude toward the theme of this entire book— that you can be delivered from the habit (or addiction) of lust and pornography? What do you see in Fred's story so far that gives you hope?

👟 EVERY YOUNG MAN'S WALK
(Your Guide to Personal Application)

   📖 One of the most difficult assignments you'll ever have is to integrate your sexuality with the emotional, spiritual, social, and relational person you want to be. Many have the tendency to see their sexuality as something shamefully separate and distinct from themselves, but that shouldn't be the case at all. 📖

📖 Within twelve short months, I'd gone from being able to say no in a secluded camper on a moonlit night to being able to say yes in any bed on any night. Just one year out of college in California, I found myself with four "steady" girlfriends simultaneously. I was sleeping with three of them and was essentially engaged to marry two of them. None knew of the others. 📖

📖 This was a different experience for me. Oh, I knew who God was and had even prayed on occasion that I wanted Him closer in my life, but nevertheless I'd be right back in bed the following evening with the French graduate student—or one of the others. I never really meant those prayers. Then again, my word never meant much back then, and I knew it. 📖

9. What does Steve mean by integrating your sexuality with the rest of your life? How do you think this would help you in the battle against impure thoughts and sexual temptation? What would be a smart first step for you to begin integrating sexuality with life?

10. Fred talks about his swift increase in sexual behavior—from saying no to being unable to stay out of bed with various girls! What have you noticed about the "mushrooming" effect of lust and sexual sin? How willing are you to stop this chain reaction in your own life? Why do you think it's vital to do so?

11. If you've prayed about this area of your life in the past, how has God answered—or seemed not to answer? Review what was required for Fred to really mean his prayers? What do you think the same change might require of you?

12. In quietness, review what you have written and learned in this week's study. If further thoughts or prayer requests come to your mind and heart, you may want to write them down.

13. What for you was the most meaningful concept or truth in this week's study? What do you believe God wants you to do in response?

14. How would you talk this over with God? Write down your response as a prayer to Him.

EVERY YOUNG MAN'S TALK
(Constructive Topics and Questions for Group Discussion)

Key Highlights from the Book to Read Aloud and Discuss

📖 It's sad that in the Christian community, where we have access to God's truth, we operate with so many lies and myths about sex. 📖

📖 Melissa looked up at me with a deep sadness in her big brown eyes, the moonlight framing her innocent face. "You know that I'm saving myself for marriage—hopefully ours," she said. "If you push forward with this, I want you to know that I won't stop you. But I will never be able to respect you as much as I do right now, and that would make me very sad for a very long time."

Laying her virginity on the line, she had delivered the ultimate pop quiz. How would I answer? Who did I love most—her or me? 📖

📖 Shocked by the centerfolds? No, I was shocked by my revulsion. *Where in the world did this reaction come from?*

I wondered. After all, we're talking Fred Stoeker, the guy who'd memorized the dates when porn magazines hit the local drugstore. The one who skipped class to lust over the pages. The one who *lived* for centerfolds, saving them for last like some sweet dessert. I'd never been repulsed by a centerfold in my life. 📖

Discussion Questions

(Note: If you're meeting in a group, begin your session by raising the issue of "comfort levels." The point is, the topic and themes in this book might be a little difficult to discuss at first. That's only natural; each of you will be a little uneasy in the beginning. Nevertheless, take courage and move forward. The Lord cares about every part of your life, including your sexuality. And sexual lust is best battled with help from other Christian men who can talk and pray together in a spirit of frank and open communication. So begin with prayer, inviting the Holy Sprit to be in your midst and to guide you in your sharing. It will take some guts, but it will be worth your effort!)

A. In the introduction, Steve talked about a friend's son who said, "Dad, I just feel like taking off my clothes and standing in front of a girl naked." Can you understand that statement coming from a twelve-year-old? How might you have stated it—that hormonal rush that kicked in when you hit puberty?

B. This book freely admits that there are many lies and myths about sex in the Christian community. Talk this over. What things would you identify as lies and myths? How have these affected your attitude about sex, lust, and pornography so far?

C. Fred talks about a turning point in his life with his girlfriend Melissa. He had to ask, "Who do I love most—her or me?" Have you BTDT (been there, done that)? What kinds of decisions have you made in the past, and what kind of impact did they make in your life—and in the life of another? How would you like to decide in the future? Why?

D. Fred was eventually amazed at his reaction against porn—the bathroom wallpaper episode. Can you believe this really happened? How do you explain the change in Fred's heart? What does this event say to your own heart right now?

E. Fred talks about the time he couldn't get aroused with an old girlfriend. Why was that such a profound spiritual turning point for him? Have you ever thought of the Holy Spirit working in this practical way? What does this story say to you personally?

F. Fred says: "I immediately fell in love with the Holy Spirit's whisper in my life." What does this mean to you? Can you think of a time when you have "heard the whisper"? When do you need to hear it the most? Share about this in the most practical terms possible.

oneness and maleness

This week's reading assignment:

chapters 3–6 of *Every Young Man's Battle*

I recall how the Holy Spirit whispered to me, "This practice can't be tolerated any-more in your life. You are Christ's now, and He loves you." The implication was that continued sexual activity would hurt my intimacy with Christ.

When you break His standards, the Lord doesn't reject you, but you can't be as close to Him.... [Yet] this new life in me was moving me His way. I had a desire to be closer to Him. And in order to get closer to Him, I had to be not so close to those women in my life.

—Fred Stoeker, from chapter 3 of *Every Young Man's Battle*

📖 EVERY YOUNG MAN'S TRUTH
(Your Personal Journey into God's Word)

In your first session, you focused on Bible passages talking about God's great love for you. It is a perfect love that lasts forever because of Christ's eternal work on the cross. The awesome Bible passage below is a reminder that God's love has also given you a special identity as His beloved child. You've been adopted as His own, and this should have a powerful and prac-tical effect on your self-image. In other words, when you are tempted to sin—remember who you are! When you are tempted and fail to resist—

remember who you are! Ask for God's forgiveness, and move ahead in the power of His never-ending love.

> Praise be to the God and Father of our Lord Jesus Christ, who has blessed us in the heavenly realms with every spiritual blessing in Christ. For he chose us in him before the creation of the world to be holy and blameless in his sight. In love he predestined us to be adopted as his sons through Jesus Christ, in accordance with his pleasure and will—to the praise of his glorious grace, which he has freely given us in the One he loves. In him we have redemption through his blood, the forgiveness of sins, in accordance with the riches of God's grace that he lavished on us with all wisdom and understanding. And he made known to us the mystery of his will according to his good pleasure, which he purposed in Christ, to be put into effect when the times will have reached their fulfillment—to bring all things in heaven and on earth together under one head, even Christ.
>
> In him we were also chosen, having been predestined according to the plan of him who works out everything in conformity with the purpose of his will, in order that we, who were the first to hope in Christ, might be for the praise of his glory. (Ephesians 1:3-12)

1. According to this passage, God chose you—but for what purpose?
2. What is your identity in Christ? Let this identity seep into your soul right now. How does it feel?
3. In what types of situations are you most likely to forget about your identity in Christ and all the spiritual blessings that come with it? Why do you think this happens?

4. When you are in the midst of temptation, how could recalling the truths of this scripture passage help you? What one sentence or phrase stands out to you with the most personal impact?

☑ EVERY YOUNG MAN'S CHOICE
(Questions for Personal Reflection and Examination, Chapters 3 and 4)

📖 Regardless of where you stand right now, let me use my story as a starting point to lay a foundation for the rest of this book. It's an underpinning of six basic truths upon which we all need to agree. 📖

📖 As young men we often treat ourselves as kids. If we viewed ourselves as men like God does, we'd always view our sexual decisions today as having an impact on our tomorrows. But we usually don't do that. There remains this huge gap between the *physical* ability to do sexual things (which happens during puberty) and the *legal* ability to do sexual things (at least in God's eyes), which is ours only at marriage. Facing this enormous chasm, it's easy to view the physical and the legal as two thoroughly separate realms. 📖

5. Go back to chapter 3 and review the six basic truths about sex and your spiritual life. Which of them reveals new information to you? Which of them would you like to learn more about? Why?

6. Think about how you would describe the idea of bifurcation to another guy. Why is it considered a myth? What are some of its destructive effects on young men? On you personally?

📖 EVERY YOUNG MAN'S WALK

(Your Guide to Personal Application, Chapters 3 and 4)

> 📖 If you don't ram a stake into the ground and declare, "This is as far as I go,' and I won't go any further," then you'll lose your footing on the slippery slope of sex. Remember how I let myself go in college? Because of the pleasure, sexual escalation was natural. 📖

> 📖 Maybe you aren't concerned. Maybe you think God will forgive you and that everything will be over once you marry. He'll forgive you, all right, but it's not over. Sin comes with inescapable consequences that follow you. You'll have to pay the price at the same toll bridge as the rest of us. Jim told us this… 📖

7. What is your experience during the past year with sexual escalation? Do you agree that it is a slippery slope?

8. What are you currently doing to "ram a stake into the ground"?

9. If God has forgiven you through Christ, then why should you be concerned about sin in your life?

10. What might be some of the consequences of sexual sin that the authors speak about? What price(s) at the "toll bridge" could you imagine having to pay someday?

11. Think about the case of Jim, who was sexually active since he was twelve (now in his late twenties). How did his young-teen actions contribute to his struggles as an adult? Do you see any similar patterns in your own life?

12. What for you was the most meaningful concept or truth in chapters 3 and 4? What do you believe God wants you to do in response to this week's study?

13. How would you talk this over with God? Write down your response as a prayer to Him.

EVERY YOUNG MAN'S TALK
(Constructive Topics and Questions for Group Discussion, Chapters 3 and 4)

Key Highlights from the Book to Read Aloud and Discuss

> When I was fourteen, my sister's boyfriend, Brock, said to me with a wicked little grin, "Once you taste the candy, you'll never say no again. So you better not taste it!"
>
> Brock was right. Once you travel down the freeway of premarital sex, you can't back up. If you want your purity back, then you'll have to exit that freeway entirely.

> Let's go to the source and check out what the Bible has to say on the subject of sexual impurity. Did you know that in nearly every book of the New Testament we're commanded to avoid sexual impurity? Here's a selection of passages that teach God's concern for our sexual purity...

> Like Pinocchio, maybe you think Adventure Island will bring you great amusement at no charge, although you know you're not supposed to go there. But there *will* be a price to pay at the end of the day, and it will be a heavy one.

Discussion Questions for Chapters 3 and 4

A. Which parts of chapters 3 and 4 were most helpful or encouraging to you, and why?

B. Go back to the beginning paragraphs of chapter 3. Would you say that

you are most like Tyler, Brad, John, or the good kid at church? Explain
your response to the other guys in the group.

C. Think about Brock's statement for a moment. If you've "tasted the
candy," do you agree that you can't back up? What, in practical terms,
does it mean to "exit the freeway"?

D. Together, review the Bible passages presented toward the end of chapter 3. Pick your favorite—the scripture that means the most to you
right now—and share why it has such an impact on you.

E. Talk about the experience of Pinocchio as described in chapter 4. As
you feel comfortable doing so, tell about any kinds of "prices" you
may have had to pay for sexual sin in your life. (Perhaps it's just a feeling of guilt or lowered self-esteem. Talk about it!)

F. The second half of chapter 4 reveals the fact that even marriage is no
sexual nirvana. Does this surprise you? What practical application(s)
for young men do you find in this truth?

Note: If you're following a twelve-week track,
save the rest of this lesson for the next session.
If you are on an eight-week track, keep going.

☑ EVERY YOUNG MAN'S CHOICE
(Questions for Personal Reflection and Examination, Chapters 5 and 6)

📖 Something was gripping me, something relentless, something I couldn't shake. And my friendship with Christ? Our
relationship had changed. He hadn't changed, but I had. I
had stopped short of His standard, and I had stopped moving closer into intimacy. I'd said no in my spirit too often,
and that stopped the flow of His inner power. I was in
bondage. 📖

📖 Our very maleness—and three male tendencies in particular—represents the second main reason (in addition to
"stopping short") for the pervasiveness of sexual impurity
among men. 📖

14. Can you relate to Fred's description of bondage to sexual sin? Think
about your own experience: What forms of no have you said to the
Spirit in the past? What kinds of yes would you like to be saying
instead?

15. Review the three male tendencies outlined in chapter 6. Reflect on
how you have experienced these in your own life. Also consider: How
have you been receiving sexual gratification through your eyes lately?

👟 EVERY YOUNG MAN'S WALK
(Your Guide to Personal Application, Chapters 5 and 6)

📖 So often there's no challenging voice calling us to obedience and authenticity. Instead, we move nearer our peers,
often sitting together on the middle ground, a good distance
from God. When challenged by His higher standards, we're
comforted that we don't look too different from other Christians around us. Trouble is, as we've seen, we don't look
much different from non-Christians either. 📖

📖 Your "addictive behaviors" are not rooted in some deep,
dark, shadowy mental maze or weakness. Rather, they're
based on pleasure highs that enter through the eyes. Men
receive a chemical high from sexually charged images when a
hormone called epinephrine is secreted into the bloodstream.
This locks into the memory whatever stimulus is present at
the time of the emotional excitement.

Therefore, our "mind's eye" can cause the same chemical high through fantasy. 📖

16. Who is challenging you to obedience these days? How hard or easy is it for you to respond to God's higher standard?

17. Have you ever thought that your repeated misbehaviors meant there was something "deep, dark, and shadowy" about you? According to the authors, what is the basic message that goes against this idea? What is the status of your "mind's eye" lately? Is it doing what you want it to do?

18. What is the difference between maleness and manhood? Which are you choosing?

19. What for you was the most meaningful concept or truth in chapters 5 and 6? What do you believe God wants you to do in response to this week's study?

20. How would you talk this over with God? Write down your response as a prayer to Him.

👤👤 EVERY YOUNG MAN'S TALK

(Constructive Topics and Questions for Group Discussion, Chapters 5 and 6)

Key Highlights from the Book to Read Aloud and Discuss

📖 When I confided in a close friend, he replied, "Oh, come on! Nobody can control his eyes and mind, for heaven's sakes! God loves you! It must be something else." But I knew differently.

I finally made the connection between my sexual immorality and my distance from God. Having eliminated the visible adulteries and pornography, and having avoided physical adultery, I looked pure on the outside to everyone else. But to God, I had stopped short.... I'd merely found a comfortable middle ground somewhere between paganism and obedience to God's standard. 📖

📖 So...are you being authentic? I once asked Thomas, a youth pastor, to describe the level of authenticity he saw within his young flock.

"Not much," was his terse reply.

I asked him to expound. "They seem to have great intentions," he noted. "They desire to be used by God. Trouble is, they won't step out. When I ask them, 'Why aren't you hungrier for God?' I know the answer already. They don't want to stand out. They don't want to put out the effort. They just want to be accepted." 📖

📖 Prayer alone is often not enough for total victory. We can go to the altar of prayer and be freed, but if we stop short and never fully close the gates of our eyes to sensual pollution, the sewage seeps right back in, day in and day out. The chemical highs return, and we're captured again.

So while we're to pray about sexual sin on the *spiritual* front, we have our orders on the *physical* battlefront as well. 📖

Discussion Questions for Chapters 5 and 6

G. How can you tell if you are stopping short of God's standard for sexual purity? What does this mean for you in practical terms?

H. How hard would it be for you to stand out in your youth or other type of group at church? Why? Is being authentic worth the potential rejection by your peers?

I. Do you agree that prayer alone will not keep you from sexual sin? What else is needed? Why?

J. Look again at the case of Kerry, described toward the end of chapter 6. If he were your best friend, what would be your advice to him?

K. What does it mean for a guy to pursue manhood over maleness? What encouragement or support can your group members give each other? List some practical actions you are willing to commit to together.

choosing authentic manhood

This week's reading assignment:

chapters 7–8 of *Every Young Man's Battle*

"How long will you be unclean?" (Jeremiah 13:27). That's the question for you as well: How long will you choose to be sexually unclean? How long will you keep shutting down the new life within you?

We've seen what God expects…. We've seen it can be done. Jesus and Job were authentic men, and they didn't mix standards even when their lives were on the line. Are you God's man, hearing the Word and doing it? If you want to turn things around, authenticity with God is the place to start.

—from chapter 7 of *Every Young Man's Battle*

📖 EVERY YOUNG MAN'S TRUTH
(Your Personal Journey into God's Word)

Before you jump into this study, take some time with your Bible. Below you'll find three passages of scripture that speak directly of God's will for your sexuality. Basically, they say: *Stay pure!* This can't be accomplished by sheer willpower, however. Read carefully and with an open heart. Ask the Lord to show you exactly what it means for you to rely on His strength in the challenge to live each day in a way that pleases Him. Be assured: He *will* answer and reward your commitment to purity.

> Blessed are they whose ways are blameless,
>> who walk according to the law of the LORD.
> Blessed are they who keep his statutes
>> and seek him with all their heart.
> They do nothing wrong;
>> they walk in his ways.
> How can a young man keep his way pure?...
>> By living according to your word. (Psalm 119:1-3,9)

> Among you there must not be even a hint of sexual immorality, or of any kind of impurity, or of greed, because these are improper for God's holy people. Nor should there be obscenity, foolish talk or coarse joking, which are out of place, but rather thanksgiving. For of this you can be sure: No immoral, impure or greedy person—such a man is an idolater—has any inheritance in the kingdom of Christ and of God. Let no one deceive you with empty words, for because of such things God's wrath comes on those who are disobedient.... Be very careful, then, how you live—not as unwise but as wise. (Ephesians 5:3-6,15)

> It is God's will that you should be sanctified: that you should avoid sexual immorality; that each of you should learn to control his own body in a way that is holy and honorable, not in passionate lust like the heathen, who do not know God.... For God did not call us to be impure, but to live a holy life. (1 Thessalonians 4:3-5,7)

1. According to the psalmist, how can a young man stay pure? What would this look like in your life?

2. In Ephesians, the apostle Paul went into detail about the things a Christian is to avoid. Make your own list of contemporary things to avoid, based upon this passage. Ask the Lord to keep you free from each item.

3. The word *sanctified* means to be dedicated for God's use. Since God's will is that you be sanctified, what changes might be needed in your daily lifestyle?

4. Think about what living a sanctified life would be like—and then prayerfully invite the Spirit of God to help you live it!

☑ EVERY YOUNG MAN'S CHOICE
(Questions for Personal Reflection and Examination)

📖 Don't be discouraged. Instead, learn from Job.

First, we need to learn more about how Job did it. In Job 31:1, we see Job making this startling revelation: "I made a covenant with my eyes not to look lustfully at a girl." A covenant with his eyes! You mean he made a promise with his eyes to not gaze upon a young woman? 📖

📖 If you aren't trustworthy in handling fleshly passions, how can you be trusted to handle things of greater value? Jesus said that if you were faithful in the little things, He would entrust you with bigger things. In this, God isn't primarily referring to what He's called you to *do* in His kingdom. He's primarily concerned with what He's called you to *be* in your character. 📖

5. How does the idea of a covenant with your eyes strike you? Do you think you could make this kind of covenant before God?
6. What is the difference between seeing and gazing? What specific steps should we commit to ahead of time, in order to prevent one from becoming the other?
7. Think through the distinction between what you do and what you are. Why is your growth in character so important to the Lord?

EVERY YOUNG MAN'S WALK
(Your Guide to Personal Application)

📖 "Oh, don't be so hard on yourself," you might say. "It's natural for guys to look. That's part of our nature." But what you're doing is stealing. The impure thought life is the life of a thief. You're stealing images that aren't yours. 📖

📖 A few years back, Cyndi was known throughout her church as a girl who lived purely and radically for God, a high school student with high standards. I'll never forget a conversation I had with her. "Is it hard to hold such high standards like you do?" I asked.
"Oh, I don't mind being mocked," she replied. "Christ was mocked plenty. That's just part of it." 📖

📖 At Calvary, He purchased for you the freedom and authority to live in purity. That freedom and authority are His gifts to you through the presence of His Spirit, who took up residence within you when you gave your life to Christ. The freedom and authority are wrapped up in our new inner connection to His divine nature, which is the link that gives us His power and the fulfillment of His promises. 📖

8. Explain the logic behind the idea that looking is actually stealing. Do you agree or disagree? During the past week, have you been a thief in this manner?

9. What is your attitude toward someone like Cyndi? Do you respect her? Why or why not?

10. How would you describe to a non-Christian what Christ's death means to you? How does what happened at Calvary make a difference in how you will act today and tomorrow?

11. Think on the story of high school sophomore Ben (chapter 8). He came to the conclusion that he hadn't yet reached the point of hating his sin. Honestly consider: "Is that where I am too?"

12. In quietness, review what you have written and learned in this week's study. If further thoughts or prayer requests come to your mind and heart, you may want to write them down.

13. What for you was the most meaningful concept or truth in this week's study? What do you believe God wants you to do in response?

14. How would you talk this over with God? Write down your response as a prayer to Him.

👀 EVERY YOUNG MAN'S TALK
(Constructive Topics and Questions for Group Discussion)

Key Highlights from the Book to Read Aloud and Discuss

> 📖 You may be thinking, *Who in their right mind would ever make a covenant with his eyes like this? It seems crazy.* What I did on Merle Hay Road may seem odd to you. But remember, acts of obedience often appear strange, even illogical. 📖

> 📖 Have you had it with the running? In his early twenties, author and pastor Jack Hayford once sat in his car after a

banking transaction with a lovely bank teller and said to himself, "I'm either going to have to purify my mind and consecrate myself unto God, or I'm going to have to masturbate right here." That Jack could say this in front of tens of thousands of men at a Promise Keepers conference was inspirational. How about you? 📖

📖 Each one of us has been manipulated by our sexual culture; each of us has made choices to sin. To varying degrees, each of us became ensnared by these choices, but we can overcome this affliction. Far too often, however, we ignore our own responsibility in this. We complain, "Well, of course I want to be free from impurity! I've been to the altar 433 times about it, haven't I? It just doesn't seem to be God's will to free me." 📖

Discussion Questions

A. Fred resolved to make a covenant with his eyes, just as Job did in ancient times. Talk together about how guys can follow Job's example. Discuss all the obstacles that everyone would have to overcome.

B. Pastor Jack Hayford came to a point of decision. Have you been there yet? If so, what encouragement or advice can you give the other guys? If you haven't reached this point, what do you think it will take to reach bottom?

C. The authors point out that sex is everywhere—even in the church. Have you found this to be the case? Talk about it; how do you handle it in a way that is pleasing to God?

D. Discuss what the authors mean by having a low-grade sexual fever (chapter 8). Then respond to the three bulleted questions they suggest a feverish guy should ask himself.

E. How many in the group have prayed over and over again for deliverance from lust? What is the authors' answer to this situation? (Refer to the final six paragraphs of chapter 8).

Steve's long slide

This week's reading assignment:

chapter 9 of *Every Young Man's Battle*

I must stress this important truth. If you base your life on wanting to feel good, any time something feels good, you'll believe it's acceptable. Every time there are no consequences, you'll believe that it's even more acceptable. It's so tempting to live that way! The world is always screaming at you to do what you want when you want. If it makes you feel the way you want to feel, then go ahead.

So I never delayed gratification. Feeling good was the ultimate goal of my life.

—Steve Arterburn, from chapter 9 of *Every Young Man's Battle*

EVERY YOUNG MAN'S TRUTH
(Your Personal Journey into God's Word)

As soon as you make a covenant with your eyes and begin to live authentic manhood, temptations will likely increase. What will you do? Will you be able to stand your ground? The Bible passages below can help. Invite the Lord to speak to your heart as you claim these scriptures for guidance and rely on His strength in the battles ahead.

> So [Potiphar] left in Joseph's care everything he had…and
> after a while his master's wife took notice of Joseph and said,
> "Come to bed with me!"

But he refused.... "My master has withheld nothing from me except you, because you are his wife. How then could I do such a wicked thing and sin against God?" And though she spoke to Joseph day after day, he refused to go to bed with her or even be with her.

One day he went into the house to attend to his duties, and none of the household servants was inside. She caught him by his cloak and said, "Come to bed with me!" But he left his cloak in her hand and ran out of the house. (Genesis 39:6-12)

Count yourselves dead to sin but alive to God in Christ Jesus. Therefore do not let sin reign in your mortal body so that you obey its evil desires. Do not offer the parts of your body to sin, as instruments of wickedness, but rather offer yourselves to God, as those who have been brought from death to life; and offer the parts of your body to him as instruments of righteousness. For sin shall not be your master, because you are not under law, but under grace. (Romans 6:11-14)

His divine power has given us everything we need for life and godliness through our knowledge of him who called us by his own glory and goodness. (2 Peter 1:3)

1. What was the key to Joseph's success with sexual temptation? How would you apply this Bible passage to the temptations of pornography? lust? sex outside of marriage?
2. What does it mean that, as a believer, you are "dead to sin"? How does "offering yourself to God"—all the parts of your body—play a key role in making this a reality? Have you asked God how you can do this?

3. You have everything you need from God to resist temptation. So—what will you do the next time you are faced with sexual temptation?

☑ EVERY YOUNG MAN'S CHOICE
(Questions for Personal Reflection and Examination)

📖 While they were eight years older than I was, something happened when I found myself woven into the arms of these two roller-rink goddesses. I hadn't felt anything so intense, so magnificent since I walked down to the front of the church to accept Christ. 📖

📖 I had little to offer a girl, but I wanted everything from her. It didn't register with me that this was someone's future wife, or that she was a real human with real needs that I could meet. Instead, it was all about me and making me feel good. Had I been godly, she could have become *more* because of her relationship with me. Too often, she was *less* because I took from her only what a husband should take. 📖

4. Can you recall having an early experience like Steve's—when your sexuality was first awakened? What attitudes or patterns of behavior did that experience set in motion in your life?

5. What do you have to offer a young woman? Do you normally focus on what you have to give or—as Steve did—consider only what you can take?

6. What does it mean to help a girl become more rather than less because of her relationship with you? Are you willing, before God and the guys in your group, to make such a commitment?

🥾 EVERY YOUNG MAN'S WALK
(Your Guide to Personal Application)

📖 Compromise is a killer that seems so innocent in the beginning. Yet when you compromise and do a small thing you know isn't right, it rarely stays small or ends there. It becomes easier and easier to choose the wrong path the next time around.

Then it feels as if the wrong path begins to choose you. 📖

📖 All I wanted to do was to feel good, and I had decided long ago that I was willing to compromise to feel good. 📖

📖 If you connect the dots of my life—the cheating, the compromise, the masturbation, the early exposure to pornography, the objectification of women, and the promiscuity—you end up with an abortion.…

Examine the dots in your life. What picture forms behind you as you connect these dots on your walk to your future? 📖

7. Where do you find areas of killer compromise in your life these days? What steps do you need to take to stop the bleeding?
8. What are some of the destructive consequences of only wanting to feel good?
9. Take some time to connect the dots in your life so far. What patterns have they formed? Why?
10. Still thinking about your dots, consider: What kind of man do you want to become? Are the things you're doing today leading you to, or away from, that goal?

11. In quietness, review what you have written and learned in this week's study. If further thoughts or prayer requests come to your mind and heart, you may want to write them down.

12. What for you was the most meaningful concept or truth in this week's study? What do you believe God wants you to do in response?

13. How would you talk this over with God? Write down your response as a prayer to Him.

EVERY YOUNG MAN'S TALK
(Constructive Topics and Questions for Group Discussion)

Key Highlights from the Book to Read Aloud and Discuss

    📖 I thought nothing could feel as good as becoming a Christian, but rolling around the rink with those two perfect "10s" was the discovery that there are some things in this world that can make a person feel *really* good. After that night, I decided I wanted to feel really good. And I decided that night to begin a search of all things that felt good. 📖

    📖 When you learned to masturbate, you didn't learn how to commit the unpardonable sin. You didn't engage in some perversion or do what only mentally ill people do. You did what almost everyone learns to do. For a few, the practice is of little consequence, but for many, it becomes a destructive habit or dependency.

    It certainly became a problem for me. 📖

    📖 The relationship broke up, as is usually the case, but the abortion didn't buy me peace. A simple thought continued to haunt me mercilessly. I hadn't simply purchased an abortion—I had killed my own child! That so-called glob of tissue was bone of my bone and flesh of my flesh. I had it snuffed out. 📖

Discussion Questions

A. Steve decided early in his life to search for what felt good. What are your reactions to this? Can you relate? Do you have a story to tell similar to Steve's roller-rink event?

B. Steve talks about not getting caught when cheating on a school test. How did that shape his future attitudes about sexual activity? What did he fail to realize in those early years?

C. How do you think Steve's grandfather's attitude toward pornography influenced Steve? Who, in your life, seems to have similar influence? How are you coping with that?

D. Consider Steve's thought (on the previous page) regarding masturbation. Is it true that it's of little consequence for some guys? How do you think the act become a self-destructive habit, as in Steve's case? What is your basic advice to other Christian guys about masturbation?

E. Steve's attitude about just feeling good eventually caused him great pain and loss. He even pushed a girl to get an abortion. How does his experience seem to fulfill what the Bible says in Galatians 6:8? What does this mean to you personally, and how would you apply it to your determination to live as God's man?

the M word

This week's reading assignment:

chapters 10–13 of *Every Young Man's Battle*

Since God didn't address masturbation directly in Scripture, the questions can seem endless. Theologians will argue over this until Christ returns, and maybe that's how it should be whenever Scripture is silent. Even we coauthors have found it difficult to decide together what to label masturbation and where to draw the lines of sin.

—from chapter 10 of *Every Young Man's Battle*

📖 EVERY YOUNG MAN'S TRUTH

(Your Personal Journey into God's Word)

The Bible passages below show an amazing contrast. In Romans 7, the apostle Paul wrote of his struggle with sin. He apparently had an ongoing battle with some kind of habit or addiction. Maybe he was too ashamed to name exactly what it was. But we do know that he felt powerless to overcome it by sheer willpower alone—until he found a way out *apart* from willpower, something he described in Romans 8.

So consider the role of willpower in your own life as you confront sexual temptation. First, feel Paul's pain in Romans 7. Surely you can relate to his sense of hopelessness as habitual sin threw him against the wall, time after time. Then move to Romans 8, and rejoice with Paul in his victory through Christ. Everything for him, and for you, depends on what is done with the mind. Is it given over to the sinful nature or to the Spirit of God?

> I do not understand what I do. For what I want to do I do not do, but what I hate I do. And if I do what I do not want to do, I agree that the law is good. As it is, it is no longer I myself who do it, but it is sin living in me. I know that nothing good lives in me, that is, in my sinful nature. For I have the desire to do what is good, but I cannot carry it out. For what I do is not the good I want to do; no, the evil I do not want to do—this I keep on doing. Now if I do what I do not want to do, it is no longer I who do it, but it is sin living in me that does it.
>
> So I find this law at work: When I want to do good, evil is right there with me…. What a wretched man I am! Who will rescue me from this body of death? (Romans 7:15-21,24)

> There is now no condemnation for those who are in Christ Jesus, because through Christ Jesus the law of the Spirit of life set me free from the law of sin and death. For what the law was powerless to do in that it was weakened by the sinful nature, God did by sending his own Son in the likeness of sinful man to be a sin offering. And so he condemned sin in sinful man, in order that the righteous requirements of the law might be fully met in us, who do not live according to the sinful nature but according to the Spirit.
>
> Those who live according to the sinful nature have their minds set on what that nature desires; but those who live in

accordance with the Spirit have their minds set on what the Spirit desires. The mind of sinful man is death, but the mind controlled by the Spirit is life and peace. (Romans 8:1-6)

1. Think about the habits in your life that you have tried and tried to overcome. When the great apostle Paul thought about his own sinful habits, he felt "wretched." Can you relate?

2. What does the passage in Romans 7 tell you about the strength of willpower? Why can't it break a sinful habit?

3. What awesome insight did the Lord give Paul in Romans 8? How does this apply to you when you face your destructive habits and addictions?

4. What is the key to overcoming the "law of sin and death"?

☑ EVERY YOUNG MAN'S CHOICE
(Questions for Personal Reflection and Examination, Chapters 10 and 11)

📖 What's so great with men I've worked with, who have been masturbating with pornography since they were teens, is that when they stop, they find there's a different world out there. They find that they can handle stress differently. When they go without masturbating for a month, they feel so clean and good about themselves. 📖

📖 When we masturbate, some of us come to our Father and say, "I've masturbated again, and I'm not worthy to be called Your son." He brushes that aside, saying, "No one but Jesus is *worthy* to be called My Son, but I love you and forgive you." He demonstrates that love by presenting us with a ring, robe, and shoes. Then He says, "In case you forgot, Jesus picked these up at Calvary for you. That makes you worthy enough for me. Now let's celebrate and enjoy each other!" 📖

5. How do you react to the statement that without masturbating, guys start feeling clean and good? Have you found this to be true in your own life? Why or why not?

6. What do the authors mean by saying that no one is worthy to be called God's son? How does their explanation help you when you're feeling guilty about falling to temptation?

👟 EVERY YOUNG MAN'S WALK
(Your Guide to Personal Application, Chapters 10 and 11)

> 📖 Many other issues besides family problems can prompt a young male to pleasure himself in order to mask the pain felt elsewhere in his life. Maybe a guy has acne problems or big ears or a lisp. Whatever. The point is, it doesn't do any good to pile a bucket-load of "You ain't no good" on top of him. Self-condemnation only sets the cycle of masturbation into a downward spiral, causing deeper embarrassment and humiliation. 📖

> 📖 This is what God is most concerned with. You're already His son. What He wants now is for you to move back closer to Him. 📖

7. What self-esteem issues might cause Christian guys to masturbate? Would you be willing to cite an example from your own life that could help the others in your group? Have you noticed the "downward spiral" that the authors speak of?

8. Take a long, careful look at how masturbation may be affecting your

relationship with God. What is required for you to move back closer to Him?

9. What for you was the most meaningful concept or truth in chapters 10 and 11? What do you believe God wants you to do in response?

10. How would you talk this over with God? Write down your response as a prayer to Him.

EVERY YOUNG MAN'S TALK

(Constructive Topics and Questions for Group Discussion, Chapters 10 and 11)

Key Highlights from the Book to Read Aloud and Discuss

In the last analysis, splitting hairs over what we call masturbation is silly. There are only two questions that matter. If you're in bondage to masturbation, should you try to break free? The answer is yes. Is it possible to break free? We believe it is.

When we sin, God doesn't shout, "Hell and damnation on you!" Since we're saved, He knows full well that there's now no more condemnation for us because of Christ. Remember, He personally had the apostles write that into the Bible! Jesus paid it all. Our Father isn't interested in making us pay further by adding shame after another orgasmic failure in cyberspace.

God, your Father, is *for* you.

We hope that thousands of readers of this book will decide to stop pouring gasoline on a hot fire of passion, desire, and lust. We're about to show you how, and we believe that those who take this path will never regret it. We don't expect anyone, after having applied the forthcoming advice, to later declare, "Gee, I just wish I had masturbated more." 📖

Discussion Questions for Chapters 10 and 11

A. Which parts of these chapters were most helpful or encouraging to you? Why?

B. Talk about the themes the authors raise at the beginning of chapter 10 (pages 107–8). Where do you tend to land in your view of masturbation—is it sin or not?

C. Do you agree that the key question is not whether masturbation is sin but rather: "If you're in bondage to masturbation, should you try to break free"? Why or why not?

D. What does "Jesus paid it all" mean to you? Tell how this biblical truth can apply to a guy's struggles with lust—and with guilt.

E. How do guys tend to pour gasoline on their sexual desire? Do you believe this habit can be stopped? How?

F. Together, turn to the four requirements to stop masturbating offered at the end of chapter 11 (under "Being Free from Sexual Fevers"). Talk about the practical applications of each step. Discuss the difficulties a guy might face in putting these requirements into practice.

Note: If you're following a twelve-week track,
save the rest of this lesson for the next session.
If you are on an eight-week track, keep going.

☑ EVERY YOUNG MAN'S CHOICE

(Questions for Personal Reflection and Examination, Chapters 12 and 13)

    📖 Loneliness, insecurity, and broken family relationships are often the steppingstones to masturbation. We replace that lost intimacy with the false intimacy of masturbation. A close relationship with God and our friends will make the false intimacy of masturbation unnecessary. 📖

    📖 Perhaps you've felt the same type of anger and pain in your family relationships. Such anger often opens a door to pornography and masturbation. The desire to become close to *somebody* can also drive you quickly into the arms of women or one-sided friendships. Rather than turn to God, you truly can begin looking for love in all the wrong places, hoping for something, anything, to take the place of that loss. 📖

11. Right now, prayerfully search your life: Where do you find loneliness? Insecurity? Broken relationships? Lost intimacy? What lost intimacy in your relationships do you tend to replace with masturbation?

12. Have you noticed that you tend to move toward pornography when you are angry, tired, hungry, or frustrated in some way? In what ways might you tend to "look for love in all the wrong places"? How have you felt inside, spiritually, when you've done so?

👟 EVERY YOUNG MAN'S WALK

(Your Guide to Personal Application, Chapters 12 and 13)

    📖 I'll never forget the day when I (Fred) came home from elementary school, tripping quickly down the school bus steps with my sisters and rushing into the house to eat cookies, then to go outdoors to play army and float boats down the creek. When we entered the house, however, my mother called the three of us into the living room to talk. She *never* did that, so I sensed that something serious had happened. 📖

📖 Once you decide to starve Mr. Sex Drive, however, his weight and heft will shrink. He'll shed pounds overnight. All you have to do is stop feeding him the cable TV, videos, Internet, magazines, and fantasy. 📖

13. Think carefully about the impact his parents' divorce had on Fred. How did he react to his pain and loss? In what negative ways might you be reacting to pain and loss in your own life?

14. Why do you think inner pain and sexual desire are so related? How do you notice this in your actions?

15. What first step could you take to begin starving your sumo sex drive?

16. What for you was the most meaningful concept or truth in chapters 12 and 13? What do you believe God wants you to do in response?

17. How would you talk this over with God? Write your response here as a prayer to Him.

👤👤 EVERY YOUNG MAN'S TALK

(Constructive Topics and Questions for Group Discussion, Chapters 12 and 13)

Key Highlights from the Book to Read Aloud and Discuss

📖 Another episode occurred when I was fourteen. Dad called Mom early one week and gave her the following order: "Have Freddie ready for me to pick up Friday night at seven o'clock. I've got a clean prostitute arranged for the evening. It's time for him to learn about love." He didn't understand why my mother and I were repulsed by the bizarre idea. 📖

📖 God turns to you and says, "Get into the ring." So you obey, but Mr. Sex Drive knocks you clean into the wall again.

Turning to God with pleading eyes, you cry, "See, God? Save me from this monster! Don't You love me?"

"Of course I love you," says the Creator of the universe. "Don't you love Me?"

"Lord, you know that I do!"

"Then starve the sumo!" 📖

📖 If you can't control your sex drive, whose fault is it? Is it God's, for giving you the sex drive? Or is it yours, because you've jumped on the gas pedal and sped past the red line far too often? 📖

Discussion Questions for Chapters 12 and 13

G. What do you think Fred's father's prostitute arrangement would do in the heart of a young man? What problems did this cause for Fred?

H. Consider the benefit of forming accountability relationships. Together, read through the part in chapter 12 in which Ron checks up on Nathan (page 126). What do you think of this form of accountability? Would it work for you? Why or why not?

I. What does it really take to starve the sumo? Generate a list of practical actions guys can take to make this powerful wrestler lose weight.

J. Have you ever been tempted to blame God for your lack of sexual control? According to the authors, what is wrong with the logic behind that approach? What is the better way?

setting your defenses

[Satan's] greatest attack weapon will be deception. He knows Jesus has already pur-
chased your freedom. He also knows that once you understand how to starve Mr.
Sex Drive, you'll probably push the big fellow right out of the ring in short order. So
he deceives and confuses. He tricks you into thinking that you're a helpless victim.
He tells you that sexual sin is just part of being a man and that there's nothing you
can or should do about it. He tells you that you don't need to live a life of obedience
because obedience *is just another word for legalism.*

—from chapter 14 of *Every Young Man's Battle*

📖 EVERY YOUNG MAN'S TRUTH
(Your Personal Journey into God's Word)

The Bible passages below are excellent resources for spiritual battle and will
help you set up your defenses as you fight for personal purity. Remember
that this battle's basic strategy is simply to rely on the Lord, by faith, day by
day. But that doesn't mean you have nothing to do! In response to God's
goodness and power in your life, you are called to fill your eyes, your mind,
and your heart with all that is good. In addition, you can take up your

spiritual armor and fight off the subtle lies and temptations that are sure to hurtle your way. In other words, you have tremendous resources available for this fight; use them!

> I made a covenant with my eyes not to look lustfully at a girl. (Job 31:1)

> Be strong in the Lord and in his mighty power. Put on the full armor of God so that you can take your stand against the devil's schemes. For our struggle is not against flesh and blood, but against the rulers, against the authorities, against the powers of this dark world and against the spiritual forces of evil in the heavenly realms. Therefore put on the full armor of God, so that when the day of evil comes, you may be able to stand your ground, and after you have done everything, to stand. Stand firm then, with the belt of truth buckled around your waist, with the breastplate of righteousness in place, and with your feet fitted with the readiness that comes from the gospel of peace. In addition to all this, take up the shield of faith, with which you can extinguish all the flaming arrows of the evil one. Take the helmet of salvation and the sword of the Spirit, which is the word of God. And pray in the Spirit on all occasions with all kinds of prayers and requests. With this in mind, be alert and always keep on praying for all the saints. (Ephesians 6:10-18)

> Flee from sexual immorality. All other sins a man commits are outside his body, but he who sins sexually sins against his own body. Do you not know that your body is a temple of the Holy Spirit, who is in you, whom you have received

from God? You are not your own; you were bought at a
price. Therefore honor God with your body (1 Corinthians
6:18-20)

1. How do you define "looking lustfully" at a girl? Answer thoughtfully
   and honestly: Does your definition allow you to rationalize an improper gaze or thought? Are you clear about the boundary lines you've
   promised God you will not cross?
2. Prayerfully study the pieces of spiritual armor laid out in Ephesians 6.
   Which do you most need today? (Suggestion: Imagine taking each
   piece into your hands. Then ask God to bless you as you put it on
   and use it.)
3. The passage in 1 Corinthians can act as a powerful shield against
   temptation. For example: How does it help you to recall that your
   body is where God's Spirit lives? And what impact does this idea
   have—that your body has been bought by the Lord?

☑ EVERY YOUNG MAN'S CHOICE
(Questions for Personal Reflection and Examination, Chapters 14 and 15)

📖 For teens and young adults, sexual gratification comes
from three places: the eyes, the mind, and the body. Therefore, as in any war, you must blockade the "shipping lanes"
of the eyes and mind that drive you toward sexual sin and
that keep your enemy strong. 📖

📖 It may be useful to memorize several verses of Scripture
about purity.... But in the cold-turkey, day-to-day fight
against impurity, having several memory verses might be as
cumbersome as strapping on a hundred-pound backpack to

engage in hand-to-hand combat. You aren't agile enough to
maneuver quickly.

  That's why we recommend a single "attack verse," and
it better be quick. 📖

4. How well have you been blockading the shipping lanes to your eyes
   and mind? What helps the most? What tends to mess you up?
5. Why is it best to have a quick-and-easy verse to recall when temptation hits?
6. What is your chosen attack verse? When did you last use it? How
   well did it work? (If you have not yet selected one, prayerfully choose
   one from the passages above and begin to commit it to memory
   this week.)

👟 EVERY YOUNG MAN'S WALK
(Your Guide to Personal Application, Chapters 14 and 15)

  📖 There'll always be spiritual opposition. The enemy
constantly whispers in your ear. He doesn't want you
to win this fight, and he knows the lies that break down
a young man's confidence and will to win. You can expect
to hear lies and plenty of them. Here's a list of some of
the all-time favorites… 📖

  📖 Your first step is listing your own "greatest enemies."…
  In choosing them, remember that they must be areas
from which you visually draw sexual satisfaction. 📖

7. Review Satan's lies (and the countering truths) found on page 144.
   Which of these lies are you most often tempted to believe? What effect

have these lies had on your spiritual morale? How can you build up your truth defenses in this area?

8. Take plenty of time to consider your personal greatest enemies. Then respond to the authors' questions: What are the most obvious and prolific sources of sensual images coming your way? Where do you look most often? Where are you weakest?

9. Re-read the case of Derrick found on pages 160–61. What was his basic problem? Where have you, too, stepped outside your rights lately? How could you make a change for the better?

10. What for you was the most meaningful concept or truth in chapters 14 and 15? What do you believe God wants you to do in response?

11. How would you talk this over with God? Write down your response as a prayer to Him.

🙂🙃 EVERY YOUNG MAN'S TALK
(Constructive Topics and Questions for Group Discussion, Chapters 14 and 15)

Key Highlights from the Book to Read Aloud and Discuss

📖 You want your heart to be right and your boundaries clear. To accomplish this, you need to build three perimeters of defense into your life:

1. You need to build a line of defense with your *eyes.*

2. You need to build a line of defense in your *mind.*

3. You need to build a line of defense in your *heart.* 📖

📖 I (Fred) had no problem coming up with a list of my six biggest areas of weakness. Let me share how I dealt with them... 📖

📖 Consider a specific example. I (Fred) recall once walking down a hotel hallway to the ice machine. On top of the machine lay a *Playboy* magazine. Believing I had a right to choose my behavior, I asked myself this question: *Should I look at this* Playboy *or not?* 📖

Discussion Questions for Chapters 14 and 15

A. Which parts of these chapters were most helpful or encouraging to you, and why?

B. Of the three lines of defense you need, name the one that is strongest at this time in your life. Which is the weakest? Have the guys in your group suggest ways you can shore up this weak area.

C. The authors say that, with the habit of sexual impurity, the best method is not a gradual reduction. Instead, you must go cold turkey. Do you agree? Why or why not?

D. Take some time to let each guy talk about his own Six Biggest Areas of Weakness. Then discuss how effective Fred's methods of defense would be in your own life.

E. Ask some volunteers to talk about how they have been doing with their "eye covenant." Unite in prayer that each group member would be strong in his commitment.

F. Have a discussion about Fred's experience at the hotel with *Playboy*. What did you learn from Fred that you could add to your lines of defense in such situations?

G. At the end of chapter 15, Fred and Steve admit that maybe their plan sounds a little crazy. How do you respond to that? If you've been attempting to implement their plan, tell your group how it's going so far.

Note: If you're following a twelve-week track,
save the rest of this lesson for the next session.
If you are on an eight-week track, keep going.

☑ EVERY YOUNG MAN'S CHOICE
(Questions for Personal Reflection and Examination,
Chapters 16 and 17)

📖 You have a flood on your hands, and that flood has to settle back into its banks. This means your sex drive has to dry up to normal levels as a drought of images and orgasms has its natural effect. That will take some time—probably more than three weeks. 📖

📖 It's so important to remember that God once looked upon His only begotten Son in Gethsemane as He struggled to submit in the biggest battle of His life. Jesus' submission was precious to the Father. Now this same Father is looking down from heaven upon you, His adopted son, as you struggle to submit in *your* battle for sexual purity. Sure, He wants victory, but...the very fact that you've entered the fray is precious to Him. 📖

12. Were you expecting a quick victory against sexual impurity? If so, how do you respond to the authors' warnings about slow-downs?

13. How does God view you these days? (Suggestion: Imagine being God

for a moment; draw a picture of your adopted son. Label it with how you feel about this young man.)

👟 EVERY YOUNG MAN'S WALK
(Your Guide to Personal Application, Chapters 16 and 17)

> 📖 Another reason the process may slow down is that your commitment and discipline to this process of purity may take some time to kick in. Our society doesn't glorify discipline all that much, especially in high school. This means it may take you some time to learn a disciplined lifestyle. 📖

> 📖 Like the father in the prodigal son story, your heavenly Father is thrilled just to see you at the crest of the hill walking toward Him. If you stumble a bit as you come home, it won't change the fact that He is eagerly waiting for you to arrive. Just get up and get walking again. Reject discouragement and fall into His arms. 📖

14. How disciplined are you, in general? What about in the area of sexual purity? What is the next step for you?
15. Jot down a plan to reject discouragement the next time you fail.
16. The authors warn against viewing your sexuality as something shamefully separate and distinct from you. What would help you remember that God gave you your body, your desires, and your sexuality?
17. What for you was the most meaningful concept or truth in chapters 16 and 17? What do you believe God wants you to do in response?
18. How would you talk this over with God? Write your response here as a prayer to Him.

👀 EVERY YOUNG MAN'S TALK

(Constructive Topics and Questions for Group Discussion, Chapters 16 and 17)

Key Highlights from the Book to Read Aloud and Discuss

📖 *Eric says:* "Porn leaves a big hole of emptiness, but I cannot get myself to turn away from it when I'm the only one in my lonely apartment. I've tried bouncing my eyes, but that's as far as I can go. What happens after that is that I cannot concentrate on my work. I can't get anything done because sex constantly floods my preoccupations and thoughts." 📖

📖 While we're talking about discipline, let's go beyond our concern for our eyes. We must also be concerned with where we place ourselves in other ways. 📖

📖 For me (Steve) the most difficult part of this book is providing a standard for you that doesn't inflict needless shame but instead guides you toward a life of meaningful relationships and lays a foundation for your sexuality being fully integrated into your marriage relationship. 📖

Discussion Questions for Chapters 16 and 17

H. Consider Eric's statement about pornography. If you were his best friend, what would you advise him to do?

I. David made this comment (page 167): "I'm sorry, but telling a man he should go at his wife with great gusto and then telling the single guy to wait for a nocturnal emission is insane!" Do you agree or disagree? Why?

J. Together, read through the experiences of Tim, Mike, Dave, and Josh in the last three paragraphs of chapter 16 (pages 170–71). Talk about the places where you have trouble with increased temptation—and also talk about what has worked for you in winning this battle.

K. Take turns giving your reactions to this statement on page 173: "Don't view your sexuality as something shamefully separate and distinct from the rest of you."

L. The authors say that God knows what we're made of, and nothing surprises Him. What does this mean to you personally? In what ways does it encourage you?

M. Steve states that he wants to find a balance between (1) holding up a high standard for you to pursue, and (2) not piling on the guilt and shame. Do you think the authors have succeeded so far? Why or why not?

from mustang to honor

This week's reading assignment:

chapters 18–21 of *Every Young Man's Battle*

Can you control the mustang? Can you run him down on foot or simply wag your finger and admonish him? No, of course not....

    Your mind runs like a mustang. What's more, your mind "mates" where it wills with attractive, sensual girls. They're everywhere. With a mustang mind, how do you stop the running and the mating? With a corral around your mind.

—from chapter 19 of *Every Young Man's Battle*

📖 EVERY YOUNG MAN'S TRUTH

(Your Personal Journey into God's Word)

Before you begin this session, take some time to prepare your heart through Bible study. The passages below deal with a key aspect of successful Christian living—relying on the Holy Spirit. The great thing is, you do have an inner helper, the Spirit of God, living inside you. He wants you to succeed in your efforts to avoid impurity of any kind. If you let Him, the Spirit will give you the strength, in the midst of the most powerful temptations, to loosen your grip on lust, to ask yourself: *What do I really want?*, to just walk away.

I tell you the truth, anyone who has faith in me will do what I have been doing. He will do even greater things than these, because I am going to the Father. And I will do whatever you ask in my name, so that the Son may bring glory to the Father. You may ask me for anything in my name, and I will do it.

If you love me, you will obey what I command. And I will ask the Father, and he will give you another Counselor to be with you forever—the Spirit of truth. (John 14:12-17)

The Spirit helps us in our weakness. We do not know what we ought to pray for, but the Spirit himself intercedes for us with groans that words cannot express. And he who searches our hearts knows the mind of the Spirit, because the Spirit intercedes for the saints in accordance with God's will....

And we know that in all things God works for the good of those who love him, who have been called according to his purpose. (Romans 8:26-28)

Flee from sexual immorality. All other sins a man commits are outside his body, but he who sins sexually sins against his own body. Do you not know that your body is a temple of the Holy Spirit, who is in you, whom you have received from God? You are not your own; you were bought at a price. Therefore honor God with your body. (1 Corinthians 6:18-20)

1. Why would Jesus call the Spirit a "Counselor"?
2. When have you most needed counsel from God's Spirit? Why not take a moment right now to ask Him for guidance?
3. Ever had difficulty praying? What awesome ministry does the Holy Spirit have for you when it comes to prayer?

4. Where does the Holy Spirit dwell? How does it make you feel to know that your body is a temple for Him?

☑ EVERY YOUNG MAN'S CHOICE
(Questions for Personal Reflection and Examination, Chapters 18 and 19)

> 📖 Every battle in life is hard, but with victory comes the spoils. So what are the "spoils" if you construct that perimeter around your eyes? Well, you're going to feel great about yourself, about your life, and about your future. 📖

> 📖 Currently, your brain moves nimbly to lust and to the little pleasure-high it brings. Your brain's worldview has always included lustful thinking. Double entendres, daydreams, and other creative forms of sexual thinking are approved pathways, so your mind feels free to run on these paths to pleasure. 📖

5. If you have been attempting to keep the covenant with your eyes, do you feel as if you've experienced some of the rewards—the spoils of victory? If so, take a moment to give thanks to God!
6. The authors explain that your mind is wild and will continue to lust as you seek to retrain it. How have you noticed this? What has been your usual response during the past week?

👟 EVERY YOUNG MAN'S WALK
(Your Guide to Personal Application, Chapters 18 and 19)

> 📖 Have you "lurked at your neighbor's door"?… This can easily refer to you as a young, single male. Lurking could mean stealing glances at her rack and rear. Lurking could

mean roaming in areas you shouldn't be accessing on the
World Wide Web. 📖

📖 There are young women you know who hit every attraction key on your keyboard—like Rachel, that new student,
or maybe the new girl in the worship band who makes
you breathless every time she gets up and sings. You neigh,
drawing them toward your corral, but only in your mind....
But you must lead her out of your corral and stop lurking. 📖

7. What forms of "lurking" seem to plague you the most?
8. When it comes to girls who hit your attraction key, what is your
defense strategy? (Hint: Review the scripture attack verse you memorized a couple of sessions ago.) How well is it working?
9. What for you was the most meaningful concept or truth in chapters
18 and 19? What do you believe God wants you to do in response?
10. How would you talk this over with God? Write down your response
as a prayer to Him.

👦👦 EVERY YOUNG MAN'S TALK
(Constructive Topics and Questions for Group Discussion, Chapters 18 and 19)

Key Highlights from the Book to Read Aloud and Discuss

📖 Garrett began his story by noting that he was raised in
the church, but by the time he was a senior in high school,
he was drinking heavily, keeping a case of Bud longnecks
iced up in a cooler that he kept in his trunk.... 📖

📖 There's nothing wrong with our attractions. Many of us
have been lost in our attractions. You may be lost in one right

now. I (Fred) got lost in high school with Julie. I noticed her early in my senior year, when Julie was a junior. 📖

📖 Don't you owe it to the Lord to put up a mental defense perimeter? If not, you'll have a sad story to tell, like the one we heard from Jake. He was the student leader of a youth group, along with four others, including Gina. He was standing strong and respected throughout the church. He had no mental defense perimeter, however, because he blissfully thought he didn't need one. As a result he allowed Gina to come too close to his corral. 📖

Discussion Questions for Chapters 18 and 19

A. Which parts of these chapters were most helpful or encouraging to you? Why?

B. Together, read back through the story of Garrett. What aspects of his experience ring a bell with you? Why? What good and bad decisions do you see him making?

C. Garrett reported that when he stayed close to the Word, it was easier for him to bounce his eyes. Have you noticed something similar in your own battle? Share your thoughts with the others in your group.

D. Review Fred's story about his so-called date with Julie (pages 189–91). Name some things that any guy can learn from this story.

E. Retrace the story of Jake's downfall (pages 193–94). What poor decisions did he make? What are the things Jake should have done?

Note: If you're following a twelve-week track,
save the rest of this lesson for the next session.
If you are on an eight-week track, keep going.

☑ EVERY YOUNG MAN'S CHOICE
(Questions for Personal Reflection and Examination, Chapters 20 and 21)

📖 I know you're my Christian brother, and I want to count on you to stand shoulder to shoulder with me in this call I have from God. Yes, I'm in my early forties and you may be in your teens or early twenties, but I'm as much your brother as your buddies are, and I'm counting on you not to lay your hands on my daughter just as much as your best friend is counting on you not to lay your hands on his girlfriend. Honor me in this. 📖

📖 Look at Uriah! He was so consumed by the purposes of God that he refused to go to his house even to wash his feet. His faithfulness and honor were so strong that, even when drunk, he didn't waver and wander on home for a little sack time with his own wife! Do you honor God's purposes like that? 📖

11. How does it feel to hear from a father regarding his daughter? Are you ready to honor Fred, Steve, and the other fathers of daughters you may date? What, exactly, does *honor* mean for you?

12. Review the Bible story of Uriah, described on pages 203–5. Have you ever been called to maintain the kind of discipline this man displayed? If so, how did you respond? If not, what do you think you would do in a future situation involving similar choices?

13. Amber spoke of the insecurity of many girls, which spurs them to give in to guys who are pushing for sexual intimacy. What would keep you from taking advantage of a girl like that?

👟 EVERY YOUNG MAN'S WALK

(Your Guide to Personal Application, Chapters 20 and 21)

> 📖 One of the biggest calls God has placed on *my* life is depending upon *your* character if you're alone with my Laura. That should make me uneasy, and it does. 📖

> 📖 Too often the only leadership we take is to charge across [a girl's] sexual boundaries. "Girls want guys to take the lead in the relationship," said Cassie. "Yet often it's the guys who are pushing the boundaries. When that has happened to me, I felt very resentful. I know that it makes girls just feel used. We neither feel validated in who we are nor in what we stand for as women." 📖

14. Imagine you're with Laura in a tempting situation. How much will you allow yourself to hear father Fred's words at that point? What would help you prepare in advance?

15. Why is it so important for the guy to take leadership in setting the sexual boundaries? (Suggestion: Think through exactly what your boundaries are going to be in the future. Be specific and detailed. Then ask the Lord to help you stick to your decision.)

16. The authors say, "It's not the act of defining sexual boundaries that makes you a spiritual leader. It's the act of defending them." Why is this distinction an important one?

17. What for you were the most meaningful concepts or truths in chapters 20 and 21? What do you believe God wants you to do in response to this week's study?

18. How would you talk this over with God? Write down your response as a prayer to Him.

🙂🙂 EVERY YOUNG MAN'S TALK

(Constructive Topics and Questions for Group Discussion, Chapters 20 and 21)

Key Highlights from the Book to Read Aloud and Discuss

📖 Danny and Uriah are cut from the same cloth. Young men like Danny have real honor, courage, and love. 📖

📖 The biggest difference is that sex is not a girl's top priority in the relationship, and you need to understand this very clearly. Maybe it can most simply be said this way:

• Guys give emotions so they can get sex.
• Girls give sex so they can get the emotions.

Guys, girls want a relationship with you, but they should not have to give sex to get it. 📖

Discussion Questions for Chapters 20 and 21

F. Read aloud the first five paragraphs of chapter 20. What is your response to Fred's attitudes about his responsibilities in raising his daughter Laura? Imagine yourself the father of an attractive teenage daughter. Do you understand where Fred is coming from?

G. Discuss the various lines of defense Danny set for himself (pages 205–7). Evaluate each one based on how practical it would be for you to use. What do you like or dislike about each of Danny's decisions?

H. You may be saying, "Wait a minute. The girls I know sure look like they're all about sex." Is this really a true statement? Talk about it!

I. Discuss the differences in guys' and girls' attitudes toward sex in general. Do you agree that guys give emotions to get sex and girls give sex to get emotions? If so, what are some practical applications in your relationships with girls?

J. Toward the end of chapter 21, the question is raised: "How far can we go?" Discuss this together, taking into account everything you've learned so far in this study.

ready for the challenge?

This week's reading assignment:
chapters 22–23 of *Every Young Man's Battle*

Amber is a twenty-year-old single woman at a Bible college. When I told her that I was writing this book…she said, "I wish I would have been told more specifically what 'sexual purity' really meant when I was growing up in the church. I was always taught that sexual purity meant 'no sexual intercourse,' but then I loved [your] definition: 'Sexual purity is receiving no sexual gratification from anything or anyone outside of your husband or wife.' That's a black-and-white definition that young people need to be taught. If you don't do anything else, please stress this definition."

—Fred Stoeker, from chapter 22 of *Every Young Man's Battle*

📖 EVERY YOUNG MAN'S TRUTH
(Your Personal Journey into God's Word)

Congratulations! You've come to the final session in this study guide. We hope that you have learned, grown, and changed significantly during the past several weeks. We also hope that your relationship with God has deepened and that your sense of personal honor and integrity has generated a new level of peace and joy in your heart.

Before you launch into our final challenge to you, take a few moments to read and meditate on the following Bible passages, which focus on the theme of "Living by Faith." Take these words from God into your heart. And ask the Lord to make them real and practical to you as you continue to fight every young man's battle, day by day.

"O unbelieving generation," Jesus replied, "how long shall I stay with you? How long shall I put up with you? Bring the boy to me."

So they brought him. When the spirit saw Jesus, it immediately threw the boy into a convulsion. He fell to the ground and rolled around, foaming at the mouth.

Jesus asked the boy's father, "How long has he been like this?"

"From childhood," he answered. "It has often thrown him into fire or water to kill him. But if you can do anything, take pity on us and help us."

"'If you can'?" said Jesus. "Everything is possible for him who believes."

Immediately the boy's father exclaimed, "I do believe; help me overcome my unbelief!" (Mark 9:19-24)

The apostles said to the Lord, "Increase our faith!"

He replied, "If you have faith as small as a mustard seed, you can say to this mulberry tree, 'Be uprooted and planted in the sea,' and it will obey you. (Luke 17:5-6)

There was given me a thorn in my flesh, a messenger of Satan, to torment me. Three times I pleaded with the Lord to take it away from me. But he said to me, "My grace is sufficient for

you, for my power is made perfect in weakness." Therefore
I will boast all the more gladly about my weaknesses, so that
Christ's power may rest on me. That is why, for Christ's sake,
I delight in weaknesses, in insults, in hardships, in persecu-
tions, in difficulties. For when I am weak, then I am strong.
(2 Corinthians 12:7-10)

1. Mark tells us that Jesus healed a man's demon-possessed son. But Jesus
   seemed mildly offended by something the man said to him. What was
   it, and why do you think Jesus emphasized it?
2. If everything is possible for those who believe, what things (specifically,
   your thought life and your responses to temptation) are you believing
   God will do in your life in the year ahead? How much prayer are you
   devoting to these things? What commitment are you willing to make
   to improve your prayer life in this crucial area?
3. How much faith is required to do great things in God's kingdom?
   How much faith do you have at the moment?
4. The apostle Paul was frustrated by something in his life that just
   wouldn't go away. Do you think it may have been sexual desire
   or lust?
5. What was Paul's basic attitude toward his frustrating thorn in the flesh.
   What do you like about his view of how God uses our weaknesses?

☑ EVERY YOUNG MAN'S CHOICE
(Questions for Personal Reflection and Examination)

📖 We'd like to leave you with this challenge: We challenge
you to live without premarital sex. We challenge you to live
without masturbation. We challenge you to clean up what
you're watching and the thoughts you're thinking. 📖

📖 Today, the sexual lines have been so blurred that no one knows what's right or wrong, holy or profane. To put it bluntly, you're living in the era of masturbation. There's more masturbation today and more things to masturbate over than ever before. There are entire industries centered on the practice of masturbation. The porn industry wants you to masturbate compulsively so it can sell you products. 📖

6. Think about the four challenges the authors give in the first quotation. For each one, consider: Am I ready to commit, without compromise?

7. Do you agree that you are living in the era of masturbation? If so, have you ever thought of yourself as a pawn, or victim, of the porn industry? How does this make you feel?

8. What new insights have you gained about homosexuality from reading chapter 23, which talks to guys who have homosexual desires?

9. How are the overall principles in this entire book just as applicable to a guy with homosexual desire? List a few of those basic principles that you can recall.

👟 EVERY YOUNG MAN'S WALK
(Your Guide to Personal Application)

📖 We challenge you to stop ridiculing your friends who are trying to walk closer to God. We challenge you to let the girls in your life know that you care more about their hearts than their bodies. 📖

📖 Thanks, Aaron, for sharing your incredible story. You decided that it was time, and you slew that monster of pornography. You changed the direction of your life, saved your marriage, and became a godly parent to your children. Now that's what we call a turnaround. What about you? Isn't it time? 📖

📖 The world will tell you [as a guy with homosexual desires] that you must act on your feelings—sexualize them—and only then will you feel whole. They'll tell you that while your family or church will reject you, you'll find completion in a world where homosexual sex is good and the attention you've always craved is available. You can listen to the world, or you can hear another voice that appears fainter but grows stronger every day. 📖

10. Steve and Fred give two more man-to-man challenges in the first excerpt above. Have you ever been guilty of ridiculing someone who was trying to hold to the highest standards of sexual purity? What about caring for a girl's heart more than for her body? (If these questions produce some guilt, ask for God's forgiveness and make amends to those you have wronged.)

11. Review the story of Aaron (pages 220–23). What one or two things about his story have the most impact on you? Why? What key truth have you learned from Aaron that can help you in your quest for sexual integrity?

12. What is your reaction to the study results of Dr. Robert Spitzer? Why do you think his views on homosexuality—based on scientific research—are so rarely heard in our society today?

13. According to the authors, what is the role of personal choice when it comes to homosexual temptation?

14. In quietness, review what you have written and learned in this week's study. If further thoughts or prayer requests come to your mind and heart, you may want to write them down.

15. What for you was the most meaningful concept or truth in this week's study? What do you believe God wants you to do in response?

16. How would you talk this over with God? Write down your response as a prayer to Him.

🙂🙂 EVERY YOUNG MAN'S TALK

(Constructive Topics and Questions for Group Discussion)

Key Highlights from the Book to Read Aloud and Discuss

📖 When I told our youth pastor I was writing this book, I asked him whether there was anything he felt was absolutely critical to include. He pleaded, "Fred, they know they're going to fail. They don't have the spiritual strength to say no, and they know it. Show them how to have that strength!" 📖

📖 Porn-related Web sites are also an amazing success. While the dotcom industry is in a shambles with all sorts of Web sites going out of business, seventy thousand adult pay-for-porn sites are flourishing. Clearly, men want to masturbate, so businesses have sprung up to meet that need. For the rest of your life, you'll be bombarded with sensual television shows, horny movies, bra-and-panty ads in newspapers and magazines, and neighborhood strip joints. All of this is waiting out there for you *because men have sought out intensity rather than intimacy in their sexuality.* 📖

📖 How many of us are like Elijah? I don't have an answer, but I do know this: God wants to use you to change these days.

We'll leave you with an inspirational story of a unique young man named Aaron, a person whom God is using in these special days… 📖

Discussion Questions

A. Do you agree with the youth pastor's belief that young men "know they're going to fail"? Do you believe God has given you strength to live in sexual purity? If so, tell how.

B. Why do you think the intensity of this false intimacy of masturbation is so tempting when appropriate, real interpersonal intimacy is available?

C. How do you guys handle the temptation to go to porn Web sites? What advice can you give other guys about this?

D. Together, let's review the story of Aaron. What key truths should we learn from his experiences?

E. Briefly summarize the authors' explanation of homosexual development. Does it make sense to you? Why or why not?

F. What is your reaction to the research results of Dr. Robert Spitzer? What encouragement is there in his words for any guy who has homosexual desires?

G. Before we bring this session to an end, let's take several moments to reflect on what we've studied and discussed over the previous weeks.

- What do you want to thank God for as a result of this study?

- What do you sense God most wants you to understand at this time about your sexuality and purity?

- In what specific ways do you believe He now wants you to more fully trust and obey Him?

don't keep it to yourself

If you've just completed the *Every Young Man's Battle Workbook* on your own and you found it to be a helpful and valuable experience, we encourage you to consider organizing a group of guys and helping lead them through the book and workbook together.

You'll find more information about starting such a group in the section titled "Questions You May Have About This Workbook."

about the authors

STEPHEN ARTERBURN is founder and chairman of New Life Ministries and host of the nationally syndicated radio show, *New Life Live!* heard across the United States and on XM and Sirius satellite. Founder of the Women of Faith Conferences, he is a best-selling author and co-author of over seventy books including the Every Man and Every Woman series and his most recent book, *Being Christian*. He has been nominated for numerous writing awards and won three Gold Medallion awards for writing excellence, carries degrees from Baylor University and the University of North Texas, and obtained two honorary doctorate degrees. Steve resides with his family in Laguna Beach, California.

FRED STOEKER is a best-selling author of several books, including *Tactics* and *Hero,* the president of Living True Ministries, and a popular conference speaker who challenges men to become sexually pure, to reconnect in true intimate relationships with their wives, and to train their sons to become godly men. A graduate of Stanford University, Fred lives in Des Moines, Iowa, with his wife, Brenda, and their children.

MIKE YORKEY, a writer living in Encinitas, California, has collaborated with Fred Stoeker on all his books for the Every Man series.

Win the War on
Sexual Temptation at Every Age

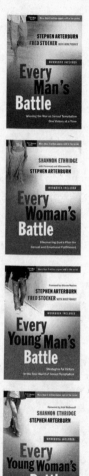

Every Man's Battle: Winning the War on Sexual Temptation One Victory at a Time
By Stephen Arterburn and Fred Stoeker
with Mike Yorkey
ISBN 978-0-307-45797-4
Ideal for ages: 18+

Every Woman's Battle: Discovering God's Plan for Sexual and Emotional Fulfillment
By Shannon Ethridge
with foreword and afterword by Stephen Arterburn
ISBN 978-0-307-45798-1
Ideal for ages: 18+

Every Young Man's Battle: Strategies for Victory in the Real World of Sexual Temptation
By Stephen Arterburn and Fred Stoeker
with Mike Yorkey
ISBN 978-0-307-45799-8
Ideal for ages: 12-17

Every Young Woman's Battle: Guarding Your Mind, Heart, and Body in a Sex-Saturated World
By Shannon Ethridge and Stephen Arterburn
with foreword by Josh McDowell
ISBN 978-0-307-45800-1
Ideal for ages: 12-17

WATERBROOK PRESS

Perfect for small group or individual study.
For additional Every Man series resources, visit www.waterbrookmultnomah.com.